THE BUTTERFLY'S BURDEN

English Translations of Books by Mahmoud Darwish

POETRY

Why Did You Leave the Horse Alone?
Translated by Jeffrey Sacks (Archipelago Books, 2006)

Unfortunately, It Was Paradise
Translated and edited by Munir Akash and Carolyn Forché
(University of California Press, 2003)

The Adam of Two Edens
Edited by Munir Akash and Daniel Moore
(Syracuse University Press and Jusoor, 2000)

PROSE

Memory for Forgetfulness
Translated by Ibrahim Muhawi (University of California Press, 1995)

The Butterfly's Burden

POEMS BY

Mahmoud Darwish

Translated from the Arabic by Fady Joudah

Copper Canyon Press

Copyright 2007 by Mahmoud Darwish

Translation and preface copyright 2007 by Fady Joudah

All rights reserved

Printed in the United States of America

Cover art: Mohammed J. Abusall, *Identity*, 2000. Ink print, 20 × 20 cm.

Copper Canyon Press is in residence at Fort Worden State Park in Port Townsend, Washington, under the auspices of Centrum Foundation. Centrum is a gathering place for artists and creative thinkers from around the world, students of all ages and backgrounds, and audiences seeking extraordinary cultural enrichment.

LIBRARY OF CONGRESS CATALOGING-IN-PUBLICATION DATA

Darwish, Mahmoud.
[Poems. English. Selections]
The butterfly's burden: poems / by Mahmoud Darwish; translated from the Arabic by Fady Joudah.
　p.　cm.
Includes bibliographical references.
ISBN-10: 1-55659-241-8
ISBN-13: 978-1-55659-241-6 (pbk.: alk. paper)
I. Joudah, Fady, 1971–　II. Title.
PJ7820.A7A212 2006
892.71'6 —dc22

2006000464

9 8 7 6 5 4 3

COPPER CANYON PRESS
Post Office Box 271
Port Townsend, Washington 98368
www.coppercanyonpress.org

ACKNOWLEDGMENTS

Beloit Poetry Journal: "Sonnet v," "Cadence Chooses Me"

Denver Quarterly: "Another Day Will Come"

Dragonfire: "Your Night Is of Lilac"

Drunken Boat: "Sonnet III," "I Waited for No One," "The Damascene Collar of the Dove," "This Is Forgetfulness"

Iowa Review: "Sonnet I," "Set Down, Here, and Now," "I Didn't Apologize to the Well," "And We Have a Land"

The Kenyon Review: "On a Day like Today," "In Jerusalem," "Don't Write History as Poetry"

Literary Imagination: "Don't Apologize for What You've Done," "They Didn't Ask: What's After Death"

The Manhattan Review: "I Have the Wisdom of One Condemned to Death," "Dream, What Is It?" "Now When You Awaken, Remember," "Nothing Pleases Me," "He's Calm, and I Am Too," "What Will Remain?" The Kurd Has Only the Wind"

Michigan Quarterly Review: "Describing Clouds," "Not as a Foreign Tourist Does"

Mississippi Review: "We Walk on the Bridge," "No Banner in the Wind," "They Don't Look Behind Them," "Murdered and Unknown," "The Coastal Road"

New American Writing: "Thanks to Tunis," "I Have a Seat in the Abandoned Theater," "In Syria," "In Egypt," "Like a Mysterious Incident"

Perihelion: "Two Stranger Birds in Our Feathers," "Sonnet VI"

Poetry: "To Our Land," "In Her Absence I Created Her Image," "If I Were Another"

Prairie Schooner: "Wedding Song," "She's Alone in the Evening," "While Waiting"

Seneca Review: "In My Mother's House," "Wednesday, Friday, Saturday"

Washington Square Review: "Low Sky," "And I, Even if I Were the Last," "A Noun Sentence"

Words Without Borders: "Housework," "Jameel Bouthaina and I"

I would like to thank Sam Hamill, Michael Wiegers, and the family of Copper Canyon for their vision and hospitality; Eleanor Wilner and Deema Shehabi for their support and love; Hana el-Sahly for supplying me with books all these years; Bouthaina Dabaja; my father, my first teacher of language, and my reference; Khaled Mattawa and all the editors of the journals in which the above poems appeared, for their generosity and insightful remarks.

Contents

xi   *Translator's Preface*

The Stranger's Bed 1998

5   We Were Missing a Present

11   Sonnet I

13   Low Sky

19   We Walk on the Bridge

23   Your Night Is of Lilac

25   Sonnet II

27   The Stranger Stumbles upon Himself in the Stranger

29   A Cloud from Sodom

31   A Doe's Young Twins

33   Sonnet III

35   Take My Horse and Slaughter It ...

37   The Stranger's Land / the Serene Land

41   Inanna's Milk

45   Sonnet IV

47   No More and No Less

51   Wedding Song

55   Housework

59   Sonnet V

61   Two Stranger Birds in Our Feathers

65   I Waited for No One

69   Drought

73   Sonnet VI

75   The Subsistence of Birds

79   Maybe, Because Winter Is Late
89   Who Am I, Without Exile?
93   Jameel Bouthaina and I
97   A Mask … for Majnoon Laila
101 A Lesson from Kama Sutra
105 The Damascene Collar of the Dove

A State of Siege 2002

121 "Here, by the downslope of hills, facing the sunset"

Don't Apologize for What You've Done 2003

I. IN THE LUST OF CADENCE

179 Cadence Chooses Me
181 I Have the Wisdom of One Condemned to Death
183 Another Day Will Come
185 And I, Even if I Were the Last
187 In My Mother's House
189 Don't Apologize for What You've Done
191 On a Day like Today
193 Set Down, Here, and Now
195 If You Return Alone
197 I Didn't Apologize to the Well
199 No Banner in the Wind
201 The Horse Fell Off the Poem
203 To Our Land
205 And We Have a Land
207 Nothing but Light
209 The Beloved Hemorrhaged Anemones

211   In Jerusalem

213   In Her Absence I Created Her Image

215   Wednesday, Friday, Saturday

217   Two Olive Trees

221   They Don't Look Behind Them

223   They Didn't Ask: What's After Death

225   Murdered and Unknown

227   The Cypress Broke

229   A Man and a Fawn Are in the Garden

233   This Is Forgetfulness

235   You'll Be Forgotten, As If You Never Were

239   As for Me, I Say to My Name

241   Dream, What Is It?

243   Now, When You Awaken, Remember

245   The Shadow

247   Nothing Pleases Me

249   He's Calm, and I Am Too

251   Describing Clouds

255   A Noun Sentence

257   Say What You Want

259   Don't Write History as Poetry

261   What Will Remain?

263   I Don't Know Your Name

265   She's Alone in the Evening

269   While Waiting

271   If I Were Another

273   Thanks to Tunis

275   I Have a Seat in the Abandoned Theater

277   In Syria

279 In Egypt

281 I Recall al-Sayyab

II. THE COASTAL ROAD

285 "A road that leads to Egypt and Syria"

III. NOT AS A FOREIGN TOURIST DOES

291 "I walked on what remains of the heart"

IV. A POETRY STANZA / THE SOUTHERNER'S HOUSE

299 "Standing together beneath a window"

V. LIKE A MYSTERIOUS INCIDENT

307 "In Pablo Neruda's home, on the Pacific"

VI. THE KURD HAS ONLY THE WIND

315 "The Kurd remembers, when I visit him, his tomorrow"

321 Notes

327 About the Author

327 About the Translator

Translator's Preface

It is tempting to describe Mahmoud Darwish's writing life through geography and history. His early poetry transformed the dispossessed land into the unattained beloved whose images inform the poet's lexicon. The features of Palestine—its flowers and birds, towns and waters—became integrated in the poet's witness to the string of tragedies, political and humanitarian, that have continued to afflict his people. Yet, over the decades, Darwish's search beyond mere place never left him. Now, in his most recent poetry, translated in this volume, his writing stands clearly at the border of earth and sky, reality and myth, love and exile, poetry and prose.

The long, circuitous journey Darwish has undertaken since his family fled his native Galilee to Lebanon in 1948 (when he was six years old) can be viewed as an odyssey. Mahmoud Darwish returned with his family to Israel months after its creation, where he grew up as a *present-absentee* who didn't return in time (from fleeing) to be recognized as an Israeli Arab. When he left for Moscow in 1970, he had already published four volumes of poetry and had known the Israeli prison system firsthand. His long life of exile had begun. One year later he moved to Cairo, and from there to Beirut. Ultimately, it was the Israeli invasion of Lebanon in 1982 that precipitated Darwish's pursuit for the sovereignty of song. Leaving Beirut to roam the Mediterranean (Greece, Cyprus, and Tunisia) proved heart wrenching for Darwish, who seemed unable, outside of his own writing, to survive another glaring mirror of exile, of dispossession. His long 1983 epic of the Beirut invasion, *Praise to the High Shadow* (*Documentary Poem*), and his 1984 collection, *A Siege to the Eulogies of the Sea*, depicted his woe, and addressed many of his close friends who had been killed or assassinated:

> My friends, do not die the way you used to die
> I beg you, do not die, wait another year for me
> one year

just one more year
we might trade ideas for walking on the street
free of the hour and the banner ...
we have other tasks beside searching for graves and elegies

In 1986 Darwish had just moved to France and published two poetry collections and his artistically brilliant prose memoir of the siege of Beirut, *Memory for Forgetfulness*. In the first of these poetry volumes, he declared his aesthetic in the title *It's a Song, It's a Song:* "Nothing concerns it other than its cadence; a wind rising for itself to rise / and a fragility that checks in on the human within his relics." It was "Time the poet killed himself," he said in another poem from the same volume, "not for a reason other than to kill himself." And pressing deeper, "Where is my humanity?"

The other collection from the same year, *Fewer Roses,* was less dialectic than its predecessor. Composed of fifty-one short lyrics (ten long lines each), *Roses* confirmed Darwish's ripe resolve to shuffle cadence, voice, and dialogue, and to maintain a transformative, restless art, as though it were borne by gusts. Darwish had discovered the necessity for perpetual renewal of his poem: a song that anchors long enough to know itself, its reason for jubilance, before departing toward another reading, another writing. This conjuring of the phoenix from the latest, cooled-off ashes of exile would become a signal for an idea of return, a sublime aesthetic of resistance that Darwish would revisit in his work: a phoenix in search of its butterfly.

Around 1988, during the first Intifada, Darwish was a member of the executive council in the Palestinian Liberation Organization (PLO). Along with Edward Said, he was assigned the task of drafting a new charter toward peace. It was a prickly and odd time for Darwish, "for what is a poet doing there, there in the executive council?" he asked himself. In an essay titled "Before Writing My Resignation," Darwish became uncomfortably aware how "the creative Palestinian is prohibited from the luxury of vacated and dedicated time for the sake of creativity, because this is bound to a direct cessation from patriotic activity. Yet prisoners grow flowers in their prison yards. And in front of the zinc huts mothers plant basil and mint. The creative person must create his flexible margin between the patriotic, the political, the daily, the cultural, and the literary. But what am I to do? What does a poet do in the executive council? Will I be able to write a book of love when color falls on the ground in autumn?"

Some time had to pass before Darwish would answer his question about a book of love. The first Intifada was another phoenix upon whose wings the poet soared higher and higher. This time Darwish was facing, as he had done before, a quintessential predicament for the poet: how to carry the "I" of the "we" without betraying one perception for the other. The result was two great epics of collective memory that display Darwish's mastery of the long poem. In *I See What I Want* (1990), he captured what is mythic and visionary about return, oscillating between, on the one hand, the dream of "a stone scratching the sun" and, on the other hand, shedding "the skin of the earth" and flying "just to fly." *Eleven Planets* (1992) expounded collective memory by invoking the voices of ancient and contemporary peoples. In it Darwish strewed the seeds of a universal voice—beginning with the Andalusian, sailing across the Atlantic to evoke the Native American, moving back in time to the Canaanite and the Greek, and ending with an Iraqi poet.

Perhaps it was what Darwish needed: to consume his self in the "we" of the "I" before leaping toward a new liberty. This emancipation came in 1996, following the bitter failure of the Oslo accords (over which he resigned from the PLO). He published his luminous, highly personalized account of place and nonplace: *Why Did You Leave the Horse Alone?* is where the longtime courtship between self and other in his poetry crystallized into mystical union. That was the year the poet came home. After twenty-six years of exile from his native Galilee, he returned to Ramallah. There, he completed *The Stranger's Bed* (1998), his book of love, the first of the three books translated in this collection. When, so soon after his return, *The Stranger's Bed* appeared, many readers were ambivalent about—some alienated by—a book of love. Perhaps many expected a glorious eulogy for the new Palestinian state yet to come. They had often imagined his poetry as *their* love poetry, but here he was singing about love as a private exile, not about exile as a public love. Eventually readers embraced the book.

The Stranger's Bed is a journey of, and through, voice. There is a delicate speech that gives birth to itself here. There is an "I" that overflows from the "you," and a duality that merges beyond the narrow constructs of language. There is dialogue between masculine and feminine, prose and poetry, self and its others.

Not enough can be said about the metaphysics of identity in this book of love. An appeal to healing begins the collection: "We came / with the wind from Babylon / and we march to Babylon," "Am I another you / and you another I?" "Then let's be kind." The subtle dialogue between tone and cadence in poems such as "Low Sky" and "We Walk on the Bridge" ushers the tender musical exchange throughout the book, where even the mythic can be treated with "one cup of hot chamomile / and two aspirins." And the sonnets — a stranger's template for another's vernacular — develop the spine that gives the book its sway as man and woman, poetry and prose, commune with each other. Duality (or the annihilation of it) becomes "the necessary clarity of our mutual puzzle." In many respects *The Stranger's Bed* is a conversation that, once begun, compels the reader through to its last utterance, uninterrupted, where the Familiar and the Stranger become "two in one." Arabic love poetry is a primary wellspring here. Whether in the Jahili night, in Majnoon Laila and Jameel Bouthaina fourteen centuries ago, in a Sufi east or an Andalusian west, it has always had its roots in an exile that slackens the bind to "the gravity of identity's land."

One year after the publication of *The Stranger's Bed*, Darwish would have died from a sudden illness, had it not been for a lengthy stay in intensive care. Subsequently, he wrote his *Mural* (2000) as if it were to be his last work. In it he celebrated life: "Green is the land of my poem, green and high." "All the arts have defeated you, Death!" "One day I will become what I want." "And I want, I want to live." Soon he began developing a more colloquial and conversational breadth in his writing. Then the terrible events of the second Intifada erupted. He was in Ramallah, and immediately found himself looking another Palestinian death in the eye, living another siege.

Comprising lyrical, journal-like entries, *A State of Siege* (2002) is witness not only to human suffering but also to art under duress, art in transmutation: "Our losses," Darwish says, "from two martyrs to eight ... / and fifty olive trees, / in addition to the structural defect /

that will afflict the poem and the play and the incomplete painting." It is difficult not to draw a parallel to twenty years ago, when the siege of Beirut exalted the poet to search for what's beyond the siege. "Besiege your siege" was his famous cry in 1983's *Documentary Poem*. Now he repeats the same words as a quiet but resolute one-line address "To poetry." In the end, it was "the butterfly light, in / this tunnel's night" that guided the poet out.

Similarly, the forty-seven short lyrics of *Don't Apologize for What You've Done* (2003) are yet another incarnation/incantation of the poet after the carnage, just as *Fewer Roses* was seventeen years earlier. These lyrics ("In the Lust of Cadence"), however, are more varied in pace, tone, and music, grouping more distinctly into twos and threes or more, in dialogue with one another. They begin by reintroducing the self, weaving through place and time, constantly looking for a new powerful center, as in the stunning pentad of death that begins with "They Don't Look Behind Them." After that, "Cadence" continues its colloquial leap, often with refreshing and playful attention to the daily and the ordinary. Darwish then concludes his "Lust" in a wonderful hovering over the body of his exile, through another pentad sequence that lands him, once more, into the twins of exile and experience, poetry and Iraq.

The beautiful poems that constitute the latter part of the book epitomize, in their discursive and lyrical conversation, the rich, incessant metamorphosis in Darwish's oeuvre. In them language is loosened from being "an adjective of place," and this language wants "from the thing only the transparency of the thing." In further contrast to the poems of 1984, language also takes "revenge on absence." Yet, whatever the transfigurations may be in Darwish's poetry, and however tempestuous the calendar of his writing life, reading Darwish has always the constant of passage through his private vocabulary. It probably would take pages to catalog the words that recur — and how they recur — in his poems: anemones and lapis lazuli, gazelles and clouds, almond blossoms and rivers, mirrors and windows, abyss and olives, endlessness and its infinite chores …

Translation should, as Darwish suggests, become more than a new poem in another language. It should expend into that language new vastness. Darwish is a songmaker whose vocabulary is accessible but whose mystery is not bashful. Finding a way to accentuate the orality of the written, that which is on the tip of the reader's tongue, is essential to translating his work. I chose to adhere to the structure of the Darwish poem in order to experience what might emerge when "physical" mimesis occurs, and to honor my faith in the harmony of the human mind. *Structure* here is *syntax* as primary tool for translating cadence and tone.

Reading the Arabic line aloud helped me achieve a transfer of the *taf'eelah* (the basic unit of prosody in Arabic) to the English meter. The syllable, of course, exists as a common denominator in the ear for both, permitting the phrase to "make its free rhythm dance." Darwish abides by the *taf'eelah*, but employs a "circular" prosody, wherein the line does not consist of a discrete whole or a fixed number of *taf'eelahs*. This is like saying that the line is often not made up of a whole number of metrical measures. Instead, the unity or wholeness (of prosody) is within the stanza or poem entire.

Perhaps it is more accurate to say that Darwish considers the whole of the poem "circular," as if it were made up of one continuous line of prosody in prose, broken up into shorter lines by the limitation of the printed page. The line is further destabilized as Darwish frequently seeks musical (and syntactic) enjambment — the former made possible in Arabic through the use of inflection. His irregular, or blithe, use of punctuation enhances this "bursting of shape /out of the frivolity of no-shape" — as if what is "circular" in his poem also draws from the mutability of clouds. The poet encouraged me to redistribute the lines and stanzas as I saw fit for the English poem, but I furthered my focus on syntax, while giving the English reader the same "view" an Arabic reader has of the page. The reader is invited to participate through the privacy of his/her eye-ear coordination — to dance and breathe, whether with consonants or vowels — to meet the curvature of the phrase in the Darwish poem.

No matter how the bifurcations of structure and syntax in translation may lead or mislead the reader, one thing is certain: Darwish does not disengage the act of writing from its subject matter. Instead, he performs a twinning. The beloved is not exclusively a woman or a land, self or other, but also poem and prose.

And now, when you awaken, remember. Did the butterfly illuminate you when it burned with the eternal light of the rose? Did the phoenix appear to you clearly, and did it call you by name? Tell me how you lived your dream in some place, and I'll tell you who you are.

Fady Joudah
7 December 2005

THE BUTTERFLY'S BURDEN

سرير الغريبة

١٩٩٨

The Stranger's Bed

1998

كان ينقصنا حاضر

لِـنَـذهَبْ كما نَـحْنُ:
سَيِّدةً حُـرَّةً
وصديقاً وفيّاً،
لنذهبْ معاً في طريقَيْن مُخْتَلِفَيْن
لنذهَبْ كما نحنُ مُـتَّحِدَيْن
ومُنْفَصِلَيْن،
ولا شيءَ يُوجِعُنا
لا طلاقُ الحمام ولا البردُ بين اليَدَيْن
ولا الريحُ حول الكنيسة تُوجِعُنا...
لم يكن كافياً ما تفتَّح من شَجَر اللوز
فابتسمي يُزْهِرِ اللوزُ أكثرَ
بين فراشات غـمازَتَيْن.

وعـمَّا قليل يكونُ لنا حاضرٌ آخَرٌ
إن نَـظَرْتِ وراءك لن تبصري
غيرَ منفى وراءك:
غُرْفَةُ نومك،
صفصافةُ الساحة،
النهرُ خلف مباني الزجاج،
ومقهى مواعيدنا... كُلُّها، كُلُّها
تَسْتَعِدُّ لتصبح منفىً، إذاً
فلنكن طيّبين!

لِـنَـذهَبْ كما نَـحْنُ:
إنسانةً حُـرَّةً
وصديقاً وفيّاً لناياتها،
لم يكن عُـمْرُنا كافياً لنشيخ معاً
ونسيرَ إلى السينما متعبين
ونَـشْهَدَ خاتمةَ الحرب بين أثينا وجاراتها
ونرى حفلة السلم ما بين روما وقرطاج
عـمَّا قليل.

We Were Missing a Present

Let's go as we are:
a free woman
and a loyal friend,
let's go together on two different paths
let's go as we are united
and separate,
with nothing hurting us
not the divorce of the doves or the coldness between the hands
nor the wind around the church …
what bloomed of almond trees wasn't enough.
So smile for the almonds to blossom more
between the butterflies of two dimples

And soon there will be a new present for us.
If you look back you will see only
the exile of your looking back:
your bedroom,
the courtyard willow,
the river behind the glass buildings,
and the café of our trysts … all of it, all
preparing to become exile, so
let's be kind!

Let's go as we are:
a free woman
and a friend loyal to her flutes.
Our time wasn't enough to grow old together
to walk wearily to the cinema
to witness the end of Athens's war with her neighbors
and see the banquet of peace between Rome and Carthage
about to happen. Because soon

فعـمّا قليلٍ ستنتقل الطَيْرُ من زَمَنٍ نحو آخَرَ،
هل كان هذا الطريقُ هباءً
على شَكْل معنى، وسار بنا
سَفَراً عابراً بين أسطورتين
فلا بُدَّ منه، ولا بُدَّ منا
غريباً يرى نَفْسَهُ في مرايا غريبته؟
«لا، ليس هذا طريقي إلى جَسَدي
«لا حُلول ثقافيَّةً لـهُمُوم وُجوديَّةٍ
«أَينما كنتَ كانت سمائي
حقيقيَّةً
«مَنْ أنا لأُعيد لَكَ الشَمْسَ والـقَمَرَ السابقين
فلنكن طيِّبين ...

لنذهبْ، كما نحن:
عاشقةً حُرَّةً
وشاعرَها.
لم يكن كافياً ما تساقط من
ثلج كانون أوَّلَ، فابتسمي
يندف الثلج قطناً على صلوات المسيحيِّ،
عـمّا قليلٍ نعود إلى غَدنا، خَلْفَنا،
حَيْثُ كُنَّا هناك صغيرين في أوَّل الحب،
نلعب قصة روميو وجولييت
كي نتعلَّم مُعْـجَمَ شكسبير...
طار الفَرَاشُ مِنَ الـنَوْم
مثل سرابِ سلام سريعٍ
يُـكَـلِّلُنا نجمتينِ
ويَقتلُنا في الصراع على الاسم
ما بين نافذتين
لنذهب، إذاً
ولنكن طيِّبين

لِـنَـذْهَبْ، كما نَحْنُ:
إنسانةً حُرَّةً
وصديقاً وفيًّا،
لنذهَبْ كما نحن. جئنا
مَعَ الريح من بابلٍ

the birds will relocate from one epoch to another:
Was this path only dust
in the shape of meaning, and did it march us
as if we were a passing journey between two myths
so the path is inevitable, and we are inevitable
as a stranger sees himself in the mirror of another stranger?
"No, this is not my path to my body"
"No cultural solutions for existential concerns"
"Wherever you are my sky
is real"
"Who am I to give you back the previous sun and moon"
Then let's be kind ...

Let's go, as we are:
a free lover
and her poet.
What fell of January snow
wasn't enough, so smile
for snow to card its cotton on the Christian's prayer,
we will soon return to our tomorrow, behind us,
where we were young in love's beginning,
playing Romeo and Juliet
and learning Shakespeare's language ...
The butterflies have flown out of sleep
as a mirage of a swift peace
that adorns us with two stars
and kills us in the struggle over the name
between two windows
so, let's go
and let's be kind

Let's go, as we are:
a free woman
and a loyal friend,
let's go as we are. We came
with the wind from Babylon

ونسيرُ إلى بابل ...
لم يَكُنْ سَفَري كافياً
ليصير الـصَّنَـوْبَرُ في أثَري
لفظةً لمديح المكان الجنوبيّ
نحن هنا طَيِّبونَ. شَماليَّةٌ
ريحُنا، والأغاني جَنُوبيَّةٌ
هل أَنا أَنت أُخرى
وأَنت أَنا آخر؟
«ليس هذا طريقي إلى أرض حُريّتي
ليس هذا طريقي إلى جَسَدي
وأَنا، لن أكون «أَنا» مَرَّتين
وقد حلَّ أَمسٍ مَحَلَّ غدي
وانقَسَمْتُ إلى امرأتين
فلا أَنا شرقيَّةٌ
ولا أَنا غربيَّةٌ،
ولا أَنا زيتونةٌ ظَلَّلَتْ آيَتَيْن
لِنَذْهَبْ، إذاً.
«لا حلولَ جماعيَّةٌ لهواجسَ شخصيَّةٍ
لم يكن كافياً أَن نكون معاً
لنكون معاً...
كان ينقُصُنا حاضرٌ لنرى
أَين نحن. لنذْهَبْ كما نحن،
إنسانةً حُرَّةً
وصديقاً قديماً
لنذهبْ معاً في طريقين مختلفين
لنذهب معاً،
ولنكن طيِّبين...

and we march to Babylon …
My travel wasn't enough
for the pines to become in my trace
an utterance of praise to the southern place.
We are kind here. Northerly
is our wind, and our songs are southerly.
Am I another you
and you another I?
"This isn't my path to my freedom's land"
this isn't my path to my body
and I won't be "I" twice
now that my yesterday has become my tomorrow
and I have split into two women
so I am not of the east
and I am not of the west,
nor am I an olive tree shading two verses in the Quran,
then let's go.
"No collective solutions for personal scruples"
it wasn't enough that we be together
to be together …
we were missing a present to see
where we were. Let's go as we are,
a free woman
and an old friend
let's go on two separate paths
let's go together,
and let's be kind …

سوناتا [I]

إذا كُنْتِ آخرَ ما قالَهُ اللهُ لي، فليكُنْ
نزولُكِ نُونَ الــ «أَنا» في الـمُـثَـنَّى. وطوبى لنا
وقد نَـوَّر اللوزُ بَعْدَ خُطَى العابرين، هنا
على ضفتيكِ، ورفَّ عليك القطا واليمامُ

بقَـرْنِ الغزال طَعَـنْتِ السماء، فسال الكلامُ
ندى في عروق الطبيعة. ما اسمُ القصيدةْ
أَمام ثُنَائيَّة الـخَـلْق والحق، بين السماء البعيدة
وأَرْزِ سريركِ، حين يحنُّ دَمٌّ لدمٍ، ويئنُّ الرخامُ؟

ستحتاجُ أسطورةٌ للتشمُّس حولك. هذا الزحامُ
إلهاتُ مصْرَ وسُومَرَ تحت النخيل يُغيِّرن أَثوابهنَّ
وأَسماءَ أيامهن، ويُـكملن رحلاتهنَّ إلى آخر القافية...

وتحتاج أنشودتي للتنفُّس: لا الشعرُ شعرٌ
ولا النثرُ نثرٌ. حلمت بأَنَّكِ آخرُ ما قالَهُ
ليَ اللهُ حين رأَيتكما في المنام، فكان الكلامُ...

Sonnet I

If you are the last of what god told me, be
the pronoun revealed to double the "I." Blessedness is ours
now that almond trees have illuminated the footprints of passersby, here
on your banks, where above you grouse and doves flutter

With a gazelle's horn you stabbed the sky, then words flowed
like dew in nature's veins. What's a poem's name
before the duality of creation and truth, between the faraway sky
and your cedar bed, when blood longs for blood, and marble aches?

A myth will need to sunbathe around you. This crowdedness,
these gods of Egypt and Sumer under palm trees change their dresses
and their days' names, and complete their journey to the end of rhyme ...

And my song needs to breathe: poetry isn't poetry
and prose isn't prose. I dreamt that you are the last of what god told me
when I saw you both in my sleep, then there were words ...

سماء منخفضة

هُنَالكَ حُبٌّ يسيرُ على قَدَمَيْهِ الْحَريريَّتَيْن
سعيداً بغُرْبَتِه في الشوارع،
حُبٌّ صغيرٌ فقيرٌ يُبَلِّلُهُ مَطَرٌ عابرٌ
فيفيض على العابرين:
«هداياَيَ أكبرُ مني
كُلوا حِنْطتي
واشربوا خَمْرَتي
فسمائي على كتفيَّ وأرضي لَكُمْ...

هَلْ شَمَمْتِ دَمَ الياسمينِ الـمَشَاعَ
وفكَّرْتِ بي
وانتظرتِ معي طائراً أخضرَ الذَّيْلِ
لا اسْمَ لَهُ؟

هُنَالكَ حُبٌّ فقيرٌ يُحدِّقُ في النهر
مُسْتَسْلِماً للتداعي: إلى أَينَ تَرْكُضُ
يا فَرَسَ الماء؟
عما قليل سيمتصُّكَ البحرُ
فامش الهوينى إلى مَوْتكَ الاختياريِّ،
يا فَرَسَ الماء!

هل كنتِ لي ضَفَّتَيْنْ
وكان المكانُ كما ينبغي أن يكون
خفيفاً خفيفاً على ذكرياتِك؟
أيَّ الأغاني تُحِبِّينَ
أيَّ الأغاني؟ أتلك التي
تتحدَّثُ عن عطشِ الـحُبِّ،
أَمْ عن زمانٍ مضى؟

هنالك حُبٌّ فقير، ومن طَرَفٍ واحدٍ
هاديةٌ هاديةٌ لا يُكَسَّرُ

Low Sky

There's a love walking on two silken feet
happy with its estrangement in the streets,
a love small and poor made wet by a passing rain
that it overflows onto passersby:
My gifts are larger than I am
eat my wheat
and drink my wine
my sky is on my shoulders and my earth is yours ...

Did you smell the jasmine's radiant blood
and think of me
then wait with me for a green-tailed bird
that has no name?

There's a poor love staring at the river
in surrender to summoning: Where do you run to
seahorse?
Soon the sea will suck you in
so walk leisurely to your chosen death,
O seahorse!

Were you as two embankments for me
and was the place as it should be
light-footed on your memories?
What songs do you love
what songs? The ones
that speak about love's thirst,
or about a time that has passed?

There's a poor love, one-sided
and quite serene it doesn't break

بلَّوْرَ أيّامِكِ الـمُنْتَقاة
ولا يُوقِدُ النارَ في قَـمَرٍ باردٍ
في سريرِكِ،
لا تشعرِيـنَ بهِ حيـنَ تبكيـنَ من هاجسٍ،
رُبّما بدلاً منه،
لا تعرفين بماذا تُحسّين حين تَضُـمّيـنَ
نفسَكِ بين ذراعيكِ!
أيَّ الليالي تريدين، أيَّ الليالي
وما لوْنُ تِلْكَ العيونِ التي تحلُمِيـنَ
بها عندما تحلمين؟
هُـنَالَكَ حُبٌّ فقيرٌ، ومن طرفين
يُقَلّلُ من عَدَد اليائسين
ويرفَعُ عَرْشَ الـحَمام على الجانبين.
عليكِ، إذاً، أن تَقُودي بنفسِكِ
هذا الربيعَ السريعَ إلى مَنْ تُحبّيـنَ
أيَّ زمانٍ تريدين، أيَّ زمان
لأصبحَ شاعرَهُ، هكذا هكذا: كُـلّما
مَضَتِ امرأةٌ في الـمساء إلى سرِّها
وَجَدَتْ شاعراً سائراً في هواجسها.
كُـلّما غاص في نفسه شاعرٌ
وَجَدَ امرأةً تتعرّى أمام قصيدتهِ...

أيَّ منفىً تريدِيـنَ؟
هل تذهبين معي، أمْ تسيرين وَحْدَكِ
في اسْمك منفىً يُكَلّلُ منفىً
بِأَلْائهِ؟

هُـنَالكَ حُبٌّ يَمُرُّ بنا،
دون أَن نَـنْتَبِهْ،
فلا هُـوَ يَـدْري ولا نحن نَـدْري
لماذا تُشرِّدُنا وردةٌ في جدارٍ قديم
وتبكي فتاةٌ على مَـوْقف الباص،
تَـقْضِم تُـفّاحَةً ثم تبكي وتضحَكُ:
«لا شيءَ، لا شيءَ أكثر
من نَـحْلَةٍ عَبَرَتْ في دمي...

your select day's crystal
and doesn't light a fire in a cold moon
in your bed,
you don't sense it when you cry from an apprehension,
which might replace it,
you don't know what to feel when you embrace
yourself between your arms!
Which nights do you want, which nights
and what color are those eyes that you dream
with when you dream?
There is a poor love, and two-sided
it diminishes the number of those in despair
and lifts the pigeons' throne on both sides.
You must, then, by yourself lead
this swift spring to the one you love.
Which time do you want, which time
that I may become its poet, just like that: whenever
a woman goes to her secret in the evening
she finds a poet walking in her thoughts.
Whenever a poet dives into himself
he finds a woman undressing before his poem ...

Which exile do you want?
Will you come with me, or walk alone
in your name as an exile that adorns exile
with its glitter?

There's a love passing through us,
without us noticing,
and neither it knows nor do we know
why a rose in an ancient wall makes us fugitives
and why a girl at the bus stop cries,
bites on an apple then laughs and cries:
Nothing, nothing more
than a bee passing through my blood ...

هُنالِكَ حُبّ فقيرٌ، يُطيلُ
التأمُّلَ في العابرين، ويختارُ
أصغَرَهُمْ قمراً: أنتَ في حاجةٍ
لسماءٍ أقلَّ ارتفاعاً،
فكن صاحبي تَـتَّسِعْ
لأَنانيّةٍ اُ ثنين لا يعرفان
لمن يُهْديان زُهُورَهُما ...
رُبَّما كان يَقْصِدُني، رُبَّما
كان يقصدُنا دون أَن نَنْتَبِهْ

هُنَالِكَ حُبّ ...

There's a poor love, it contemplates
at length the passersby, and chooses
the youngest moon among them: You are in need
of a lower sky,
be my friend and the sky will expand
for the selfishness of two who do not know
to whom they should give their flowers ...
Maybe it meant me, maybe
it meant us and we didn't notice

There is a love ...

نَمشي على الجسر

تُصابين، مثلي، برحلةِ طَيْرٍ
ويحدُثُ ذلك بعد الظهيرةِ،
حيث تقولين: خُذْني إلى النهرِ
يا أَجنبيُّ، إلى النهر خذني
فإنَّ طريقي على ضَفَّتَيْكَ طويلُ

ونُصغي إلى ما يَقُولُ الـمُشَاةُ
على الجسر:
«لي عَمَلٌ آخرٌ غيرُ هذا،
«ولي مقعدٌ في السفينة
«لي حِصَّةٌ في الحياة
«وأَمَّا أَنا،
فعليَّ اللحاقُ بمترو الضواحي
«تأخَّرْتُ عن ذكرياتي
وعن موعد الساكسفون،
وَلَيْلي قليلُ

ونُصغي إلى ما بنا من حنينٍ خفيّ
إلى شارعٍ غامض: لي حياتي هناك
حياتي التي صنعَتْها القوافلُ وانصرَفَتْ،
وهنا لي حياتي على قَدْرِ خبزي
وأَسئلتي عن مصيرٍ يُعَذّبُه حاضرٌ
عابرٌ، وغدٌ فوضويٌّ جَميلُ

صدىً للصدى، أَيُّنا قال هذا الكلام، أَنا
أَم الأَجنبيَّةُ؟ لا أَحَدٌ يستطيعُ
الرَجوع إلى أَحد. تصنع الأَبديَّةُ
أَشغالها اليدويَّةَ من عمرنا وتُعَمِّرُ...
فليكُنِ الـحُبُّ ضرباً من الغَيْب، وليكُنِ
الغيبُ ضرباً من الـحُبِّ. إني عجبتُ
لمن يعرفُ الحبَّ كيف يُحبُّ! فقد

We Walk on the Bridge

You're afflicted, like me, with a bird's journey
and this happens in the afternoon,
when you say: Take me to the river
you foreign man, to the river take me
my road upon your banks is long

And we listen to what pedestrians say
on the bridge:
"I have other things to do"
"I have a place on the ship"
"I have a share in life"
"And as for me,
I must catch the subway
I am late for memories
and for the saxophone lesson,
and my night is short"

We listen to what hidden longing for a mysterious street
is in us: I have my life over there
my life that caravans made then went on their way,
and here I have my life as my bread's worth
and my questions about a destiny a passing present
tortures, and I have a beautiful chaotic tomorrow

Echo for echo: who of us said those words, me
or the foreign woman? No one can
return to another. Eternity performs
its manual chores out of our lives then thrives ...
So let love be an unknown, and
the unknown a kind of love. How strange
to believe this and still love! Because

يتعَبُ الـحُبّ فينا من الانتظار ويمرَضُ،
لكنَّهُ لا يَقُولُ

لدى غدنا ما سيكفي من الوقت، يكفي
لنمشي على الجسر عَشْرَ دقائقَ أُخرى،
فقد نتغيَّرُ عما قليلٍ وننسى ملامح
ثالثنا/ الموت، ننسى الطريقَ إلى البيت
قرب السماء التي خذلتنا كثيراً،
خذيني إلى النهر، يا أَجنبيَّةُ،
قد نتغيَّر عـمّا قليل. وقد يحدثُ
المستحيلُ

كما في الكتابة، يأتي الضروريُّ
في حينه قمراً أُنثوياً لملء فراغ
القصيدة. لا تتركيني تماماً، ولا
تأخذيني تماماً. ضعي في المكان الصحيح
الزمانَ الصحيح. فأنتِ السبيلُ وأَنتِ الدليلُ

بلاد حقيقيَّةٌ، لا مجاز، ذراعاك
حولي... هنالك قرب الكتاب الـمُقَدَّس
أو ههنا. أيُّنا قال: قد تحفَظُ
اللغةُ الأرضَ مما يُلِمُّ بها من
غيابٍ إذا انتصر الشعرُ؟ مَنْ
قال منا: سأنسى، وأغفر للقلب
أكثر من خطأ واحد، كلما طال
هذا الرحيلُ...

love might tire in us from waiting and fall ill,
but it never says

Our tomorrow has enough time, enough
for us to walk on the bridge for ten more minutes,
we might change soon and forget the features
of our third (death), forget the way to the house
near the sky that has often failed us,
so take me to the river, foreign woman,
we might change soon. And the impossible
might happen

As in writing, the necessary comes
on time, a feminine moon to fill the poem's
emptiness. Do not leave me completely, and do not
take me completely. Put the right time
in the right place. You are the means and the guide

A real country, not a metaphor, your arms
around me ... over there by the holy book
or right here. Who of us said: Language
might preserve the land from the plight
of absence if poetry wins? Who
of us said: I will forget, and forgive the heart
more than one mistake, the longer
this departure takes ...

ليلُكِ من ليلٍ

يجلسُ الليلُ حيث تكونين. ليلُك من لَيْلَك. بين حين وآخرَ تُفْلتُ إيماءةٌ من أَشعَّة غـمّازتَيْك فتكسر كأسَ النبيذ وتُشعل ضوء النجوم. وليلُكِ ظلُّكِ ــ قطعةُ أرض خرافيَّة للمساواة ما بين أحلامنا. ما أَنا بالمسافر أو بالـمُقيم على لَيْلِك الليليِّ، أنا هُـوَ مَنْ كان يوماً أنا، كُلَّما عَسْعَسَ الليلُ فيك حَدَسْتُ بِمَـنْزِلَةِ القلب ما بين مَنْزِلَتَيْن: فلا النفسُ ترضى، ولا الروحُ ترضى. وفي جَسَدَيْنا سماءٌ تُعانق أرضاً. وكُلُّك ليلُكِ... لَيْلٌ يشعُّ كحبر الكواكب. لَيْلٌ على ذمَّة الليل، يزحف في جسدي خَدَراً كنُعاس الثعالب. ليل ينثُّ غموضاً مضيئاً على لُغَتي، كُلَّما اتَّضَحَ ازدَدْتُ خوفاً من الغد في قبضة اليد. ليلٌ يُحدِّقُ في نفسه آمناً مطمئناً إلى لا نهاياته، لا تحفُّ به غيرُ مرآته وأغاني الرُّعاة القُدامى لصيف أباطرة يمرضون من الحبِّ. ليل ترعرع في شِعْرِه الجاهليِّ على نزوات اُمرىء القيس والآخرين، ووسَّع للحالمين طريقَ الحليب إلى قمرٍ جائعٍ في أقاصي الكلام...

Your Night Is of Lilac

The night sits wherever you are. Your night
is of lilac. Every now and then a gesture escapes
from the beam of your dimples, breaks the wineglass
and lights up the starlight. And your night is your shadow—
a fairy-tale piece of land to make our dreams
equal. I am not a traveler or a dweller
in your lilac night, I am he who was one day
me. Whenever night grew in you I guessed
the heart's rank between two grades: neither
the self accepts, nor the soul accepts. But in our bodies
a heaven and an earth embrace. And all of you
is your night ... radiant night like planet ink. Night
in the covenant of night, crawling in my body
anesthetized like a fox's sleepiness. Night diffusing a mystery
that illuminates my language, whenever it is clearer
I become more fearful of a tomorrow in the fist. Night
staring at itself safe and assured in its
endlessness, nothing celebrates it except its mirror
and the ancient shepherd songs in a summer of emperors
who get sick on love. Night that flourished in its Jahili poetry
on the whims of Imru' el-Qyss and others,
and widened for the dreamers the milk path to a hungry
moon in the remoteness of speech ...

سوناتا [II]

لعلَّكِ حين تُديرِين ظلَّكِ للنهر لا تطلبين
مِنَ النهر غيرَ الـغُموض. هُناكَ خريفٌ قليلْ
يَـرُشُّ على ذَكَرِ الأَيّلِ الماءَ من غيمة شاردةْ
هُناكَ، على ما تَرَكْتِ لنا من فُتَاتِ الرحيل

غموضُكِ دَرْبُ الحليب. غبارُ كواكبَ لا اسم لها
وَلَيْلٌ غُمُوضُكِ في لُؤْلُؤٍ لا يُضيءُ سوى الماء،
أمَّا الكلامُ فمن شأنه أَن يضيء بِمفردةٍ واحدةٍ
«أُحبُّكِ» لَيْلَ المهاجر بين مُعَلَّقَتَيْن وَصَفَّيْ نخيلْ

أَنا مَـنْ رأى غَدهُ إذ رآكِ. أَنا مَنْ رأى
أَناجيلَ يكتبها الوثنيُّ الأخيرُ على سفح جلعادَ
قبل البلاد القديمَةِ أو بعدها. وأنا الغيمةُ العائدةْ
إلى تِينَةٍ تحملُ اسمي، كما يحملُ السيفُ وَجْهَ القتيلْ

لعلَّكِ، حين تُديرين ظلَّكِ لي، تمنحين المجاز
وقائعَ معنًى لما سوف يحدث عـمَّا قليلْ...

Sonnet II

Perhaps when you turn your shadow to the river you ask
of the river only obscurity. Over there a little autumn
sprinkles the stag with water from a fugitive cloud
there, on what you have left for us of departure's crumbs

Your mystery is the Milky Way. The dust of nameless planets,
and your mystery is night in pearls that illuminate only water.
Whereas speech can illuminate with one phrase
"I love you," the emigrant's night between two odes and two palm tree rows

I am who saw his tomorrow when he saw you. I am who saw
gospels the last idolater wrote on Gilead's slopes
before the ancient lands or after. And I am the returning cloud
to a fig tree that bears my name, as a sword bears the murdered's face

Perhaps, when you turn your shadow to me, you give incident
to metaphor as a meaning to what is about to happen …

وقوع الغريبة على نفسه في الغريب

واحدٌ نحن في اثنين/
لا اسمَ لنا، يا غريبةٌ، عند وُقُوع
الغريب على نفسه في الغريب. لَنَا من
حديقتنا خلفنا قُوَّةُ الظلِّ. فلتُظهري
ما تشائين من أرض ليلك، ولتُبْطني
ما تشائين. جئنا على عَجَلٍ من غروب
مكانين في زمن واحد، وبحثنا معاً
عن عناوينا: فاذهبي خَلْف ظلِّك،
شَرِّقْ نشيد الأناشيد، راعيةٌ للقطا،
تجدي نجمةً سَكَنَتْ موتها، فاصعدي جَبَلاً
مُهْمَلاً تجدي أمسِ يُكْمِلُ دورتَهُ في غدي.
تجدي أَين كنا وأَين نكون معاً،
واحدٌ نحن في اُثنين/
فاذهب إلى البحر، غَرِّبْ كتابك،
واغطُسْ خفيفاً خفيفاً كأنَّك تحمل
نَفْسَكَ عند الولادة في موجتين،
تجدْ غابةً من حشائش مائيةٍ وسماءً
من الماء خضراءَ ، فاغطسْ خفيفاً
خفيفاً كأنك لا شيء في أيِّ شيء،
تجدنا معاً...
واحدٌ نحن في اُثنين/
ينقُصُنا أن نرى كيف كنا هنا، يا
غريبةٌ، ظلِّين ينفتحان وينغلقان على ما
تشكَّل من شكلنا: جَسَداً يختفي ثم يظهَرُ
في جَسَدٍ يختفي في التباس الثنائية
الأبدية. ينقُصُنا أن نعودَ إلى اثنين
كي نتعانق أكثر. لا اسم لنا يا غريبة
عند وقوع الغريب على نفسه في الغريب!

The Stranger Stumbles upon Himself in the Stranger

We are one in two /
There's no name for us, woman, when the stranger
stumbles upon himself in the stranger. Of our
garden behind us we have the force of shadow. So show
what you want of your night's land, and conceal
what you want. We came in a hurry from the twilight
of two places at one time, and searched together
for our addresses: Go behind your shadow,
east of the Song of Songs, a shepherd of sand grouse,
you'll find a star dwelling in its death, then climb a neglected
mountain and you'll find my yesterday completing its cycle in my tomorrow.
You'll find where we were and where we'll be together,
we are one in two /
Go to the sea then, man, west of your book,
and dive lightly, lightly as if you were carrying
yourself at birth in two waves,
you'll find a wetland forest and a green sky
of water, then dive lightly
lightly as if you were nothing in anything,
and you'll find us together ...
we are one in two /
We need to see how we were here,
stranger, as two shadows opening and closing on what
has been shaped of our shape: a body disappearing then reappearing
in a body disappearing in the mystery of the eternal
duality. We need to return to being two
to embrace each other more. There's no name for us,
when the stranger stumbles upon himself in the stranger!

غيمة من سدوم

بَعْدَ لَيْلِكِ، ليلِ الشتاء الأَخير
خَلاَ شارعُ البحر من حَرَس الليل،
لا ظلَّ يتبعُني بعدما جَفَّ لَيْلُكِ
في شمس أغنيتي. مَنْ يقول لي
الآن: دعك من الأمس واحلُمْ بكامل
لا وعيك الـحُرّ؟
حُرّيتي تجلس الآن قربي، معي، وعلى
ركبتيَّ كقطٍ أليف. تُحدّق بي وبما
قد تركتِ من الأمس لي: شالك
الليلكيّ، شرائطَ فيديو عن الرقص بين الذئاب، وعقداً من
الياسمين على طُحْلُب القلب...

ماذا ستصنع حُرّيتي، بعد ليلك،
ليل الشتاء الأخير؟
«مَضَتْ غَيْمَةٌ من سَدومَ إلى بابلٍ،
من مئات السنين، ولكن شاعرها «بول
تسيلان» انتحر، اليومَ، في نهر باريس.
لن تأخذيني إلى النهر ثانية. لن يسائلني
حارسٌ: ما اسمُكَ اليومَ؟ لن نَلْعَنَ
الحربَ. لن نَلْعَنَ السِلْم. لن نتسَلَّقَ سُورَ
الحديقة بحثاً عن الليل ما بين صفصافتين
ونافذتين، ولن تسأليني: متى يفتح
السِلْمُ أبوابَ قلعتنا للحمام؟

بعد ليلك، ليل الشتاء الأخير
أقام الجنودُ معسكرهم في مكان بعيد
وحطَّ على شرفتي قمر أبيض
وجلست وحُرّيتي صامتين نُحَدِّقُ في ليلنا
مَنْ أنا؟ مَنْ أنا بعد لَيْلِكِ
ليلِ الشتاءِ الأخير؟

A Cloud from Sodom

After your night, night of the last winter,
the sea road was empty of its night guards,
no shadow follows me after your night dried up
in my song's sun. Who will say to me
now: Let go of yesterday and dream with all
of your subconscious?
My freedom sits beside me, with me, and on
my knees like a house cat. It stares at me and at
what you might have left of yesterday for me: your lilac
shawl, videotapes of dancing among wolves, and a jasmine
necklace around the algae of the heart ...

What will my freedom do, after your night,
night of the last winter?
"A cloud went from Sodom to Babylon,"
hundreds of years ago, but its poet Paul
Celan committed suicide, today, in Paris's river.
You won't take me to the river again. No guard
will ask me: What's your name today? We won't curse
war. We won't curse peace. We won't climb
the garden fence searching the night for two willows
and two windows, and you won't ask me: When
will peace open our citadel doors to the doves?

After your night, night of the last winter,
the soldiers pitched their camp in a faraway place
and a white moon alighted on my balcony
and I sat with my freedom silently staring into our night:
Who am I? Who am I after your night
night of the last winter?

شادنا ظبية توأمان

مساءً، على نَمَش الضوء ما بين
نهديك، يقتربُ الأَمسُ والغدُ مَنِّي.
وُجِدْتُ كما ينبغي للقصيدة أَن تُوَجَدَ...
ألليلُ يُولَدُ تحت لِحَافك، والظلُّ
مُرَتَّبٌ ههنا وهنالك بين ضفافك
والكلمات التي أَرْجَعَتْنا إلى نَبْرها:
«وضعتُ يميني على شَعْرها
وشمالي على شادِنَيْ ظَبْيَةٍ توأمين
وَسِرْنا إلى لَيْلنا الخاصِّ...»
هل أَنتَ حقاً هنا؟ أَم أَنا
عاشقٌ سابقٌ يتفقَّدُ أَحوالَ ماضيه؟
نامي على نفسك المطمئنَّة بين
زُهُور الملاءات. نامي يداً فوق صدري
وأُخرى على ما سَيَنْبُتُ من زَغَبٍ لفراخ
اليمامات. نامي كما ينبغي للحديقة من
حولنا أَن تنام... امتلأنا بأَمس،
امتلأنا بوسواس جيتارةٍ لا سرير لها.
يا لها... مِنْ فتاةٍ خُلاسيَّةٍ تبعت ظلَّها.
يا لها... من هياجٍ يُمَزِّقُ ما يتناثر من
وَرَق الورد حول السياج. فنامي
على نَفَسي نَفَساً ثانياً قبل أَن يفتح
الأَمسُ نافذتي كُلَّها. ليس لي طائرٌ
وطنيٌّ، ولا شَجَرٌ وطنيٌّ، ولا زَهْرَةٌ
في حديقة منفاك. لكنني ـــ ونبيذي
يُسَافِرُ مثلي ـــ أُقاسمُك الغَدَ والأَمس.
لولاك لولا الرذاذُ الذي يتلألأ في نَمَش
الضوء ما بين نهديك، لانحرفتْ لُغتي
عن أنوثتها. كم أَنا والقصيدة أُمُّك،
وابناك، نغفو على شَادِنَيْ ظَبْيَةٍ
توأَمَيْن!

A Doe's Young Twins

In the evening, by the freckled light between
your breasts, yesterday and tomorrow approach me.
I came into being as a poem should come into being ...
the night is born under your bedcover, and shadow
is fretful here and there between your riverbank
and the words that carried us back to their tone:
"I placed my right hand on her hair
and my left on a doe's young twins
then we walked into our private night ..."
Are you really here? Or am I
a previous lover who checks in on his past?
Sleep within your self secure among your
bedsheet flowers. Sleep with one hand on my chest
and the other on the down that will sprout on baby
pigeons. Sleep as the garden
around us should ... we've become filled with yesterday,
filled with wicked whispers of a bedless guitar.
(And what a mulatto she is ... following her shadow.
What a tumult ... tearing up what scatters
of rose petals around the fence.) Sleep
upon my breath as a second breath before yesterday
fully opens my window. I have no national
bird, no national tree, and no flower
in your exile garden. But I—and my wine
travels as I do—split with you yesterday and tomorrow.
If it weren't for you and for the drizzle
that glimmers in the freckled
light between your breasts, my language would have swerved
from its femininity. But the poem and I are now your mother,
and your two children, falling asleep on a doe's young
twins!

سوناتا [III]

أُحبُّ من الليل أَوَّلَهُ، عندما تأتيان معا
يداً بيد، ورويداً رويداً تَضُـمَّانني مَقْطَعاً مقطعا
تطيران بي، فوق. يا صاحبيَّ أَقيما ولا تُسْرِعا
وناما على جانبيَّ كمثل جناحيْ سُنُونُوَّة مُتْعَبَهْ

حريرُكما ساخِنٌ. وعلى الناي أَن يتأنَّى قليلا
ويصقُلَ سُوناتَةً، عندما تقعان عليَّ غموضاً جميلا
كمعنى على أُهْبَةِ الـعُزْي، لا يستطيعُ الوصولا
ولا الانتظارَ الطويلَ أَمامَ الكلام، فيختارني عَتَبَهْ

أُحبُّ من الشعر عَفْويَّةَ النثر والصورةَ الخافيةْ
بلا قَـمَر للبلاغة: حين تسرين حافيةً تترُكُ القافية
جِماعَ الكلام، وينكسرُ الوَزْنُ في ذروة التجربةْ

قليلٌ من الليل قربك يكفي لأخرج من بابلي
إلى جوهري ــ آخري. لا حديقةَ لي داخلي
وكُلُّكِ أَنتِ. وما فاض منك «أنا» الـحُرَّةُ الطيِّبةْ

Sonnet III

Of night, I love the beginning, when you two come together
hand in hand, and bit by bit embrace me one section at a time
then in flight take me, higher. Stay my friends, don't hurry
and sleep on each of my sides like the wings of a tired swallow

Both of your silks are hot. But the flute should be patient
and polish a sonnet, when you two descend on me as a lovely mystery,
like a meaning on the verge of nakedness, incapable of arrival
and of long waiting in front of speech, it chooses me as a threshold

Of poetry, I love the spontaneity of prose and the hidden image
without a moon for rhetoric: when you walk barefoot rhyme abandons
copulating speech, and meter breaks in the climax of experience

A bit of night near you is enough for me to get out of my Babylon
and into my essence — my other. No garden for me within me
and all of you is you. And what overflows from you is "I" the free and kind

خُذي فرسي واذبحيها ...

أنتِ، لا هَـوَسي بالفتوحات، عُرْسي
تَرَكْتُ لنفسي وأقرانها من شياطين نفسكِ
حُريَّةَ الامتثال لما تطلبين،
خُذي فَرَسي
واذبحيها،
لأَمشي مثلَ الـمُحَارِب بَعْدَ الهزيمة
من غَيْرِ حُلم وحسٍّ ...
سلاماً على ما تُريدين من تَعَب
للأمير الأسير، ومن ذهب لاحتفال
الوصيفات بالصيف. ألْفُ سلام عَلَيْك
جميعك حافلةٌ بالـمُريدين مِنَّ كُلِّ جنٍّ وإنسٍ،
سلاماً على ما صَنَعْت بنفسك من
أجل نفسك: دَبُّوسُ شَعْرِك يكسر
سيفي وتُرْسي
وزرُّ قميصك يحمل في ضَوْئه
لفظةَ السرِّ للطير من كُلِّ جنس،
خُذي نَفَسي أَخْذَ جيتارَة تستجيبُ
لما تطلبين من الريح. أندلسي كُلُّها
في يديك، فلا تَدَعي وَتَراً واحداً
للدفاع عن النفس في أَرْض أندَلُسي
سوف أُدرك، في زمن آخر،
سوف أدرك أني انتصرتُ بيأسي
وأني وجدت حياتي، هنالك
خارجها، قرب أمسي
خذي فَرسي
واذبحيها، لأَحمل نفسيَ حيّاً ومَيْتاً،
بنفسي...

Take My Horse and Slaughter It ...

You, and not my craze with conquest, are my wedding.
I left to myself and its match in your devil self
the freedom to comply with your demands,
take my horse
and slaughter it,
and I will walk like a warrior after defeat
without dream or sense ...
Salaam upon what you desire of fatigue
for the captive prince, and of gold for the maidens
to celebrate the summer. And salaam upon you
abounding with suitors of every jinn and man,
for what you've done to yourself for
yourself: your hairpin breaks
my shield and my sword,
and your shirt button bears in its glare
the secret word of birds of every sort,
take my breath the way a guitar responds
to what you demand of the wind. All of my Andalus
is within your hands, so don't leave a single string
for self-defense in the land of my Andalus.
I will realize, in another time,
I will realize that I have won with my despair
and that I have found my life, over there
outside itself, near my past
take my horse
and slaughter it, and I will carry myself dead and alive,
by myself ...

أَرض الغريبة/أَرض السكينة

فيّ، مثلك، أَرضٌ على حافّة الأَرض
مأهُولَةً بك أو بغيابكِ. لا أَعرفُ
الأُغنيات التي تجْهَشين بها، وأَنا سائرٌ
في ضبابك. فلتَكُنِ الأَرضُ ما
تومئين إليه... وما تفعلينَهْ

جنوبيّةٌ،
لا تكفُّ عن الدَوَران على نفسها
وعليك. لها موعدان قصيران حول
السماء: شتاءٌ وصَيْفٌ. وأَمَّا الربيعُ
وأَطوارهُ، فَهْوَ شَأْنُكِ وَحْدَك.
قُومي إلى أَيَّةِ اُ مرأةٍ فيك تنتشرِ
المرغريتا على كُلّ نافذَةٍ في المدينهْ

مُذهَّبَةٌ،
مثل صَيْفِ الأمير الصغير. وأَمّا
الخريفُ وتأويلُهُ ذَهَباً مُتْعَباً، فهو
شأني أنا، حين أُطعِمُ طَيْرَ الكنائس
خُبْزي. وأنسى وأنتِ تسيرين بين
التماثيل حريَّةَ الـحَجَرِ المرمريّ، وأَتْبَعُ
رائحةَ المندرينهْ

مسافرةٌ،
حول صُورَتها في مراياك: «لا
أُمَّ لي يا ابنَتي فَلِديني هنا»
هكذا تَضَعُ الأَرضُ في جَسَدٍ سرّها،
وتُزوّجُ أُنثى إلى ذَكَرٍ. فخذيني
إليها إليك إليّ. هُنَاكَ هُنا. داخلي
خارجي. وخُذيني لتَسْكُنَ نفسي
إليكِ، وأَسْكُنَ أرضَ السكينهْ

The Stranger's Land / the Serene Land

In me, as in you, a land on the edge of land
populated with you or with your absence. I don't know
the songs you sob, as I pass
through your fog. So let land be
what you gesture to … and what you do

Southerly,
and doesn't cease orbiting around herself
and around you. She has two brief appointments
around the sky: summer and winter. As for spring
and its phases, that's your concern alone:
rise to any woman within you and the margarite
will spread to every window in town

Gilded,
as the little prince's summer. And as
for autumn and its tired gold interpretation, that
is my concern, when I feed the church birds
my bread. And I forget, when you walk among
the statues, the freedom of marble, and I follow
the mandarin scent

Traveling,
around her image in your mirrors: "My daughter
I have no mother so give birth to me here."
That's how the land places in a body her secret,
and weds a woman to a man. Take me
to her to you to me. There here. Inside me
outside me. And take me so that my self is serene
in you, and that I reside in the serene land

سَماويَّةٌ،
لَيْس لي ما أقولُ عن الأرض فيك
سوى ما يقولُ الغريبُ: سَماويَّةٌ ...
رُبَّما يُخْطىءُ الغُرَباءُ بلفظ حُروفٍ آراميَّةٍ.
رُبَّما يَصنَعُون إلهَتَهُمْ من مَوَادَّ
بدائيَّةٍ وَجدوها على ضفَّة النهر،
لكنهُم يُتْقِنُونَ الغناءَ: سماويَّةٌ
هذه الأرضُ مِثْلُ سَحَابٍ خَفيفٍ
تَبَخَّرَ من ياسمينهْ

مجازيَّةٌ،
كالقصيدة قبل الكتابة: «لا أَبَ
لي يا بُنَيَّ، فَلِدْني» تقولُ لي الأرضُ
حين أمرُّ خفيفاً على الأرض، في
لَيْلِ بلُّوْرِك المتلالىء بين الفراشات.
لا دَمَ فوق المحاريثِ. عُذْريَّةٌ تتجدَّدُ
لا اسمَ لما ينبغي أن تكون عليه
الحياةُ سوى ما صَنَعْتِ بروحي وما تصنعينه...

Heavenly,
I have nothing to say about the land in you
other than what the stranger says: Heavenly ...
The strangers might err in pronouncing Aramaic letters,
they might make their gods out of primitive
elements they found on the riverbank,
but they master singing: Heavenly
this land like weightless clouds
evaporated out of jasmine

Metaphorical,
like the poem before writing: "I have no father
my son so give birth to me," the land says to me
when I pass lightly upon the land, in
your shimmering crystal night amid the butterflies.
No blood on the plows. A virginity renewing itself.
There is no name for what life should be
other than what you've made of my soul and what you make ...

حليب إنانا

لَكِ التَوْأمان: لَكِ النثرُ والشعرُ يَتَّحدان، وأَنتِ
تطيرين من زَمَنٍ نحو آخَرَ، سالمةً كاملةٌ
على هَوْدَجٍ من كواكبِ قَتْلاكِ ـــ حُرَّاسِكِ الطّيبين
وَهُمْ يحملّون سماواتِكِ السَبْعَ قافلةً قافلةً.
رُعاةُ خُيُولِكِ بين نخيلِ يَدَيْكِ ونَهرَيْكِ يقتربون
منَ الماء «أُولى الإلهات أكثرُهُنَّ اُ متلاءاً
بنا». خالقٌ عاشقٌ يَتَأَمَّلُ أفعالَهُ، فيُجَنُّ
بها ويَحِنُّ إليها: أأَفعَلُ ثانيةً ما فَعَلْتُ؟
وكُتَّابُ بَرْقِكِ يحترقون بجبْرِ السماء، وأَحفادُهُمْ
يَنْشُرون السنونو على مَوْكبِ السُومريَّةِ...
صاعدةً كانتِ السومريَّةُ، أَمْ نازلة

لَكِ، أَنتِ الـمَديدَة في البَهْو
ذاتِ القميصِ الـمُشَجَّر، والبنطلونِ
الرماديِّ، لا لمِجازِكِ، أُوقِظُ
برِّيَتي، وأَقولُ لنفسي: سيطلع
من عَتْمتي قَـمَـرُ...

دَعي الماءَ ينزلْ من الأُفق السومريّ
علينا، كما في الأَساطير. إنْ كانَ
قلبي صحيحاً كهذا الزجاج المحيطِ بنا
فامْلئيه بغيمِكِ حتى يَعُودَ إلى أهله
غائماً حالماً كصلاةِ الفقير. وإنْ كانَ
قلبي جريحاً فلا تَطْعَنيه بقَرْنِ الغزال،
فلم تَبْقَ حول الفُرَاتِ زهورٌ طبيعيَّةٌ
لـحُلُولِ دمي في الشقائق بعد الحروب.
ولم تَبْقَ في معبدي جَـرَّةٌ لنبيذ الإلهاتِ
في سُومَرَ الأَبديَّة، في سُومَرَ الزائلةْ

لَكِ، أَنتِ الرشيقة في البَهْو
ذاتِ اليَدَيْنِ الـحَريريَّـتَـيْنِ

Inanna's Milk

For you the twins: for you poetry and prose unite, as you
fly from one epoch to another, safe and sound
on a howdah made of your murdered victims' planets—your kind guards
who carry your seven heavens one caravan at a time.
And between the palm trees and your hands' two rivers, your
horse-keepers approach the water: The first goddess is the one most filled
with us. And an infatuated creator contemplates his work, becomes mad
with her and longs for her: Shall I make again what I did before?
The scribes of your lightning burn in the sky's ink, and their offspring
strew the swallows over the Sumerian woman's parade ...
be she ascending, or descending

For you, the one stretched out in the hall
in the forest shirt, and the ashen
pants, not for your metaphor, I awaken
my wilderness, and say to myself: A moon
will rise from my darkness ...

Let the water flow down from the Sumerian horizon
upon us, as in the myths. If my heart
is as straight as this glass surrounding us
then fill it up with your clouds until it returns to its folk
overcast and dreamy like a poor man's prayer. And if my heart
is wounded, don't stab it with a gazelle's horn,
there are no natural flowers left around the Euphrates
for my blood to incarnate in the anemones after the wars.
And there isn't a jar left in my temple for the wine of the goddesses,
in Sumer the eternal, in Sumer the ephemeral

For you, the slender one in the hall
with the silken hands

وخاصرة اللَّهْو،
لا لرموزك،
أُوقظُ بريَّتي، وأقول:
سأستلُّ هذي الغزالَةَ من سرْبها
وأطعن نفسي... بها!

لا أُريد لأُغنيَّة أَن تكون سريرك،
فليَصْقُل الثورُ، ثورُ العراق
الـمُجَنَّحُ قَرْنَيْه بالدَهر والـهَيْكَل الـمُتَصَدِّع
في فضَّة الفجر. وليَحْمِل الموتُ آلَتَهُ
المعدنيَّةَ في جَوْقة المنشدين القُدامى
لشمسٍ نَبُوخَذنَصَّر. أما أنا، المتحدِّر
من غير هذ الزمان، فلا بُدَّ لي
من حصَانٍ يُلائم هذا الزفاف. وإنْ كانَ
لا بُدَّ من قَـمَر فَليكُنْ عالياً... عالياً
ومن صُنع بَـغْدادَ، لا عربيّاً ولا فارسيّاً
ولا تدَّعيه الإلهاتُ من حولنا. وليَكُنْ خالياً
من الذكريات وَخَـمْر الـمُلُوك القدامى،
لنُكْملَ هذا الزفافَ الـمُقَدَّسَ، نكملُهُ يا ابْنَةَ
القمر الأَبَديِّ هنا في المكان الذي نَزَّلْتَهُ
يداكِ على طَرَف الأرض من شُرْفَة الجنَّة الآفلة! ...

لكِ، أنت التي تَـقْرَئيـنَ
الجريدةَ في البَهْو،
أنتِ الـمُصَابة بالإنفلوَنْزا
أقولُ: خُذي كأسَ بابُونج ساخنٍ
وَخُذي حَبَّتَيْ «أسبرين»
ليهدأ فيكِ حليبُ إنانا،
ونعرفَ ما الـزَمَنُ الآن
في مُـلْتَقى الرافدَيْن!

and the frolicking waist,
not for your symbols,
I awaken my wilderness and say:
I will draw this gazelle out of her flock
and stab myself … with it!

I don't want a song to be your bed,
so let the Bull, Iraq's winged Bull, burnish
his horns with the ages on the fissured altar
in the silver of dawn. And let death carry its metal
instrument amid the ancient choir
of Nebuchadnezzar's sun. As for me, the descendant
from without this time, I must have
a suitable horse for this procession. And if
there must be a moon let it be high … high
and made in Baghdad, not Arabic or Persian
and not claimed by any of the gods around us. And let it be empty
of memories and of ancient kings' wine,
for us to complete this holy procession, together, you daughter
of the eternal moon, in this place that your hands brought down
to the edge of the earth from the balcony of the fading paradise! …

For you, the one reading
the newspaper in the hall,
the one sick with influenza
I say: Take one cup of hot chamomile
and two aspirins
for Inanna's milk to quiet in you,
and for us to know what time it is now
at the confluence of the two rivers!

سوناتا [VI]

بِبُطءٍ أمسِّدُ نومَكِ. يا اسمَ الذي أنا فيهِ
من الـحُلْم نامي. سيلتحفُ الليلُ أشجارَهُ، وسيغفو
على أَرضه سيّداً لغياب قليل. ونامي لأُطفو
على نُقَط الضوء ترشَحُّ من قَـمَرٍ أحتويهِ...

يُخيّمُ شَعْرُكِ فوق رُخَامك بَدْواً ينامون سَهْواً
ولا يحلمون. يُضيئُك زَوْجا يَمَامك من كَتِفَيْكِ
إلى أقحوان منامك. نامي عليك وفيك. عليك
سلامُ السماوات والأرض تفتحُ أَبهاءها لَكِ بَهْواً فبهوا

يُغَلِّفُك النوم بي. لا ملائكةٌ يحملون السرير
ولا شَبَحٌ يُوقِظ الياسمينة. يا اسميْ المؤنَّثَ، نامي
فلا نايَ يبْكي على فَرَسٍ هاربٍ من خيامي

كما تحلمين تكونين، يا صَيْفَ أرضٍ شماليَّةٍ
يُخَدِّرُ غاباته الألفَ في سَطْوَة النوم. نامي
ولا توقظي جَسَداً يشتهي جَسَداً في منامي

Sonnet IV

Slowly I massage your sleep. You're the name of what's in me
of dream, so sleep. The night will blanket its trees, and will doze off
on its earth as a master of a brief absence. Sleep and I will float
on drops of light that leak from a moon I enclose ...

Your hair above your marble is a tent for bedouins who absently sleep
and don't dream. Your pair of doves illuminates you from your shoulders
to your daisy sleep. Sleep upon and in yourself. Upon you
the salaam of heaven and earth opening up their halls one by one

Sleep wraps you up with me. No angels carry the bed
and no ghost awakens the jasmine. O my feminine name, sleep
since no flute cries over a mare that escapes my tents

You are as you dream, the summer of a northerly land
anesthetizing its thousand forests in the pounce of sleep. Sleep
and don't awaken a body desiring a body in my sleep

لا أَقل، ولا أكثر

أنا أُمرأةٌ. لا أقلَّ ولا أكثرَ
أعيشُ حياتي كما هِيَ
خَيْطاً فَخَيْطاً
وأغزِلُ صُوفي لألبسَهُ، لا
لأكملَ قصّةَ «هُوميرَ»، أو شمسَهُ
وأرى ما أَرى
كما هُوَ، في شَكْله
بيد أَنّي أُحدّقُ ما بين حينٍ
وآخرَ في ظلّه
لأُحسَّ بنبض الخسارةِ،
فاكتُبْ غداً
على وَرَقِ الأمس: لا صَوْتَ
إلّا الصدى.
أحبُّ الغموضَ الضروريَّ في
كلمات المسافر ليلاً إلى ما اختفى
من الطير فوق سُفُوح الكلام
وفوق سُطُوح القُرى
أنا امرأة، لا أقلَّ ولا أكثرَ

تُطيِّرُني زَهرَةُ اللوز،
في شهر آذار، من شرفتي
حنيناً إلى ما يقول البعيدُ:
«أُلمسيني لأُوردَ خيليَ ماء الينابيع»
أبكي بلا سَبَب واضح، وأُحبُّكَ
أنْتَ كما أنتَ، لا سَنَداً
أو سُدَى
ويطلع من كتفيَّ نهارٌ عليك
ويهبط، حين أضُمُّكَ، ليلٌ إليك
ولستُ بهذا ولا ذاك
لا، لستُ شمساً ولا قمراً
أنا امرأةٌ، لا أقلَّ ولا أكثرَ

No More and No Less

I am a woman. No more and no less
I live my life as it is
thread by thread
and I spin my wool to wear, not
to complete Homer's story, or his sun.
And I see what I see
as it is, in its shape,
though I stare every once
in a while in its shade
to sense the pulse of defeat,
and write tomorrow
on yesterday's sheets: there's no sound
other than echo.
I love the necessary vagueness in
what a night traveler says to the absence
of birds over the slopes of speech
and above the roofs of villages
I am a woman, no more and no less

The almond blossom sends me flying
in March, from my balcony,
in longing for what the faraway says:
"Touch me and I'll bring my horses to the water springs."
I cry for no clear reason, and I love you
as you are, not as a strut
nor in vain
and from my shoulders a morning rises onto you
and falls into you, when I embrace you, a night.
But I am neither one nor the other
no, I am not a sun or a moon
I am a woman, no more and no less

فكُنْ أَنتَ قَيْس الحنين،
إذا شئتَ. أَمَّا أَنا
فيُعجِبُني أَن أُحَبَّ كما أنا
لا صُورَةً
مُلَوَّنَةً في الجريدة، أو فكرةً
مُـلَـحَّنةً في القصيدة بين الأَيائلِ...
أَسْمَعُ صرخة ليلى البعيدة
من غرفة النوم: لا تتركيني
سجينةَ قافيةٍ في ليالي القبائلِ
لا تتركيني لهم خبرا...
أَنا اُ مرأةٌ، لا أَقَلَّ ولا أَكثرَ

أَنا مَن أَنا، مثلما
أَنت مَنْ أَنت: تسكُنُ فيَّ
وأَسكُنُ فيك إليك ولَكْ
أُحبَّ الوضوح الضروريَّ في لغزنا المشترك
أَنا لَكَ حين أَفيضُ عن الليل
لكنني لَسْتُ أَرضاً
ولا سَفَراً
أَنا اُ مرأةٌ، لا أَقَلَّ ولا أَكثرَ

وَتُتْعِبُني
دَوْرَةُ القَمَر الأُنثويّ
فتمرضُ جيتارتي
وَتَراً
وَتَراً
أَنا اُ مرأةٌ،
لا أَقَلَّ
ولا أَكثرَ!

So be the Qyss of longing,
if you wish. As for me
I like to be loved as I am
not as a color photo
in the paper, or as an idea
composed in a poem amid the stags ...
I hear Laila's faraway scream
from the bedroom: Do not leave me
a prisoner of rhyme in the tribal nights
do not leave me to them as news ...
I am a woman, no more and no less

I am who I am, as
you are who you are: you live in me
and I live in you, to and for you
I love the necessary clarity of our mutual puzzle
I am yours when I overflow the night
but I am not a land
or a journey
I am a woman, no more and no less

And I tire
from the moon's feminine cycle
and my guitar falls ill
string
by string
I am a woman,
no more
and no less!

أُغنية زفاف

وانتقلتُ إليكَ، كما انتقل الفلكيّونَ
من كوكبٍ نحو آخرَ. روحي تُطِلُّ
على جسدي من أصابعك العَشْر.
خُذني إليك، انطلق باليمامة حتى
أقاصي الهديل على جانبيك: المدى
والصدى. وَدَع الـخَيْلَ تركُضْ ورائي
سدى. فأنا لا أَرى صورتي، بَعْدُ،
في مائها... لا أَرى أحدا

لا أَرى أَحداً، لا أَراكَ. فماذا
صنعتَ بحريتي؟ مَنْ أنا خلف
سُور المدينة؟ لا أُمٌّ تعجنُ شَعْري
الطويلَ بحنّائها الأبديّ، ولا أُخْتَ
تضفرهُ. مَنْ أنا خارج السور بين
حقول حياديّة وسماء رماديّةٍ. فلتكن
أَنتَ أُمِّيَ في بَلَد الغُرَبَاء. وخذني
برفق إلى مَنْ أكونُ غدا

مَنْ أكونُ غداً؟ هل سأُولَدُ من
ضلعك اُ مرأةً لا هُمُومَ لها غيرُ زينةِ
دُنْيَاكَ. أمْ سوف أبكي هناك على
حَجَرٍ كان يُرْشِدُ غيمي إلى ماء بئرك؟
خذني إلى آخر
الأرض قبل طلوع الصباح على قَمَرٍ كان
يبكي دماً في السرير، وخُذْني برفق
كما تأخُذُ النجمةُ الحالمين إليها سُدىً
وسُدى

وسدىً، أتطلّعُ خلف جبال مُؤَابٍ،
فلا ريح تُرْجِعُ ثوب العروس. أُحبُّكَ
لكنَّ قلبي يرنّ برجع الصدى ويحنُّ
إلى سَوْسَنٍ آخر. هل هنالك حُزْنٌ أشَدُّ

Wedding Song

And I moved into you, as astronomers move
from one planet to another. My soul looks upon
my body through your ten fingers.
Take me to you, dash off with the dove to
the remoteness of cooing on your two sides: expanse
and echo. And let the horses run after me
in vain. Because I do not, yet, see my image
in its water ... I see no one

I see no one, I do not see you. What
have you done with my freedom? Who am I
behind the city wall? No mother kneads my long
hair with her eternal henna, and no sister
braids it. Who am I outside the wall between
neutral fields and an ashen sky. Be
my mother in the stranger's land. And take me
gently to who I become tomorrow

Who do I become tomorrow? Will I be born
out of your rib a woman without worry except to adorn
your life. Or will I cry over there on a rock
that used to guide my clouds to your water well?
Take me to the end
of the earth before morning rises on a moon that used
to cry blood in bed, and take me gently
as a star takes the dreamers in vain

And in vain, I look behind Moab's mountains,
since no wind brings back the bride's dress. I love you
but my heart resonates with echo's return and longs
for another iris. Is there a sorrow more

التباساً على النفس من فَرَح البنت
في عُرْسها؟ وأُحبك مهما تذكّرْتُ
أمسٍ، ومهما تذكرتُ أني نسيتُ
الصدى في الصدى

أَلصدى في الصدى، وانتقلتُ إليكَ
كما انتقلَ الاسمُ من كائنٍ نحو آخر.
كنا غريبين في بلدين بعيدينِ قبل قليل،
فماذا أكون غداةَ غد عندما أُصبحُ
اثنين؟ ماذا صَنَعْتَ بحُريَّتي؟ كلما
ازداد خوفَ منك اندفعتُ إليك،
ولا فضل لي يا حبيبي الغريب سوى
وَلَعي، فلتكن ثعلباً طيّباً في كرومي،
وحدِّق بخُضْرة عينيك في وجعي. لن
أعود إلى اُ سمي وبرِّيتي، أَبداً
أَبداً
أَبدا.

confusing than a woman's happiness
on her wedding night? And I love you no matter how often I remember
my yesterday, no matter how often I remember that I forget
the echo in echo

Echo in echo, and I moved into you
as a name moves from one creature to another.
We were two strangers in two faraway lands a while ago,
so what will I be tomorrow when I become
two? What have you done with my freedom? Whenever
my fear of you mounts I rush into you,
my beloved stranger, since my ardent desire
is my only credit. So be a kind fox in my vineyard
and stare with the green of your eye into my ache. I
won't return to my name and my wilderness, never
never
never.

تدبير منزلي

١

كم أَنا
في الصباح ذهبتُ إلى سوق يوم
الخميس. اشتريتُ حوائجنا المنزليّة،
واخترتُ أُوركيدَةً وبعثتُ الرسائل.
بلّلني مَطرٌ فامتلأتُ برائحة البرتقالة.
هل قُلْتَ لي مَرَّةً إنني نَخْلَةٌ حاملٌ،
أَم تخيّلْتُ ذلك؟ إن لم تجدني
أَرِفُّ عليك، فلا تَخْشَ ضَعْفَ الهواءِ،
وَنَمْ يا حبيبيَ نَوْمَ الهنا...

٢

كم أَنا؟
في الظهيرة، لَمّعْتُ كُلَّ مراباي. أَعددتُ
نفسي لعيدٍ سعيدٍ. ونهدايَ، فَرْخا
حمام لياليك ممتلئان بشهوة أَمس.
أَرى في عُروق الرخام حليبَ الكلام
الإباحي يجري ويصرخ بالشُّعَراء
أُكتبوني، كما قال ريتسوس. أَين
اختفيت وأَخفيت منفايَ عن رغبتي؟
لا أَرى صُورَتي في المرايا، ولا صُورَةَ
أُ مرأةٍ من نساء أَثينا تُديرُ تَدَابيرَها
العاطفيّةَ مثلي هُنا.

٣

كم أَنا؟
في المساء، ذهبتُ إلى السينما
مع إحدى الصديقات. كان الـهُنُودُ
القدامى يطيرون في زمن الحرب والسلم

Housework

1

How often
did I go in the morning to Thursday's
market. I bought our house supplies,
and chose an orchid and mailed the letters.
A rain made me wet and filled me with the scent of oranges.
Did you tell me once that I was a pregnant palm tree,
or did I imagine that? If you don't find me
fanning you, don't fear the feeble air,
and sleep, my love, a blissful sleep …

2

How often?
At noon, I brandished my mirrors. I prepared
myself for a happy feast. And my breasts, your nights'
baby doves, were filling with yesterday's lust.
I see in the marble veins the milk of licentious
talk running and screaming at the poets:
Write me, as Ritsos said. Where
have you hidden yourself
and hidden my exile from my desire?
I do not see my image in mirrors, or the image
of a woman from Athens running her emotional
errands as I do here

3

How often?
In the evening, I went to the cinema
with one of my girlfriends. The ancient American Indians
were flying in the time of war and peace

كالشُّهُب الأَثريَّة، مثلي ومثلك.
حدَّقْتُ في طائرٍ فرأيتُ جناحَيْكَ
يرتديان جناحيَّ في شجر الأكاليبتوس.
ها نحن ننجو نجاة الغبار من
النهر. مَنْ كان فينا الضحيّةَ فليُحلُم
الآن أكثرَ من غيره، بيننا.

٤

كم أَنا؟
بعد مُنْتَصفِ الليل، أَشْرَقَت
الشمسُ في دمنا
كم أنا أنْتَ، يا صاحبي
كم أنا! مَنْ أَنا!

like antique meteors, like you and me.
I stared at a bird and I saw your wings
wearing my wings in eucalyptus trees.
We are rescued here the way dust is rescued
from the river. Whoever the victim is between us should dream
now, more than the other

4

How often?
After midnight, the sun rose
in our blood,
how much of me is you, my love
how often! Who am I!

سوناتا [V]

أَمسُّكِ مَسَّ الكمان الوحيد ضواحي المكان البعيد
على مَهلٍ يطلب النهرُ حصّته من رذاذ المطرْ
ويدنو، رويداً رويداً، غَـدٌ عابرٌ في القصيد
فأحملُ أرضَ البعيد وتحملني في طريق السفرْ

على فَرَسٍ من خصالك تنسجُ روحي
سماء طبيعيّة من ظلالك، شرنقةً شرنقةْ
أنا اُبن فعالك في الأرض، و إبنُ جروحي
وقد أَشعلَتْ وحدها جُـلَّـنَارَ بساتينك المغلقة

من الياسمين يسيل دمُ الليل أَبيضَ. عطرُكِ
ضعفي وسرُّكِ، يتبعني مثل لدغة أفعى. وشَعْرُكِ
خيمةُ ريح خريفيّة اللونِ. أمشي أَنا والكلامْ
إلى آخر الكَلمات التي قالها بدويٌّ لزوجي حمام

أجسُّكِ جَسَّ الكمان حريرَ الزمان البعيدْ
وينبت حولي وحولك عُشْبُ مكانٍ قديمٍ ــ جديدْ

Sonnet V

I touch you as a lonely violin touches the suburbs of the faraway place
patiently the river asks for its share of the drizzle
and, bit by bit, a tomorrow passing in poems approaches
so I carry faraway's land and it carries me on travel's road

On a mare made of your virtues, my soul weaves
a natural sky made of your shadows, one chrysalis at a time.
I am the son of what you do in the earth, son of my wounds
that have lit up the pomegranate blossoms in your closed-up gardens

Out of jasmine the night's blood streams white. Your perfume,
my weakness and your secret, follows me like a snakebite. And your hair
is a tent of wind autumn in color. I walk along with speech
to the last of the words a bedouin told a pair of doves

I palpate you as a violin palpates the silk of the faraway time
and around me and you sprouts the grass of an ancient place—anew

طائران غريبان في ريشنا

سمائي رماديَّةٌ. حُكَّ ظهري. وفُكَّ
على مَهَلٍ، يا غريبُ، جدائلَ شعري. وقُلْ
ليَ في مَ تَّفَكِّرُ. قُلْ ليَ ما مَرَّ
في بال يُوسُفَ. قل ليَ بعضَ الكلام
البسيط... الكلام الذي تشتهي اُمرأةٌ
أن يُقَالَ لها دائماً. لا أريدُ العبارةَ
كاملةً. أكتفي بالإشارة تنثُرُني في مَهَبِّ
الفراشاتِ بين الينابيع والشمس. قل لي
إنِّي ضروريَّةٌ لَكَ كالنوم، لا لامتلاء
الطبيعة بالماء حولي وحولك. وأبسُطْ
عليَّ جناحاً من الأزرق اللانهائيِّ...
إنَّ سمائي رماديَّةٌ،
ورماديَّةٌ مثل لَوْح الكتابة، قبل
الكتابة. فاُكتُبْ عليها بحبر دمي أَيَّ
شيء يُغيِّرُها: لفظةً... لفظتين بلا
هَدَفٍ مُشرِف في المجاز. وقُلْ إنَّنا
طائرانِ غريبانِ في أرض مصرَ وفي
الشام.
قل إننا طائرانِ غريبان في
ريشنا. واكتُبْ اُسميَ و اُسمَكَ تحت
العبارة. ما الساعة الآن؟ ما لَوْنُ
وجهي ووجهك فوق المرايا الجديدة؟
ما عُدْت أملكُ شيئاً ليُشْبِهَني. هل
أحبَّتك سيِّدةُ الماء أكثرَ؟ هل راوَدَتْك
على صخرة البحر عن نفسِكَ، اُعْتَرِف
الآن أَنَّكَ مَدَّدْتَ تِيهَكَ عشرين عاماً
لتبقى أَسيرَ يديها. وقُلْ ليَ في مَ
تُفَكِّرُ حين تصيرُ السماءُ رماديَّة اللون...
إنَّ سمائي رماديَّةٌ
صرتُ اُشْبهُ ما ليس يشبهني.
هل تريدُ الرجوع إلى ليل منفاك

Two Stranger Birds in Our Feathers

My sky is ashen. Scratch my back. And undo
slowly, you stranger, my braids. And tell me
what's on your mind. Tell me what crossed
Youssef's mind. Tell me some simple
talk ... the talk a woman always desires
to be told. I don't want the phrase
complete. Gesture is enough to scatter me in the rise
of butterflies between springheads and the sun. Tell me
I am necessary for you like sleep, and not like nature
filling up with water around you and me. And spread
over me an endless blue wing ...
My sky is ashen,
as a blackboard is ashen, before
writing on it. So write with my blood's ink anything
that changes it: an utterance ... two, without
excessive aim at metaphor. And say we are
two stranger birds in Egypt
and in Syria. Say we are two stranger birds
in our feathers. And write my name and yours
beneath the phrase. What time is it now? What color
are my face and yours in new mirrors?
I own nothing for anything to resemble me.
Did the water mistress love you more? Did she seduce you
by the sea rock? Confess now
that you have extended your wilderness twenty years
to stay prisoner in her hands. And tell me of what
you think when the sky is ashen ...
My sky is ashen
I resemble what no longer resembles me.
Do you want to return to your exile night
in a mermaid's hair? Or do you want to return

في شَعْر حُوريّةٍ؟ أَم تريد الرجوع
إلى تين بيتك. لا عَسَلٌ جارحٌ للغريب
هنا أو هناك. فما الساعَةُ الآن؟
ما اُ سمُ المكان الذي نحن فيه؟ وما
الفرق بين سمائي وأرضك. قل لِيَ
ما قال آدَمُ في سره. هل تَـحَرَّرَ
حين تَذَكَّرَ. قل أيِّ شيء يُغَيِّر لون
السماء الرمادي. قُلْ لِيَ بعضَ الكلام
البسيط، الكلام الذي تَشتهي اُ مرأةٌ
أَن يُقال لها بين حيـنٍ وآخرَ. قُلْ
إنَّ في وسع شخصين، مثلي ومثلك،
أَن يحملا كل هذا التشابه بين الضباب
وبين السراب، وأَن يَرْجِعا سالمين. سمائي
رماديَّةٌ، فبماذا تفكِّرُ حين تكونُ السماءُ
رماديَّةً؟

to your home figs. For no honey wounds a stranger
here or there. What time is it now?
What's the name of this place we're in? And what's
the difference between my sky and your land. Tell me
what Adam said in secret to himself. Was he emancipated
when he remembered. Tell me anything that changes the sky's
ashen color. Tell me some simple
talk, the talk a woman desires
to be told every now and then. Say
that two people, like you and me,
can carry all this resemblance between fog
and mirage, then safely return. My sky
is ashen, so what do you think of when the sky
is ashen?

لم أَنتظر أحداً

سأعرفَ، مهما ذَهَبْتَ مَعَ الريح، كيفَ
أعيدُكَ. أَعرفُ من أَين يأتي بعيدُكَ.
فاذهَبْ كما تذهبُ الذكرياتُ إلى بئرها
الأَبديّة، لن تَجِدَ السومريّةَ حاملةً جَرّة
للصدى في انتظارك
أمّا أنا، فسأَعرف كيف أُعيدُكَ
فاذهبْ تقودُكَ ناياتُ أهل البحار القدامى
وقافلةُ الملح في سَيْرها اللانهائيِّ. واذهبْ
نشيدُكَ يُفْلِتُ منّي ومنك ومن زَمَني،
باحثاً عن حصان جديد يُرَقِّصُ إيقاعَهُ
الـحُرّ. لن تجد المستحيلَ، كما كان يَوْمَ
وَجَدْتُكَ، يوم وَلَدْتُكَ من شهوتي
جالساً في انتظارك،
أمّا أنا، فسأَعرف كيف أُعيدُكَ،
واذهب مع النهر من قَدَرٍ نحو
آخر، فالريحُ جاهزةٌ لاقتلاعك من
قمري، والكلامُ الأَخيرُ على شجري جاهزٌ
للسقوط على ساحة التروكاديرو. تَلَفَّتْ
وراءك كي تجد الـحُلْمَ، واذهب
إلى أيِّ شَرقٍ وغرب يزيدُك منفىً،
ويُبْعِدُني خطوةً عن سريري وإحدى
سماوات نفسي الحزينة. إنَّ النهاية
أختُ البداية، فاذهبْ تَجِدْ ما تركتَ
هنا، في انتظارك
لم أنتظرْكَ، ولم أنتظر أحداً.
كان لا بُدَّ لي أَن أُمشّطَ شعري
على مَهَلٍ أُسْوةً بالنساء الوحيدات
في ليلهنَّ، وأَن أَتدبّرَ أَمري، وأَكسرَ
فوق الرخام زجاجةَ ماء الكولونيا، وأَمنعَ
نفسي من الانتباه إلى نفسها في
الشتاء، كأَني أَقولُ لها: دَفِّئيني

I Waited for No One

I'll know, no matter how often you go with the wind, how
to bring you back. I'll know from where your faraway comes.
So go as memories go to their endless
wells, you won't find a Sumerian woman carrying an urn
of echo waiting for you.
    As for me, I'll know how to bring you back
so go led by the flutes of ancient sea peoples
and by salt caravans in their endless march. And go
while your anthem slips away from me and you and from my time,
and search for a new horse that makes its free rhythm
dance. You won't find the impossible, as it was
the day I found you, the day my passion birthed you,
waiting for you,
    as for me, I'll know how to bring you back.
And go with the river from one fate
to another, the wind is ready to uproot you
from my moon, and the last words on my trees
are ready to fall on Trocadero square. And look
behind you to find the dream, go
to any east or west that exiles you more,
and keeps me one step farther from my bed
and from one of my sad skies. The end
is beginning's sister, go and you'll find what you left
here, waiting for you.
    I did not wait for you, I waited for no one.
I should have combed my hair
slowly in the manner of lonely women
in their nights, pondered my needs, broken
a bottle of perfume over the marble, and prevented
myself from attention to herself
in winter, as if I were telling her: Warm me up

أُدفِّئْكِ يا اُ مرآتي، واُعْتَني بيديك،
فما هو شأنُهما بنزول السماء إلى
الأرض أو رحْلةِ الأرض نحو السماء،
اُ عتني بيديك لكي تَحْملاكِ «يَدَاكِ
هُما سَيِّداك» كما قال إيلوار.. فاذهب
أريدُكَ أو لا أريدُك.

لمْ أنتظِرْكَ، ولم أنتظر أحداً.
كان لا بُدَّ لي أَن أَصبَّ النبيذَ
بكأسين مكسورتين، وأَمنعَ نفسي من
الانتباه إلى نفسها في انتظارك!

my woman and I'll warm you up, take care of your hands,
for what's their concern with heaven's descent
to earth or earth's journey to heaven,
take care of your hands so that they carry you: "Your hands
are your masters" as Éluard said … So go
I want you or I don't want you

    I did not wait for you, I waited for no one.
I should have poured some wine
in two broken glasses, and prevented myself
from attention to herself while waiting for you!

جفاف

هذه سَنَةٌ صَعْبَةٌ
لم يَعِدْنا الخريف بشيءٍ
ولم ننتظرْ رُسُلاً
والجفافُ كما هُوَ: أرضٌ مُعَذَّبَةٌ
وسماءٌ مُذَهَّبَةٌ،
فليكُنْ جَسَدي مَعْبَدي

... وَعَلَيْكَ الوُصُولُ إلى خبز روحي
لتعرف نفسَكَ. لا حدَّ لي
إن أَردتُ:
أُوَسِّعُ حقلي بسنبلةٍ
وأوسِّعُ هذا الفضاء بَتَرْغَلَّةٍ،
فليكن جَسَدي بَلَدي

والجفاف يُحَدِّقُ في النهر،
أو يتطلَّعُ نحو النخيلِ
ويُخْطِىءُ بئري العميقة،
لا حَدَّ لي بكَ...
إنَّ السماءَ حقيقيَّةٌ في الخريف
تخيَّلْ، ولو مَرَّةً، أنَّكَ اُ مرأةٌ
لترى ما أرى.
جسدي سيِّدي

والجفافُ على حاله:
كُلَّما جَفَّتِ الفكرةُ ازدهَرَتْ جوقةُ
المنشدين المريدين: ماء، وماء
فما حاجتي للنُّبوءةِ؟ إنَّ الملائكةَ
الطيِّبين ضيوفٌ على غيمة الحالمين.
وما حاجتي لكتابِكَ ما دام ما بكَ... بي؟
جَسَدي يَتَفَتَّحُ في جَسَدي

Drought

This is a difficult year
autumn promised us nothing
we waited for no messengers
and the drought remains the same: a tortured land
and a gilded sky,
so let my body be my temple

… but you must arrive to my soul's bread
to know yourself. There is no limit to me.
If I want:
I widen my field with a grain of wheat
and widen this space with a turtledove,
let my body be my country

And the drought stares into the river,
or looks toward the palm trees
and misses my deep well,
there is no limit to me with you …
the sky is real in autumn.
Just imagine, if only once, you were a woman
to see what I see.
My body is my master

And the drought remains the same: whenever
the idea dries up, the choir
of suitors prospers: water, water
so what's my need for prophecy? The kind
angels are the guests of the dreamer's cloud.
And what's my need for your book
as long as what's in you … is in me?
My body blooms in mine

والجفافُ يودِّعُ سَبْعَ السنين العجاف
فلا بُدَّ من هُـدْنَة في المدينة،
لا بُدَّ من ماعز يَقْضِمُ العُشْبَ
من كُتُب البابليين أو غيرهم،
كي تصير السماءُ حقيقيةً...
فأُضيءْ عَتْمتي ودمي بنبيذكَ
وأسْكُنْ، معي، جسدي!

And the drought bids the seven emaciated years farewell
because there must be a truce in the city,
there must be goats that gnaw at the grass
of Babylonian and other books,
for the sky to become real ...
So light up my darkness and blood with your wine
and reside, in my body, with me!

سوناتا [IV]

صُنَـوْبَرَةٌ في يمينك. صَفْصَافَةٌ في شمالك. هذا
هُوَ الصيفِ: إحدى غزالاتك المائة استسلمت للندى
ونامت على كَتِفي، قُرْبَ إحدى جهاتك، ماذا
لو انتبَهَ الذئبُ، واحترقتْ غابةٌ في المدى

نعاسُك أقوى من الخوف. بريَّةٌ من جمالك
تغفو، ويصحو ليحرس أشجارَها قمرٌ من ظلالك
ما اُ سمُ المكان الذي وَشَمَتْهُ خُطاك على الأرض
أرضاً سماويَّة لسلام العَـصَافير، قرب الصدى؟

وأقوى من السيف نومُك بين ذراعيك مُـنْسَابَتَيْن
كنهريـنِ في جنّة الحالميـنَ بما تصنعيـنَ على الجانبين
بنفسِك محمولةً فوق نفسك. قد يحمل الذئبُ ناياً
ويبكي على ضفّة النهر: ما لم يُـؤَنَّثْ... سُـدَى

قليلٌ من الضعف في الاستعارة يكفي غدا
لينضج توتُ السياج، وينكسرَ السَـيْفُ تحت الندى

Sonnet VI

A pine tree in your right hand. A willow in your left. This
is summer: one of your hundred gazelles has surrendered to the dew
and slept on my shoulder, near one of your regions, and what
if the wolf notices, and a forest burns in the distance

Your sleepiness is stronger than fear. A wilderness of your beauty
dozes off, and a moon out of your shadows wakes to guard its trees.
What's the name of the place your footsteps tattooed on the ground
a heavenly ground for the salaam of the birds, near echo?

And stronger than the sword is your sleep between your streamlined arms,
like two rivers, in the dreamer's paradise, of what you do on the banks
to yourself carried above yourself. The wolf might carry a flute
and cry by the river: What isn't feminized ... is in vain

A bit of weakness in metaphor is enough for tomorrow
for the berries to ripen on the fence, and for the sword to break beneath
        the dew

رزق الطيور

رُزقتُ مع الخبز حُبَّـك
ولا شأن لي بمصيريَ،
ما دام قُرْبَك
فخُذهُ إلى أيِّ معنى تريدُ
معي، أو وحيداً
ولا بَيْتَ أقرَبَ مـمَّا أُحِسُّ به
هـهُنا في الربيع السريع
على شجر الآخرين...

رُزقْتُكَ أُمّاً، أَباً، صاحباً
وأَخاً للطريق، ولا تحمل الطَّيْرُ
أكثرَ من وُسْعها: ريشَها والحنين
وحبَّةَ قمح ضروريَّةً للغناء، فكن
في سمائي كِّما
أنا في سمائك، أو بعض ذلك،
كُنْ يا غريب الـمُوَشَّح لي. مثلما
أنا لَكَ: مائي لمائك، ملحي
لملحك، و أُسمي على اسمكَ تعويذةٌ
قد تُقَرِّبنا من تلال سَمَرقَنْدَ
في عصرها الذهبيِّ. فلا بُدَّ مني
ولا بُـدَّ منك، ولا بُـدَّ من آخرين
لنسمع أبواق إخوتنا السابقين
وهم يمتطون ظهور الخيول، من الجانبين
ولا يرجعون. فكن يا غريبُ سلامَ
الغريبةِ في هُـدْنَةِ الـمُـتْـعَبين
وكن حُلْمَ يقظتها، كُلَّما
ألَـمَّ بها قَـمَرٌ عائدٌ من أَريحا، كما
تعود الإلهاتُ بعد الحروب إلى الحالمين
فكُلُّ هُنَاكَ هنا. وأنا
لا أُحبّ الرجوع إلى نجمتي
بعدما كبرت حكمتي، هاتِ

The Subsistence of Birds

Along with bread, I was given your love to subsist on
and my fate isn't my concern
as long as you are near
so take this to any meaning you want
with me, or alone
for no home is closer than what I feel
right here in this swift spring
on others' trees ...

You were given to me as mother, father, friend
and brother for the road, and no bird
bears more than it can: its feathers and its longing
and a grain of wheat necessary for song, so be
in my sky as I am
in your sky, or something like it,
be, you stranger to the muwashah, mine. As I am
yours: my water is for your water, my salt
is for your salt, and my name upon your name is an amulet
that might draw us near the hills of Samarkand
in its golden age. Because you and I
are inevitable, and others are inevitable
for us to hear the trumpets of our previous brothers
when they mount their horses, from either side,
and never return. Be, stranger, another stranger's
salaam in the truce of the weary
and be her daydream, whenever
a moon suffers her on its way back from Jericho, the way
goddesses return after the wars to the dreamers
since every there is here. And I
don't love coming back to my star
now that my wisdom is older, so bring

هات البعيد إلى خيمتي سُـلّماً
لنصعد أعلى كـغُـضْـنَيْ بَتُولا على
حائط الآخرين [ونحن نصير غداً آخرين]
فلا بَـيْـتَ أقرَبَ مما أُحسُّ به هـهنا
وأنا حاملٌ بالربيع السريع
رَزقت مع الخبز حُبَّكْ
ولا شأن لي بمصيرِيَ
ما دام قُـرْبَكْ
ويا ليتني لم أُحبَّك
يا ليتني لم أُحبَّكْ!

the faraway to my tent as a ladder
we can climb on higher like two branches of a birch tree
on others' walls (and we'll become others tomorrow).
For no home is closer than what I feel right here
while I'm pregnant with this swift spring.
Along with bread I gave sustenance to your love
and my fate isn't my concern
as long as you are near
and I wish I never loved you
I wish I never loved you!

رُبَّما، لأَن الشتاء تأخَّر

١

أَقَلُّ من الليل تحت الـمَطَر
حنينٌ خُـمَاسِيّة
إلى أمسها الـمُنْتَظَر،
وأكثرُ مـمّا تقول يَدٌ لِيَد
على عَجَلٍ في مَهَبِّ السَفَر

٢

شماليّةٌ هذه الريحُ
فليكتب العاطفيّون، أَهـلُ الكلام الجريح،
رسائلَ أُخرى إلى ما وراءَ الطبيعةِ
أَمّا أَنا
فَسَأُرمي بنفسيْ إلى الريح.../

٣

لا لَيْلَ عنْدَك، إذ تَدْلِفيـنَ
إلى الليل وَحْدَك. أَنت هُنا
تَكسرينَ بنظرتِك الوَقْتَ. أَنتِ
هنا في مكانك بعدي وبعدك
لا أَنْتِ تنتظرين، ولا أَحَـدٌ يَنْتَظِرْ

٤

لَعَـلَّ خيالِيَ أَوضحُ من واقعي
والرياحُ شماليّةٌ. لن أُحبَّك أكْثَرَ
إنْ لم تكوني معي
هنا، الآن ما بين أَيْقُونَتَيْنِ
وجيتارةٍ فَتَحَتْ جُرْحَها للقَـمَرْ

Maybe, Because Winter Is Late

1

Less than the night beneath the rain
is a pentad's longing
for its awaited past,
but more than what a hand says to a hand
in the hurry of travel's draft

2

Northerly is the wind
so let the sentimentalists, kin of wounded talk, write
other letters to nature's beyond
as for me
I'll throw myself to the wind ... /

3

You have no night, when you saunter
toward the night alone. You are here
breaking time with your look. You
are still here in place after me and you
neither you wait, nor anyone waits

4

Perhaps my imagination is more lucid than my reality
and the winds are northerly. I won't love you more
if you are not with me
here, now between two icons
and a guitar that has opened its wound to the moon

٥

أنا والمسيحُ على حالنا:
يَموتُ ويحيا، وفي نَفْسه مريمُ
وأحيا، وأَحْلُـمْ ثانيةً أنني أَحلُـمُ
ولكنَّ حُـلمي سريعٌ كبرقيَّةٍ
تُـذَكِّرُني بالأُخُـوَّةِ بين السماوات والأرض.../

٦

مِنْ غَـيْرِ قَـصْدٍ،
يصيرُ الحصى لُغَةً أو صدى
والعواطفُ في مُـتَـنَاوَلِ كُلِّ يَدٍ.
ربما كان هذا الحنينُ طريقَـتَنا في البقاء
ورائحة العُـشْب بعد الـمَطَرْ

٧

بلا غايةٍ، وَضَـعَـتْـنَا السماءُ
على الأرض إلْـفَـيْـن مؤتلفين وباسمين مُـخْـتَـلِفَـيْنِ،
فلا اسميَ كان يُـزَيِّنُ خاتَـمَكِ الذهبيَّ
ولا اسْـمُكِ كان يَرِنُّ
كقافيةٍ في كتاب الأَساطير.../

٨

أمثالُنا لا يموتون حُـبّاً،
ولو مَـرَّةً، في الغناء الحديث الخفيف
ولا يقفون، وحيدين، فوق الرصيف
لأنَّ القطارات أكثرُ من عَـدَد الـمُـفْـرَدَات
وفي وُسْعنا دائماً أن نُـعِيدَ النظَرْ

5

Christ and I are as we've been:
he dies and lives, Mary within him
and I live, and I dream again that I dream
but my dream is quick like a telegraph
reminding me of the brotherhood between earth and sky ... /

6

Unintentionally,
pebbles become language or echo
and emotions are within every hand's reach.
Maybe this longing is our way of surviving
and the smell of grass after rain

7

Without purpose, the sky placed us
on earth as two harmonious intimates with two different names,
so that my name would not adorn your gold ring
nor would your name ring
as a rhyme in the book of myth ... /

8

The likes of us don't die, not even once,
from being in love with the nimble modern song
and they don't stand alone on the sidewalk
because trains are more numerous than words
and we can always reconsider

٩

وأمثالُنا لا يعودون إلّا
لِيَسْتَحْسِنُوا وَقْعَ أقدامهم
على أرض أحلامهم،
أو ليعتذروا للطفولة عن حِكْمَةٍ
بلغوها على حافة البئر.../

١٠

بي مثلُ ما بِكِ من وَحَم الليلِ
يصرُخُ شَخْصٌ: «أنا اُ مرأتي
في المنام. وتصرخ أُنثى: «أنا رَجُلي»
أَيُّنا أنتَ. أنت؟ نَضيقُ
نَضيقُ، ويتّسعُ الـمُنْحَدَرْ.../

١١

أَضُمُّك، حتى أعود إلى عَدَمي
زائراً زائلاً. لا حياةَ ولا
موتَ في ما أُحسُّ بهِ
طائراً عابراً ما وراء الطبيعة
حين أَضُمُّكِ.../

١٢

ماذا سنفعلُ بالـحُبِّ؟ قُلْتِ
ونحن ندسُّ ملابسنا في الحقائب
نأخذه مَعَنا، أَمْ نُعَلِّقُهُ في الخزانةِ؟
قلتُ: لِيَذهَبْ إلى حيثُ شاءَ
فقد شبَّ عن طَوْقِنا، وانتشرْ

9

And the likes of us return only
to approve of their footsteps
on their dreamland,
or to apologize to childhood about a wisdom
they reached at the edge of the well ... /

10

I have in me what's in you of night's craving.
A man screams in his sleep: "I am my woman!"
And a woman screams: "I am my man."
Which one of us are you? You? We become narrow
narrow, and the descent widens ... /

11

I embrace you, until I return to my void
as an eternal visitor. No life and no
death in what I sense
as a bird passing beyond nature
when I embrace you ... /

12

What will we do with love? you said
while we were packing our suitcases
do we take it with us, or hang it in the closet?
I said: Let it go wherever it wants
it has already outgrown our collar and spread

١٣

هَشَاشَتُنا لُؤْلُؤُ الخاسرين
وأمثالنا لا يزورون حاضرَهُمْ أبداً
لا يريدون أن يبلغوا بلداً
في الطريق إلى الريح، حيث وُلدنا
على دفعتين: أنا وجمالُك.../

١٤

قرْبَ حياتي نَبَتُّ كإحدى
حدائق قَيْصَرَ. كَمْ تَرَكَ الأقوياءُ
لنا شجراً. كَمْ قطفتُ زنابقَ
سريَّةً من سياجك. كَمْ كنتِ
معنى وصورتَه في أعالي الشَجَرْ

١٥

أضمُّك، بيضاءَ سمراءَ، حتى التلاشي
أُبَعْثِرُ لَيْلَك. ثـمَّ ألُمُّك كُلَّك...
لا شيءَ فيك يزيدُ وينقُصُ عن
جَسَدي. أنت أُمُّك وابنتُها
تُولَدِين كما تطلبين من الله.../

١٦

ماذا سنصنع بالأمس؟ قُلتِ
ونحن نُهيل الضباب على غدنا
والفُنُونُ الحديثةُ ترمي البعيدَ إلى
سلّة المهملات. سيتبعُنا الأمْسُ،
قلتُ، كما يتبع النَهَوَنْدُ الوَتَرْ

13

Our fragility is the pearl of losers.
The likes of us never visit their present
and don't want a country
on the road to the wind, where we were born
in two thrusts: your beauty and I ... /

14

Near my life you sprouted as one
of Caesar's gardens. How often have the mighty left
trees for us. How often have I picked lilies
secretly off your fence. How often were you
a meaning and its image at treetops

15

I embrace you, dark white, until vanishing
I scatter your night. Then I gather you whole ...
Nothing in you is more or less than
my body. You are your mother and her daughter
you are born as you ask of god ... /

16

What will we do with yesterday? you said
while we were heaping the fog upon our tomorrow
and the modern arts were throwing the faraway into
the trash canister. Yesterday will follow us,
I said, as the nahawand follows the string

١٧

على الجسر، قُرْب حياتِكِ، عشتُ
كما عاش عازفُ جيتارةٍ قرب نجمته.
غنِّ لي مائةً من أناشيدَ حُبِّكَ تَـدْخُلْ
حياتي! فغنِّ عن الحبِّ تسعاً
وتسعين أُغنيَّةً، وانتحرْ

١٨

يمرُّ الزمانُ بنا، أو نمرُّ به
كضيوفٍ على حنطة الله
في حاضرٍ سابقٍ، حاضرٍ لاحق،
هكذا هكذا نحن في حاجة للخرافة
كي نتحـمَّلَ عبءَ المسافة ما بَـيْن بابين.../

١٩

منفىً سخيٌّ على حافَّة الأرض
لَـوْ لم تكوني هُـنَاكَ لَـمَـا
أنشأ الـغُـرَبَاءُ القلاعَ وشاعَ التصوُّفُ،
لو لم تكوني هنا لاكتَـفَـيْـتُ بما
يصنعُ النهرُ بي... وبوجه الـحَـجَرْ

٢٠

ويكفي، لأعرفَ نفسيْ البعيدةَ، أَن
تُـرْجعي ليَ بَـرْقَ القصيدةِ حين انقسمتُ
إلى اُ ثنين في جَسَدك
أنا لَكِ مِـثْـلُ يَدكْ
فما حاجتي لغدي
بعد هذا السفر؟

17

On the bridge, near your life, I lived
as a guitar player lived near his star.
Sing for me, she said, a hundred of your love songs
and you will enter my life! So he sang ninety-
nine songs about love, then killed himself

18

Time passes through us, or we pass through it
as guests to god's wheat.
In a previous present, a subsequent present,
just like that, we are in need of myth
to bear the burden of the distance between two doors ... /

19

A generous exile on the edge of the earth.
Had you not been there the strangers would not have
built their castles nor would Sufism have spread,
had you not been here I would have been satisfied
with what the river would do with me ... and with the face of stone

20

And it is enough, to know my faraway self, that
you return to me the poem's lightning when I split
into two within your body
I am yours as your hand is yours
so what's my need for my tomorrow
after this journey?

من أَنا، دون منفى؟

غريبٌ على ضفة النهر، كالنهر ... يَرْبِطُني
باسمك الماءُ. لا شيءَ يُرْجعُني من بعيدي
إلى نخلتي: لا السلامُ ولا الحربُ. لا
شيء يُدْخِلُني في كتاب الأَناجيلِ. لا
شيء... لا شيء يُومِضُ من ساحل الجَزر
والمدّ ما بين دجْلَةَ والنيلِ. لا
شيء يُنْزِلُني من مراكب فرعون. لا
شيء يَحْملني أو يُحَـمِّلني فكرةً: لا الحنينُ
ولا الوَعْدُ. ماذا سأفعل؟ ماذا
سأفعل من دون منفى، وليلٍ طويلٍ
يُحَدِّقُ في الماء؟

يربطني
باسمك
الماءُ ...
لا شيء يأخذني من فراشات حُلْمي
إلى واقعي: لا الترابُ ولا النارُ. ماذا
سأفعل من دون وَرْد سَمَرْقَنْدَ؟ ماذا
سأفعل في ساحةٍ تصقُلُ المُنشدين بأحجارها
القمرّية؟ صِرْنا خَفِيفَيْن مثلَ منازلنا
في الرياح البعيدةِ. صِرنا صَديقَيْن للكائنات
الغريبةِ بين الغيوم... وصِرنا طَليقَيْن من
جاذبيّة أرض الـهُويّةِ. ماذا سنفعل... ماذا
سنفعل من دون منفى، وليلٍ طويلٍ
يُحَدِّقُ في الماء؟
يربطني
باسمك
الماءُ ...
لم يبقَ منّي سواكِ، ولم يبق منك
سِواي غريباً يُـمَسِّدُ فَخْذَ غريبتِه: يا

Who Am I, Without Exile?

A stranger on the riverbank, like the river ... water
binds me to your name. Nothing brings me back from my faraway
to my palm tree: not peace and not war. Nothing
makes me enter the gospels. Not
a thing ... nothing sparkles from the shore of ebb
and flow between the Euphrates and the Nile. Nothing
makes me descend from the pharaoh's boats. Nothing
carries me or makes me carry an idea: not longing
and not promise. What will I do? What
will I do without exile, and a long night
that stares at the water?

Water
binds me
to your name ...
Nothing takes me from the butterflies of my dreams
to my reality: not dust and not fire. What
will I do without roses from Samarkand? What
will I do in a theater that burnishes the singers with its lunar
stones? Our weight has become light like our houses
in the faraway winds. We have become two friends of the strange
creatures in the clouds ... and we are now loosened
from the gravity of identity's land. What will we do ... what
will we do without exile, and a long night
that stares at the water?

Water
binds me
to your name ...
There's nothing left of me but you, and nothing left of you
but me, the stranger massaging his stranger's thigh: O

غريبةٌ! ماذا سنصنع في ما تبقَّى لنا
من هُدوءٍ... وقَيْلُولَةٍ بين أسطورتين؟
ولا شيء يحملُنا: لا الطريقُ ولا البيتُ.
هل كان هذا الطريق كما هُوَ، منذ البداية،
أم أَنَّ أحلامنا وَجَدَتْ فرساً من خيول
الـمَغُول على التلِّ فَاُسْتَبْدَلَتْنا؟
وماذ سنفعلُ؟
ماذا
سنفعلُ من
دون
منفى؟

stranger! what will we do with what is left to us
of calm ... and of a snooze between two myths?
And nothing carries us: not the road and not the house.
Was this road always like this, from the start,
or did our dreams find a mare on the hill
among the Mongol horses and exchange us for it?
And what will we do?
What
will we do
without
exile?

أَنا، وجميلُ بُثَيْنة

كَبِرْنا، أَنا وجميلُ بُثَيْنَةَ، كُلٌّ
على حِدَة، في زمانين مُخْتَلِفَيْنْ...
هُوَ الوقتُ يفعل ما تفعل الشمس
والريحُ: يَصْقُلُنا ثم يقتلُنا حينما
يحملُ العقلُ عاطفةَ القلب، أو
عندما يبلُغُ القلبُ حكمتَهُ

يا جميلُ! أتكبَرُ مِثْلَكَ، مثلي،
بُثينةُ؟

تكبَرُ، يا صاحبي، خارجَ القلب
في نَظَر الآخرين. وفي داخلي تستحمُّ
الغزالةُ في نبعها المتدفّق من ذاتها

هيَ، أَم تلك صُورَتُها؟

إنها هيَ يا صاحبي. دَمُها، لحمُها،
واسمُها. لا زمان لها. رُبَّما استَوْقَفَتْني
غداً في الطريق إلى أَمسها

هل أَحبّتْكَ؟ أَم أَعْجَبَتْها استعارتُها
في أَغانيك، لؤلؤةً كُلَّما حدّقتْ في
لياليكَ واغرورقتْ ... أَشرقَتْ قمراً قلبُهُ
حَجَر يا جميل؟

هو الحُبُّ، يا صاحبي، موتُنا الـمُنْتَقَى
عابرٌ يَتَزَوَّجُ من عابر مُطلقاً ...
لا نهايةَ لي، لا بدايةَ لي. لا
بُثَيْنَةُ لي أَو أَنا لبثينةَ. هذا
هو الحبُّ، يا صاحبي. ليتني كُنْتُ
أَصغرَ منّي بعشرين باباً لكان

Jameel Bouthaina and I

We grew older, Jameel Bouthaina and I, each
alone, in two separate eras ...
It is time that does what sun
and wind do: it polishes us then kills us whenever
the mind bears the heart's passion, or
whenever the heart reaches its wisdom

Jameel! does she grow old, like you, like me,
Bouthaina?

She grows old, my friend, outside the heart
in others' eyes. But inside me
the gazelle bathes in the spring that pours out of her being

Is that her, or is that her image?

That's her, my friend. Her flesh, her blood,
and her name. Timeless. She might stop me
tomorrow on her road to her yesterday

Did she love you, Jameel? Or did she like being a metaphor
in your songs, a pearl ... whenever she stared
into your nights and welled up, she rose easterly as a moon
with a heart of stone?

It's love, my friend, our chosen death
one passerby marrying the absolute in another ...
No end for me, no beginning for me. No
Bouthaina for me or me for Bouthaina. This
is love, my friend. I wish I were
twenty doors younger than myself

الهواءُ خفيفاً عليَّ، وصورتُها الجانبيَّةُ
في الليل أوضحَ من شامةٍ فوق
سُرّتها...

هل هَمَمْتَ بها، يا جميل، على عكس
ما قال عنك الرُواةُ، وهَمَمْتْ بكَ؟

تزوَّجتُها. وهَزَزْنا السماءَ فسالَتْ
حليباً على خُبْزنا. كُلّما جئتُها
فَتَّحَتْ جَسَدي زهرةً زهرةً، وأراق غدي
خمرهُ قطرةً قطرةً في أباريقها

هل خُلِقْتَ لها، يا جميل،
وتبقى لها؟

أُمِرْتُ وعُلِّمْتُ. لا شأنَ لي
بوجودي الـمُراقِ كماءٍ على جلدها
الـعِنَبيّ. ولا شأنَ لي بالخلود
الذي سوف يتبعُنا ككلاب الرعاة.
فما أنا إلاّ كما خَلَقَتني بُـثَيْنَةُ

هل تشرَحُ الـحُبَّ لي، يا جميلُ،
لأحفظَهُ فكرةً فكرةً؟

أَعْرَفُ الناس بالـحُبِّ أكثرُهُمْ حَـيْـرَةً،
فاحترقْ، لا لتعرف نفسك، لكن
لتُشْعِلَ لَيْلَ بُـثَيْنَةَ ...

أعلى من الليل، طار جميل
وكسّر عُكّازتَيْه. ومال على أُذُني
هامساً: إن رأيت بثينةَ في امرأةٍ
غيرها، فاجعل الموت، يا صاحبي،
صاحباً. وتلألأ هنالك، في اسم
بثينة، كالنون في القافيةْ!

for the air to be light on me, and for her side-profile
at night to be clearer than a mole
above her navel ...

Did you seduce her, Jameel, contrary to what
the narrators have said about you, and did she seduce you?

I married her. And we shook the heavens and they streamed
milk on our bread. Whenever I came to her my body
bloomed flower by flower, and my tomorrow spilled
its wine drop by drop into her jugs

Were you created for her, Jameel,
and will you remain for her?

I was ordered and tutored. I have no concern
for my spilled presence like water on her grape
skin. And no concern for the immortality
that will follow us like shepherd dogs.
I am only as Bouthaina created me

Would you explain love to me, Jameel,
to remember it one idea at a time?

People who know love best are the most perplexed,
you must burn, not to know yourself, but
to illuminate Bouthaina's night ...

Higher than the night, Jameel flew
and broke his crutches. And leaned into my ear
and whispered: If you see Bouthaina in another
woman, make of death, my friend,
a friend. And shimmer over there, in Bouthaina's
name, like the nūn in rhyme!

قناع ... لمجنون ليلى

وجدتُ قناعاً، فأعجَبَني أَنْ
أكون أَنا آخَري. كنتُ دُونَ
الثلاثين، أَحَسَبُ أَنَّ حدودَ
الوجود هيَ الكلماتُ. وكنتُ
مريضاً بليلى كأيِّ فتىً شَعَّ
في دَمِهِ المِلحُ. إنْ لم تكُنْ هيَ
موجودةً جسداً فلها صُورَةُ الروح
في كُلِّ شيء. تُقَرِّبُني من
مدار الكواكب. تُبْعِدُني عن حياتي
على الأرض. لا هيَ مَوْتٌ ولا
هي ليْلى. «أَنا هُـوَ أنت،
فلا بُدَّ من عَدَم أزرق للعناق
النهائيِّ». عَالجني النهرُ حين
قذفتُ بنفسي إلى النهر مُنْتَحِراً،
ثم أَرجعني رَجُلٌ عابر، فسألتُ:
لماذا تُعيد إليَّ الهواء وتجعلُ
موتيَ أطولَ؟ قال: لتعرف
نفسك أفَضَلَ... مَنْ أنتَ؟
قلتُ: أَنا قَيْسُ ليلى، وأنتَ؟
فقال: أَنا زوجُها

ومَشَيْنا معاً في أزِقَّة غرناطةٍ،
نَـتَـذَكَّرُ أَيَّامَنا في الخليج... بلا أَلم
نتذكَّر أيّامنا في الخليج البعيد.

أَنا قَيْسُ ليلى
غريبٌ عن اسمي وعن زمني
لا أَهزُّ الغيابَ كجذع النخيل
لأَدفع عني الخسارةَ، أو استعيدَ
الهواء على أرض نَجْدٍ. ولكنني،
والبعيدُ على حالهِ وعلى كاهلي،

A Mask ... for Majnoon Laila

I found a mask, so I liked that
I can become my other. I was less
than thirty years old, thinking the boundaries
of existence were words. And I was
sick with Laila like any other young man
when salt beams in his blood. When she wasn't
present as body she was the soul's image
in everything. Drawing me closer
to the orbits of planets. Distancing me from life
on earth. She is neither death
nor is she Laila. "I am you, Laila,
there must be a blue void for the endless
embrace." The river doctored me
when I threw myself to the river as suicide,
but a passerby brought me back, so I asked:
Why do you give me back the air and prolong
my death? He said: To know
yourself better ... Who are you?
I said: I am Qyss Laila, and you?
He said: I am her husband

And we walked together in Granada's alleys
remembering our days in the Gulf ... painlessly
remembering our days in the faraway Gulf

I am Qyss Laila
a stranger to my name and to my time
I do not shake absence like a palm tree trunk
to push away loss, or to bring back
the air on the ground of Najd. But I—
and the faraway is as it has been on my shoulder—

صوتُ ليلى إلى قلبها
فلتكن للغزالة بريَّةٌ
غيرُ دربي إلى غَيْبها
هل أُضيِّقُ صحراءها أم أوسِّعُ لَيْلي
لتجمعنا نجمتان على دربها؟
لا أَرى في طريقي إلى حُبِّها
غيرَ أمسٍ يُسَلِّي بشِعري القديم
نُعَاسَ القوافل في ليلها، ويُضيءُ
طريقَ الحرير بجرحي القديم
لعلَّ التجارةَ في حاجةٍ هيَ أيضاً
لما أَنا فيه. أَنا من أولئك،
مـمَّـنْ يموتون حين يُحبُّونَ. لا شيءَ
أَبعدُ من فَرَسي عن معلَّقة الجاهليّ
ولا شيءَ أَبعدُ من لُغَتي عن أمير
دَمَشْقَ. أَنا أوَّلُ الخاسرين. أَنا
آخرُ الحالمين وعَبْدُ البعيد. أَنا
كائنٌ لم يكن. وأَنا فكرةٌ للقصيدة
ليس لها بَلَدٌ أو جَسَدْ
وليس لها والدٌ أو وَلَد.

أَنا قيس ليلى، أَنا
وأَنا ... لا أَحَدْ!

am Laila's voice to her heart
so let there be a wilderness for the gazelle
other than my path to her unknown.
Shall I diminish her desert or expand my night
for two stars on her path to unite us?
I only see on my road to her love
a yesterday amusing with my ancient poetry
the sleepiness of caravans in her night, and lighting
the Silk Road with my ancient wound.
Perhaps commerce also has a need
for what I'm in. I am of those
who die when they love. Nothing
is further than my name from the Jahili's ode
and nothing is further than my language from the prince
of Damascus. I am the first of losers. I am
the last of dreamers and faraway's slave. I am
a being who never was. And I am an idea for the poem
without land or body
without father or son

I am Qyss Laila, I am
and I am ... no one!

درس من كاما سوطرا

بكأس الشراب المرصَّع باللازوردِ
انتظرها،
على بركة الماء حول المساء وزَهر الكُولُونيا
انتظرها،
بصبر الحصان الـمُعَـدّ لـمُـنْـحَدرات الجبالِ
انتظرها،
بذَوْقِ الأمير الرفيع البديع
انتظرها،
بسبع وسائدَ مَـحْـشُـوَّةٍ بالسحابِ الخفيفِ
انتظرها،
بنار البَـخُور النسائيِّ ملءَ المكانِ
انتظرها،
برائحة الصَنْدَلِ الذَكَرِيَّةِ حول ظُهُور الخيولِ
انتظرها،
ولا تتعجَّلْ، فإن أقبلَتْ بعد موعدها
فانتظرها،
وإن أقبلتْ قبل موعدها
فانتظرها،
ولا تُجْفِل الطيرَ فوق جدائلها
وانتظرها،
لتجلس مرتاحةً كالحديقة في أَوْج زِينَتِها
وانتظرها،
لكي تتنفَّسَ هذا الهواء الغريبَ على قلبها
وانتظرها،
لترفع عن ساقها ثَـوْبَها غيمةً غيمةً
وانتظرها،
وخُـذْها إلى شرفة لترى قمراً غارقاً في الحليبِ
انتظرها،
وقدِّمْ لها الماءَ، قبل النبيذ، ولا
تتطلَّعْ إلى تَوْأَمَيْ حَجَلٍ نائمَين على صدرها
وانتظرها،

A Lesson from Kama Sutra

With the drinking glass studded with lapis
wait for her,
by the pool around the evening and the rose perfume
wait for her,
with the patience of the horse prepared for mountain descent
wait for her,
with the manners of the refined and marvelous prince
wait for her,
with seven pillows stuffed with light clouds
wait for her,
with burning womanly incense filling up the place
wait for her,
with the sandalwood male scent around the backs of horses
wait for her,
and don't hurry, so if she arrives late
wait for her,
and if she arrives early
wait for her,
and don't startle the birds in her braids
and wait for her,
so that she sits comfortably in her beauty's summit in the garden
and wait for her,
so she may breathe this strange air upon her heart
and wait for her,
so that she lifts her dress off her calf cloud by cloud
and wait for her,
take her to a balcony to see a moon drowning in milk
and wait for her,
offer her water, before wine, and don't
look at twin partridges sleeping on her chest
and wait for her,

ومُسَّ على مَهَل يَدَها عندما
تَضَعُ الكأسَ فوق الرخام
كأنَّكَ تحملُ عنها الندى
وانتظرها،
تحدَّثْ إليها كما يتحدَّثُ نايٌّ
إلى وَتَرٍ خائفٍ في الكمان
كأنكما شاهدانِ على ما يُعدُّ غَدٌ لكما
وانتظرها
ولَـمِّع لها لَـيْـلَها خاتِماً خاتِماً
وانتظرها
إلى أَن يقولَ لَكَ الليلُ:
لم يَبْقَ غيرُكما في الوجودِ
فخُـذْها، برِفْقٍ، إلى موتكَ الـمُـشـتَهى
وانتظرها!...

slowly touch her hand
when she places the glass on the marble
as if you were carrying dew for her
and wait for her,
talk to her as a flute talks
to a frightened violin string
as if you two were witnesses to what tomorrow prepares for you
and wait for her
brighten her night ring by ring
and wait for her
until the night says to you:
You are the only two left in the universe
so take her, gently, to your desired death
and wait for her! …

طوقُ الحمامة الدمشقيّ

أ.

في دِمَشـقَ،
تطيرُ الحماماتُ
خَلْفَ سياجِ الحرير
اُثْنَتَيْن ...
اُثْنَتَيْن ...

ب.

في دِمَشـقَ:
أرى لُغَتي كُلَّها
على حبَّةِ الـقَـمْحِ مكتوبةً
بـإبرةِ أُنثى،
يُـنَـقِّـحُها حَجَـلُ الرافدَيْن

ت.

في دِمَشْقَ:
تُـطَـرِّزُ أَسماءُ خَيْلِ العَرَبْ،
مِنَ الجاهليّةِ
حتى القيامة،
أو بَعْدَها،
... بخُيُوطِ الذَهَبْ

ث.

في دِمَشْقَ:
تسيرُ السماءُ
على الطُرُقاتِ القديمةِ
حافيةً، حافيةٌ

The Damascene Collar of the Dove

A

In Damascus,
   the doves fly
      behind the silk fence
         two ...
            by two ...

B

In Damascus:
   I see all of my language
      written with a woman's needle
         on a grain of wheat,
            refined by the partridge of the Mesopotamian rivers

C

In Damascus:
   the names of the Arabian horses have been embroidered,
      since Jahili times
         and through judgment day,
           or after,
               ... with gold threads

D

In Damascus:
   the sky walks
      barefoot on the old roads,
         barefoot

فما حاجةُ الشُّعَراءِ
إلى الوَحْيِ
والوَزْنِ
والقافِيَةْ؟

ج.

في دِمَشْقَ:
ينامُ الغريبُ
على ظلّه واقفاً
مثل مِئْذَنَة في سرير الأَبد
لا يَحِنُّ إلى بَلدٍ
أو أَحَـدْ ...

ح.

في دِمَشْقَ:
يُواصِلُ فعْلُ الـمُضَارِع
أَشغالَـهُ الأُمويَّـةَ:
نمشي إلى غَدنا واثقينَ
من الشمس في أَمسنا.
نحن والأَبديَّـةُ،
سُـكَّانُ هذا البَـلَـدْ!

خ.

في دِمَشْقَ:
تَدُورُ الحوارات
بين الكَـمَـنْـجَةِ والعُود
حَـوْلَ سؤال الوجود
وحول النهايات:
مَنْ قَتَـلَـتْ عاشقاً مارقاً
فَـلَـهَا سِدْرَةُ المنتهى!

so what's the poet's use
of revelation
and meter
and rhyme?

E

In Damascus:
the stranger sleeps
on his shadow standing
like a minaret in eternity's bed
not longing for a land
or anyone ...

F

In Damascus:
the present tense continues
its Umayyad chores:
we walk to our tomorrow certain
of the sun in our yesterday.
Eternity and we
inhabit this place!

G

In Damascus:
the dialogue goes on
between the violin and the oud
about the question of existence
and about the endings:
whenever a woman kills a passing lover
she attains the Lotus Tree of Heaven!

د.

في دِمَشْقَ:
يُقَطِّعُ يوسُفُ،
بالنايِ،
أَضْلُعَهُ
لا لشيءٍ،
سوى أَنَّهُ
لم يَجِدْ قلبَـهُ مَعَـهُ

ذ.

في دِمَشْقَ:
يَعُودُ الكلامُ إلى أَصلِه،
الماءِ:
لا الشعْرُ شعْرٌ
ولا النَّثْرُ نَـثْرٌ
وأنتِ تقولين: لن أَدَعَـكْ
فـخُـذْني اليكَ
وخُـذْني مَعَـكْ!

ر.

في دِمَشْقَ:
ينامُ غزالٌ
إلى جانب امرأةٍ
في سرير النَدى
فتخلَعُ فُسْـتانَها
وتُـغَـطّي بِـهِ بَـرَدَى!

ز.

في دِمَشْقَ:
تُـنَـقِّـرُ عُـصْـفُـورَةٌ
ما تركتُ من القمح
فوق يدي

H

In Damascus:
    Youssef tears up,
        with the flute,
            his ribs
                not for a reason,
                    other than that
                        his heart isn't with him

I

In Damascus:
    speech returns to its origin,
        water:
            poetry isn't poetry
                and prose isn't prose
                    and you say: I won't leave you
                  so take me to you
                    and take me with you!

J

In Damascus:
    a gazelle sleeps
        beside a woman
            in a bed of dew
                then the woman takes off her dress
                and covers Barada with it!

K

In Damascus:
    a bird picks
        at what is left of wheat
            in my palm

وتركُ لي حَبَّةً
لتُريني غداً
غَدِي!

س.

في دِمَشْقَ:
تـدَاعِبُني الياسمينةُ:
لا تَبْتَعِدْ
وامش في أَثَري
فَتَغارُ الحديقةُ:
لا تقترِبْ
من دَمِ الليل في قَمَري

ش.

في دِمَشْقَ:
أُسامِرُ حُـلْمي الخفيفَ
على زَهْرة اللوز يضحَكُ:
كُـنْ واقعياً
لأُزْهِرَ ثانيةً
حول ماء اسمها
وكُـنْ واقعياً
لأُعبِر في حُلْمها!

ص.

في دِمَشْقَ:
أُعرِّفُ نفسي
على نفسها:
هـهنا، تحت عَيْنَـيْن لوزِيَّتَـيْن
نطيرُ معاً تَوْأَمَـيْن
ونُـرْجىء ماضينَا المشترك

and leaves for me a single grain
to show me my tomorrow
tomorrow!

L

In Damascus:
the jasmine dallies with me:
Don't go far
and follow my tracks.
But the garden becomes jealous:
Don't come near
the blood of night in my moon

M

In Damascus:
I keep my lighthearted dream company
and laughing on the almond blossom:
Be realistic
that I may blossom again
around her name's water
and be realistic
that I may pass in her dream!

N

In Damascus:
I introduce myself
to itself:
Right here, beneath two almond eyes
we fly together as twins
and postpone our mutual past

ض.

في دِمَشْقَ:
يرقُّ الكلامُ
فأسمع صَوْتَ دَم
في عُرُوق الرَّخام:
اخْتَطِفْني مِنَ ابني
تقولُ السجينةُ لي
أو تحـجَّرْ معي!

ط.

في دِمَشْقَ:
أعدُّ ضُلُوعي
وأُرْجِعُ قلبي إلى خَبَبه
لعلَّ التي أَدْخَلَتْني
إلى ظلِّها
قَتَلَتْني،
ولم أَنْتَبِهْ ...

ظ.

في دِمَشْقَ:
تُعيدُ الغريبةُ هَوْدَجَها
إلى القافلَةْ:
لن أعودَ إلى خيمتي
لن أُعلِّقَ جيتارتي،
بَعْدَ هذا المساء،
على تينة العائلةْ ...

ع.

في دِمَشْقَ:
تَشِفُّ القصائدُ
لا هِيَ حِسِّيَّةٌ

O

In Damascus:
    speech softens
        and I hear the sound of blood
            in the marble veins:
                Snatch me away from my son
                    (she, the prisoner, says to me)
                or petrify with me!

P

In Damascus:
    I count my ribs
        and return my heart to its trot
            perhaps the one who granted me entry
            to her shadow
                has killed me,
                    and I didn't notice …

Q

In Damascus:
    the stranger gives her howdah back
        to the caravan:
            I won't return to my tent
            I won't hang my guitar,
                after this evening,
                    on the family's fig tree …

R

In Damascus:
    poems become diaphanous
        they're neither sensual

ولا هيَ ذهْنيّةٌ
إنّها ما يقولُ الصدى
للصدى...

غ.

في دِمَشْقَ:
تجفُّ السحابةُ عصراً،
فتحفُرُ بئراً
لصيف المحبِّينَ في سَفْح قاسْيُون،
والنايُ يُكـمِلُ عاداته
في الحنين إلى ما هُوَ الآن فيه،
ويبكي سدى

ف.

في دِمَشْقَ:
أُدوِّنُ في دَفْتَرِ امرأةٍ:
كُلُّ ما فيك
من نَرْجِسٍ
يَشتَهيك
ولا سُورَ، حَوْلَك، يحميك
مِنْ ليل فِتْنَتِك الزائدةْ

ق.

في دِمَشْقَ:
أرى كيف ينقُصُ ليلُ دِمَشْقَ
رويداً رويداً
وكيف تزيدُ إلهاتُنا
واحدةْ!

nor intellectual
they are what echo says
to echo ...

S

In Damascus:
the cloud dries up by afternoon,
then digs a well
for the summer of lovers in Qasyoon Valley,
and the flute completes its habit
of longing to what is present in it,
then cries in vain

T

In Damascus:
I write in a woman's journal:
All that's in you
of narcissus
desires you
and no fence, around you, protects you
from your night's excess allure

U

In Damascus:
I see how the Damascus night diminishes
slowly, slowly
and how our goddesses increase
by one!

ك.

في دِمَشْقَ:
يغني المسافر في سره:
لا أعودُ من الشام
حياً
ولا ميتاً
بل سحاباً
يخفِّفُ عبءَ الفراشة
عن روحي الشاردة

v

In Damascus:
　the traveler sings to himself:
　　I return from Syria
　　　neither alive
　　　　nor dead
　　　　　but as clouds
　　　　　　that ease the butterfly's burden
　　　　　　from my fugitive soul

حالة حصار

٢٠٠٢

A State of Siege

2002

هنا، عند مُنْحَدرات التلالِ، أمامَ الغروبِ
وفُوَّهَةِ الوقت،
قُرْبَ بساتينَ مقطوعةِ الظلِّ،
نفعَلُ ما يفْعَلُ السُجَناءُ،
وما يفعلُ العاطلونَ عَن العَمَل:
نُرَبِّي الأَمَل.

ڡ

بلادٌ على أُهْبَة الفجر،
صِرنا أَقَلَّ ذكاءً،
لأنَّا نُحملقُ في ساعة النصر:
لا لَيْلَ في ليلنا المُتَلألِىء بالمدفعيّةِ
أعداؤنا يسهرونَ،
وأعداؤنا يُشعلون لنا النورَ
في حلكة الأَقبيةْ.

ڡ

هنا، بعد أشعار «أيوب» لم ننتظر أحداً...

ڡ

هنا، لا «أنا»
هنا يتذكرُ «آدمُ» صلصالَهُ

ڡ

سيمتدُّ هذا الحصار إلى أن نُعَلِّم أعداءنا
نماذجَ من شعرنا الجاهليِّ.

ڡ

ألسماءُ رصاصيّةٌ في الضُّحى
برتقاليَّةٌ في الليالي. وأما القلوبُ
فظلَّت حياديَّةً مثل ورد السياج

Here, by the downslope of hills, facing the sunset
and time's muzzle,
near gardens with severed shadows,
we do what the prisoners do,
and what the unemployed do:
we nurture hope

            ⌒

A country on the verge of dawn,
we have become less intelligent,
because we stare into victory's hour:
no night in our artillery-glistened night
our enemies are sleepless,
and our enemies ignite the light for us
in the blackness of shelters

            ⌒

Here, after Job's poems we waited for no one ...

            ⌒

Here, no "I"
here "Adam" recalls his clay

            ⌒

This siege will extend until we teach our enemies
paradigms of our Jahili poetry

            ⌒

The sky is leaden at twilight
orange at night. As for the hearts
they've remained neutral like fence flowers

؎

في الحصار، تكون الحياةُ هي الوقتُ
بين تذكُّر أوَّلها
ونسيان آخرها...

؎

ألحياةُ.
الحياةُ بكاملها،
الحياةُ بنُقْصَانها،
تستضيفُ نجوماً مُجاورةً
لا زمانَ لها...
وغيوماً مُهاجرةً
لا مكانَ لها.
والحياةُ هنا
تتساءلُ:
كيف نُعيدُ إليها الحياةُ

؎

يقولُ على حافة الموت:
لم يَبْقَ بي مَوطىء للخسارةِ،
حُرٌّ أنا قُرْبَ حُرّيتي
وغدي في يدي...
سوف أدخُلُ، عما قليلٍ، حياتي
وأولَدُ حُرّاً بلا أبَوين،
وأختارُ لاسمي حروفاً من اللازَوَرْد...

؎

هنا، عند مُرتفعات الدُّخان، على دَرَج البيت
لا وَقْتَ للوقتِ،
نفعَلُ ما يفعَلُ الصاعدونَ إلى اللهِ:
نَنْسَى الألَمْ

؎

❦

In siege, life becomes the time
between remembering life's beginning
and forgetting its end ...

❦

Life.
Life in its entirety,
life with its shortcomings,
hosts neighboring stars
that are timeless ...
and immigrant clouds
that are placeless.
And life here
wonders:
How do we bring it back to life!

❦

On the brink of death he says:
I have no foothold in me left to lose,
I am free near my freedom
and my tomorrow is in my hand ...
I will enter, in a little while, my life
and become born free and parentless,
and choose for my name letters of lapis ...

❦

Here, by upslopes of smoke, on the house steps
there is no time for time,
we do what ascenders to Allah do:
forget pain

❦

الألَم
هُوَ: أن لا تُعَلِّق سيِّدةُ البيت حَبْلَ الغسيل
صباحاً، وأن تكتفي بنظافةِ هذا العَلَمْ

ـۍ

لاَ صدىً هوميريّ لشيء هنا.
فالأساطيرُ تطرُقُ أبوابنا حين نحتاجُها
لا صدىً هوميريّ لشيءٍ...
هنا جنرالٌ يُنَقِّبُ عن دَوْلة نائمةٌ
تحت أنقاضٍ طروادةَ القادمةْ

ـۍ

يقيسُ الجنودُ المسافةَ بين الوجود
وبين العَدَمْ
مِنظار دَبَّابةٍ...

ـۍ

نقيسُ المسافةَ ما بينَ أجسادنا
والقذيفةِ... بالحاسّة السادسةْ

ـۍ

أيُّها الواقفون على العَتَبات ادخلوا،
وإشربوا مَعَنا القهوةَ العربيَّةَ
[قَدْ تَشْعُرونَ بأنَّكُمْ بَشَرٌ مثلنا]
أيُّها الواقفون على عَتَبات البيوتِ،
اخرجوا من صباحاتنا،
نطمئنَّ إلى أنّنا
بَشَرٌ مثلكُمْ!

ـۍ

Pain
is: that a housewife doesn't hang up her clothesline
in the morning, and that she's satisfied with this flag's cleanliness

⌒

No Homeric echo to a thing here.
Myths knock on our doors when we need them
no Homeric echo to a thing ...
Here a general excavates for a country sleeping
beneath the rubble of the upcoming Troy

⌒

The soldiers measure the distance between being
and nonbeing
with a tank's scope ...

⌒

We measure the distance between our bodies
and mortar shells ... with the sixth sense

⌒

You standing at the doorsteps, enter
and drink Arabic coffee with us
(you might sense you're human like us)
you standing at the doorsteps of houses,
get out of our mornings,
we need reassurance that we
are human like you!

⌒

نجدُ الوقتَ للتسليةْ:
نلعب النَّرْد، أو نتصفَّحُ أخبارَنا
في جرائدِ أمسِ الجريح،
ونقرأُ زاويةَ الحظِّ: في عامِ
ألفينِ واثنينِ تبتسمُ الكاميرا
لمواليدِ بُرْج الحصارُ

ـ๑ـ

كُلَّما جاءني الأمس، قُلْتُ لَهُ:
ليس موعدنا اليوم، فلتبتعدْ
وتعالَ غدا!

ـ๑ـ

قال لي كاتبٌ ساخرٌ:
لو عرفتُ النهايةَ، منذ البداية،
لم يَبْقَ لي عَمَلٌ في اللُّغَةْ

ـ๑ـ

كُلُّ مَوْتٍ،
وإنْ كانَ مُنْتَظَراً،
هُوَ أوَّلُ موتٍ
فكيف أرى
قمراً
نائماً تحت كُلِّ حَجَرٍ؟

ـ๑ـ

أفكِّرُ، من دون جَدْوَى:
بماذا يفكِّرُ مَنْ هُوَ مثلي، هُنَاكَ
على قمَّةِ التلِّ، مُنْذُ ثلاثةِ آلافِ عامٍ،
وفي هذه اللحظة العابرةْ؟
فتوجعني الخاطرةُ
وتنتعشُ الذاكرة.

We find time for entertainment:
we throw dice or flip through our papers
for news of yesterday's wounded,
and read the horoscope column: In the year
two thousand and two the camera smiles
for those born in the sign of siege

&

Whenever yesterday arrives, I tell it:
Our appointment is not today, so go away
and come back tomorrow!

&

A satirist said to me:
Had I known the ending, from the start,
I would have had no work left in language

&

Every death,
even if anticipated,
is a first death
so how can I see
a moon
sleeping beneath each stone?

&

I think, to no avail:
What would another like me think, there
on the hilltop, three thousand years ago,
of this fleeting moment?
Then the notion pains me
and the memory revives

ى~

عندما تختفي الطائراتُ تطيرُ الحماماتُ،
بيضاءَ، بيضاءَ. تغسلُ خدَّ السماء
بأجنحةٍ حُرَّةٍ، تستعيدُ البهاءَ وملكيَّةَ
الجوِّ واللَهوِ. أعلى وأعلى تطيرُ
الحماماتُ، بيضاءَ بيضاءَ. لَيْتَ السماءَ
حقيقيَّةٌ [قال لي رجلٌ عابرٌ بين قنبلتيْن].

ى~

الوميضُ، البصيرةُ، والبرقُ
قَيْدَ التشابُه...
عمَّا قليلٍ سأعرف إن كان هذا
هو الوَحْيُ...
أو يعرفُ الأصدقاءُ الحميمونَ
أنَّ القصيدةُ مَرَّتْ،
وأودتْ بشاعرِها...

ى~

[إلى ناقد:] لا تُفَسِّرْ كلامي
بمِلْعَقَةِ الشاي أو بفخاخ الطيور!
يحاصرني في المنام كلامي،
كلامي الذي لم أقُلْهُ،
وَيكتُبُني ثم يتركني باحثاً
عن بقايا منامي...

ى~

شَجَرْ السَرو، خلف الجنود، مآذنُ
تحمي السماءَ من الانحدار. وخلف سياج
الحديد جنودٌ بيولون ـ تحت حراسة دبَّابةٍ ـ
والنهارُ الخريفيُّ يُكمِلُ نزهتَهُ الذهبيَّةَ
في شارعٍ واسعٍ كالكنيسةِ
بعد صلاة الأَحَدْ...

When the fighter planes disappear, the doves fly
white, white. Washing the sky's cheek
with free wings, reclaiming splendor and sovereignty
of air and play. Higher and higher
the doves fly, white white. I wish the sky
were real (a man passing between two bombs told me)

Flash, perception, and lightning
are under simile's consideration ...
In a little while I'll know if this is
revelation ...
or the intimate friends will know
the poem had passed,
and perished its poet ...

(To a critic:) Do not interpret my words
with a teaspoon or a bird snare!
My speech besieges me in sleep,
my speech that I have not yet said,
it writes me then leaves me searching
for the remnants of my sleep ...

The cypress trees, behind the soldiers, are minarets
that protect the sky against declivity. And behind the iron
fence the soldiers are urinating—under a tank's guard—
and the autumn day completes its golden stroll
in a street spacious like church
after Sunday prayer ...

ــؤ

بلادٌ على أُهْبَةِ الفجرِ،
لن نختلفْ
على حصَّة الشُّهَداءِ من الأرضِ،
ها هُمْ سَوَاسِيَةٌ
يفرشون لنا العُشْبَ
كي نأتلفْ!

ــؤ

نُحبُّ الحياةَ غداً
عندما يصل الغَدُ سوف نحبُّ الحياة
كما هيَ، عاديةٌ ماكرةٌ
رماديَّةٌ أو مُلَوَّنَةٌ،
لا قيامةَ فيها ولا آخرةْ.
وإن كان لا بُدَّ من فَرَحٍ
فليكُنْ
خفيفاً على القلب والخاصرةْ!
فلا يُلْدَغُ المُؤْمِنُ المتمرِّنُ
من فَرَحٍ... مَرَّتَيْن!

ــؤ

[إلى قاتلٍ:] لو تأمَّلْتَ وجهَ الضحيَّةْ
وفكَّرتَ، كُنْتَ تذكَّرْتَ أُمَّكَ في غُرْفَةِ
الغازِ، كُنْتَ تحرَّرتَ من حكمة البندقيَّةْ
وغيَّرتَ رأيَكَ: ما هكذا تُسْتَعادُ الهُويَّة!

ــؤ

[إلى قاتلٍ آخر:] لو تَرَكْتَ الجَنينَ
ثلاثين يوماً، إذاً لتغيَّرتِ الاحتمالاتُ:
قد ينتهي الاحتلالُ ولا يتذكَّرُ ذاك
الرضيعُ زمان الحصار،
فيكبر طفلاً مُعَافًى، ويصبحُ شاباً

⌒

A country on the verge of dawn,
we won't disagree
on the martyrs' share of the land,
they are equals here
furnishing us with grass
so that we'd get along!

⌒

We love life tomorrow
when tomorrow arrives we will love life
as it is, ordinarily shrewd
gray or colored,
no resurrection in it or end.
And if there must be a joy
let it be
light on the heart and hip!
For no faithful veteran is stung
from a joy ... twice!

⌒

(To a killer:) If you'd contemplated the victim's face
and thought, you would have remembered your mother in the gas
chamber, you would have liberated yourself from the rifle's wisdom
and changed your mind: this isn't how identity is reclaimed!

⌒

(To another killer:) Had you left the fetus
for thirty days, the possibilities would have changed:
the occupation might end and that suckling
would not remember the time of siege,
and he'd grow up a healthy child, become a young man

ويَدْرُسُ في معهدٍ واحدٍ مَعَ إحدى بَنَاتِكَ
تاريخَ آسيا القديمَ
وقد يَقَعَانِ معاً في شباك الغرامِ
وقد يُنْجِبانِ ابنةً [وتكونُ يهوديّةً بالولادةِ]
ماذا فعلتَ إذاً؟
صارت ابنتُكَ الآن أرملةً
والحفيدةُ صارت يتيمةٌ؟
فماذ فَعَلْت بأُسْرَتِكَ الشاردة
وكيف أصبتَ ثلاثَ حمائمَ بالطلقة الواحدةْ؟

ح

لم تكن هذه القافيةْ
ضروريّةً، لا لضبط النغمْ
ولا لاقتصاد الألمْ
إنها زائدةٌ
كذبابٍ على المائدةْ

ح

الضبابُ ظلامٌ، ظلامٌ كثيفُ البياضِ
تُقَشِّرهُ البرتقالةُ والمرأةُ الواعدةْ

ح

وحيدون، نحن وحيدون حتى الثمالة،
لولا زياراتُ قَوْسِ قُزَحْ

ح

هل نُسيء إلى أحدٍ؟ هل نُسيء إلى
بَلَدٍ، لو أُصِبنا، ولو من بعيدٍ،
ولو مرةً، برذاذ الفَرَحْ؟

ح

and study in the same institution with one of your daughters
the ancient history of Asia
and they might fall together in passion's net
and beget a girl (and she'd be Jewish by birth)
so what have you done then?
Now your daughter has become a widow
and your granddaughter an orphan?
What have you done to your fugitive family
and how did you strike three doves with one shot?

꧁

This rhyme was not
necessary, not for melody
or for the economy of pain
it is additional
like flies at the dining table

꧁

The fog is darkness, thick white darkness
peeled by an orange and a promising woman

꧁

Alone, we are alone to the dregs,
had it not been for the visits of the rainbow

꧁

Do we harm anyone? Do we harm any
country, if we were struck, even if from a distance,
just once, with the drizzle of joy?

꧁

الحصارُ هو الانتظار
هو الانتظارُ على سُلّم مائلٍ وَسَطَ العاصِفَةْ

۵

لنا أخوةٌ خلف هذا المدى
أخوةٌ طيّبون، يُحبُّوننا، ينظرون إلينا
ويبكون، ثُمَّ يقولون في سِرِّهمْ:
«ليت هذا الحصار هنا عَلنيٌّ...»
ولا يُكمِلُون العبارةَ: «لا تتركونا
وحيدين.. لا تتركونا»

۵

ألقبائلُ لا تستعينُ بكسرى
ولا قَيْصَرٍ، طَمَعاً بالخلافة،
فالحُكُمُ شُورى على طَبَقِ العائلةْ
ولكنَّها أُعجِبَتْ بالحداثةِ
فاستبدلَتْ
بطائرةٍ إبِلَ القافلةْ

۵

سأصرُخُ في عُزْلتي،
لا لكَيْ أُوقظَ النامِّينْ.
ولكنْ لتُوقِظَني صَرْختي
مِنْ خيالي السجينْ!

۵

أنا آخر الشعراء الذين
يؤرِّقُهُمْ ما يُؤَرِّقُ أعداءَهم:
رُبَّما كانت الأرضُ ضيِّقَةً
على الناس،
والآلهة

Siege is the waiting
the waiting on a ladder leaning amid the storm

᷍

We have brothers behind this expanse
kind brothers, who love us, look at us
and cry, then say to themselves in secret:
"We wish this siege were public …"
But they don't finish the phrase: "Do not leave us
alone … do not leave us"

᷍

The tribes ask, in their greed
over khilafah, neither Khosrau nor Caesar for help,
because rule is through council at the family plate.
Yet modernity awed them
and so they exchanged
the camels of the caravan for a plane

᷍

I will scream in my solitude,
not to wake up the sleeping.
But for my scream to wake me
from my imprisoned imagination!

᷍

I am the last of the poets who
are insomniac by what makes their enemies insomniac:
perhaps the earth is too narrow
for people,
and for the gods

ـمـ

هُنا، تتجمّعُ فينا التواريخُ حمراءَ،
سوداءَ. لولا الخطايا لكان الكتابُ
المُقَدَّسُ أصغَرَ. لولا السرابُ لكانت
خُطى الأنبياء على الرمل أقوى، وكان
الطريقُ إلى الله أقْصَرَ
فَلْتُكمِل الأبديّةُ، أعمالها الأزليّةَ...
أمّا أنا، فسأهمسُ للظلّ: لو
كان تاريخُ هذا المكان أقلَّ زحاماً
لكانت مدائحُنا للتضاريس في
شَجَر الحَوْر... أكثْرُ!

ـمـ

خَسَائرُنا: من شهيدَيْن حتى ثَمَانيةٍ
كُلَّ يوم،
وعشرةُ جَرْحَى
وعشرونَ بيتاً
وخمسونَ زيتونةً،
بالإضافة للخَلَل البنيويِّ الذي
سيُصيبُ القصيدةَ المسرحيةَ واللوحةَ الناقصةُ

ـمـ

نُخَزّنُ أحزاننا في الجِرار، لئلّا
يراها الجنودُ فيحتفلوا بالحصار...
نُخَزّنُها لمواسمَ أُخرى،
لذكرى،
لشيء يفاجئنا في الطريق.
فحين تصيرُ الحياةُ طبيعيّةً
سوف نحزن كالآخرين لأشياءَ شخصيّةٍ
خَبّأتَهَا عَنَاوينُ كبرى،
فلم نَنْتَبِهْ لنزيف الجُروح الصغيرة فينا.
غداً حين يَشْفَى المكانُ
نُحسُّ بأعراضِه الجانبيّةْ

❧

Here, histories gather in us red,
black. If it weren't for the sins the holy book would've been
smaller. If it weren't for the mirage
the prophets' footsteps on the sand would've been stronger, and
the road to god shorter
so let endlessness complete its infinite chores ...
As for me, I'll whisper to the shadow: If
the history of this place were less crowded
our eulogies to the topography of
poplar trees ... would've been more!

❧

Our losses: from two martyrs to eight
every day,
and ten wounded
and twenty homes
and fifty olive trees,
in addition to the structural defect
that will afflict the poem and the play and the incomplete painting

❧

We store our sorrows in our jars, lest
the soldiers see them and celebrate the siege ...
We store them for other seasons,
for a memory,
for something that might surprise us on the road.
But when life becomes normal
we'll grieve like others over personal matters
that bigger headlines had kept hidden,
when we didn't notice the hemorrhage of small wounds in us.
Tomorrow when the place heals
we'll feel its side effects

في الطريقِ المُضَاءِ بقنديلِ منفى
أرى خيمةً في مَهَبِّ الجهاتْ:
الجنوبُ عَصيٌّ على الريح،
والشرقُ غَرْبٌ تَصَوَّفَ،
والغربُ هُدْنَةُ قَتْلى يسكُّون نَقْدَ السلام.
وأمَّا الشمالُ، الشمال البعيد
فليس بجغرافيا أو جِهَةٌ
إنه مجمع الآلهةْ!

۲

يقولُ لها: انتظريني على حافّة الهاويةْ
تقول: تَعَالَ... تَعَالَ! أنا الهاويةْ

۲

قالت امرأةٌ للسحابة: غَطِّي حبيبي
فإن ثيابي مُبَلَّلةٌ بِدَمِهْ!

۲

إذا لم تَكُنْ مَطراً يا حبيبي
فكُنْ شجراً
مُشْبعاً بالخُصُوبَةِ... كُنْ شَجَرا
وإن لم تَكُنْ شَجَراً يا حبيبي
فكُنْ حجراً
مُشْبعاً بالرطوبة... كُنْ حجرا
وإن لم تكن حَجراً يا حبيبي
فكُنْ قمراً
في مَنَام الحبيبة... كُنْ قمرا
[هكَذا قالت امرأةٌ
لابنها في جنازته

۲

On the road lit with an exile lantern
I see a tent in leaping directions:
the south too stubborn for the wind,
the east a Sufi west,
and the west a truce of the dead who stamp the coins of peace.
As for the north, the far north
is neither geography nor direction
it is the assembly of the gods!

He tells her: Wait for me by chasm's edge
She says: Come ... come! I am the chasm

A woman told a cloud: Cover my lover
because my clothes are wet with his blood!

If you're not a rain my love
be a tree
soaked with fertility ... be a tree
and if you're not a tree my love
be a stone
soaked with humidity ... be a stone
and if you're not a stone my love
be a moon
in the lover's sleep ... be a moon
    (that's what a woman said
    to her son at his funeral)

[إلى الليل:] مهما ادَّعَيْتَ المُسَاواةَ
«كُلُّكَ للكُلِّ»... للحالمِينَ وحُرَّاس
أحلامهم، فلنا قَمَرٌ ناقصٌ، ودَمٌ
لا يُغَيِّرُ لَوْنَ قميصكَ يا لَيْل...

‏٭

نُعزِّي أباً بابنه: «كرَّم اللهُ وَجْهَ الشهيدْ»
وبعد قليلٍ، نُهَنِّئُهُ بوليدٍ جديدْ.

‏٭

[إلى الموت:] نعرف من أيِّ دَبَّابةٍ
جئْتَ. نعرف ماذا تريدُ... فَعُدْ
ناقصاً خاتَماً. واعتذرْ للجنود وُضبّاطهم،
قائلاً: قد رآني العروسان أنظُرُ
نحوهما، فترَدَّدتُ ثم أَعَدْتُ العروسَ
إلى أهلها... باكيةً!

‏٭

إلهي... إلهي! لماذا تخلَّيْتَ عنّي
وما زلتُ طفلاً... ولم تَمْتَحِنْي؟

‏٭

قالت الأُمُّ:
لم أرهُ ماشياً في دَمهْ
لم أرَ الأُرْجوانَ على قَدَمهْ
كان مُسْتَنِداً للجدارِ
وفي يَدِه
كأسُ بابونج ساخنٍ
ويُفَكِّرُ في غَدِه...

‏٭

(To the night:) No matter how much you claim equality
"Your all is for all" … for the dreamers and the guards
of their dreams, we still have a missing moon, and blood
that doesn't change the color of your shirt O night …

We console a father for his son: "May god honor the martyr's face"
and after a while, we congratulate him on his newborn

(To death:) We know from which tank
you came. We know what you want … so go back
missing one ring. And apologize to the soldiers and their officers,
and say: The newlyweds caught me looking
their way, so I hesitated then returned the tearful bride
to her kin … alone

My lord … my lord! why have you forsaken me
while I'm still a child … and you haven't tested me yet?

The mother said:
I did not see him walking in his blood
I did not see the purple flower on his foot
he was leaning against the wall
and in his hand
a cup of hot chamomile
he was thinking of his tomorrow …

قالت الأُمُّ: في بادىءِ الأمرِ لم
أفهمِ الأمرَ. قالوا: تزوَّجَ منذ
قليلٍ. فَزَغْرَدْتُ، ثُمَّ رَقَصْتُ وَغَنَّيْتُ
حتى الهزيعِ الأخيرِ من الليلِ، حيث
مضى الساهرون ولم تبقَ إلاَّ سلالُ
البَنَفْسَج حَوْلي. تساءلتُ: أين العروسانِ؟
قيل: هنالك فوق السماء مَلاَّكانِ
يَسْتَكْملانِ طُقُوسَ الزواج. فَزَغْرَدْتُ،
ثُمَّ رَقَصْتُ وغنَّيْتُ حتى أُصِبْتُ
بداء الشَلَلْ
فمتى ينتهي، يا حبيبي، شَهْرُ العَسَلْ؟

❧

سيمتدُّ هذا الحصارُ إلى أن
يُحِسَّ المُحَاصِرُ، مثل المُحَاصَرِ،
أن الضَجَرْ
صِفةٌ من صِفاتِ البَشَرْ

❧

أيُّها الساهرونَ! ألم تتعبوا
من مراقبةِ الضوءِ في مِلْحِنا؟
ومن وَهَجِ الوردِ في جُرْحِنا
ألم تتعبوا أيُّها الساهِرُونْ؟

❧

واقفون هنا. قاعدون هنا. دائمُون هنا.
خالدون هنا. ولنا هَدَفٌ واحدٌ واحدٌ:
أن نكون.
ومن بعدِه نحن مُخْتَلِفُونَ على كُلِّ شيءٍ:
على صورةِ العَلَمِ الوطنيِّ
[سَتُحْسِنُ صُنعاً لو اخْتَرْتَ يا
شعبيَ الحيَّ رَمْزَ الحمارِ البسيط]
وَمُخْتَلِفُونَ على كلماتِ النشيدِ الجديد

The mother said: In the beginning of the matter I didn't
comprehend the matter. They said: He just got married
a little while ago. So I let out my zaghareed, then danced and sang
until the last fraction of the night, when
the sleepless were gone and only baskets of purple flowers
remained around me. Then I asked: Where are the newlyweds?
Someone said: There, above the sky, two angels
are consummating their marriage ... So I let out my zaghareed,
then danced and sang until I was struck
with a stroke.
When then, my beloved, will this honeymoon end?

This siege will extend until
the besieger feels, like the besieged,
that boredom
is a human trait

O you sleepless! have you not tired
from watching the light in our salt?
And from the incandescence of roses in our wounds
have you not tired, O sleepless?

We stand here. Sit here. Remain here. Immortal here.
And we have only one goal:
to be.
Then we'll disagree over everything:
over the design of the national flag
(you would do well my living people
if you choose the symbol of the simpleton donkey)
and we'll disagree over the new anthem

[سَتُحْسِنُ صُنعاً لو أُخْتَرْتَ أغنيَّةً عن زواج الحمام]
ومُخْتَلِفُون على وَاجبات النساء
[سَتُحْسَنُ صنعاً لو اخترْتَ سيِّدةً لرئاسة أجهزة الأمن]
مختلفون على النِسْبَةِ المئوية، والعامِّ والخاصِّ،
مختلفون على كُلَّ شيء. لنا هَدَفٌ واحدٌ:
أن نكون...
ومن بعده يجد الفَرْدُ مُتَّسعاً لاختيار الهَدَف

ح

عميقاً، عميقاً
يُواصلُ فعلُ المضارع
أشغالَهُ اليدويَّةَ،
في ما وراء الهَدَفْ...

ح

قال لي في الطريق إلى سِجْنِه:
عندما أتحَرَّرُ أعرفُ
أنَّ مديحَ الوَطَنْ
كهجاء الوَطَنْ
مهنةٌ مثل باقي المِهَنْ

ح

بلادٌ على أُهْبَة الفجرِ،
أيقظْ حصانَكَ
وأصعَدْ
خفيفاً خفيفاً،
لِتَسْبقَ حُلْمَكَ،
واجلس ــ إذا مأطَلَتْكَ السماءُ ــ
على صَخْرةٍ تَتَنَهَّدْ

ح

(you would do well if you choose a song about the marriage of doves)
and we'll disagree over women's duties
(you would do well if you choose a woman to preside over security)
we'll disagree over the percentage, the private and the public,
we'll disagree over everything. And we have one goal:
to be ...
After that one finds room to choose other goals

Deeply, deeply
the present tense continues
its manual chores,
past the goal ...

He told me on his way to his prison:
When I liberate myself I'll know
that praising the land
is like scoffing the land
a profession like any other profession

A country on the verge of dawn,
awaken your horse
and ascend lightly,
lightly
to surpass your dream,
then sit—when the sky paints you—
on a rock and sigh

كيف أحملُ حُرّيتي، كيف تحملُني؟ أين
نسكُنُ من بعد عَقْد النكاح، وماذا
أقول لها في الصباح: أَمْتِ كما ينبغي
أن تنامي إلى جانبي؟ وحَلُمتِ بأرض السماء؟
وهمْتِ بذاتك. هل قُمْتِ سالمةً من منامك
هل تشربين معي الشايَ أم قهوةً بالحليبِ؟
وهل تؤثرين عصيرَ الفواكه، أم قُبَلي؟
[كيف أجعل حُرّيتي حُرّةً؟] يا غريبةُ!
لَسْتُ غريبَكِ. هذا السريرُ سريرُك. كوني
إباحيّةً، حُرّةً، لا نهائيّةً، وانثري جَسَدي
زهرةً زهرةً بلهاثك. حُرّيتي! عَوِّديني
عليك. خُذيني إلى ما وراء المفاهيم كي
نصبح اثنين في واحد!
كيف أحملها، كيف تحملني، كيف أصبح سيِّدها
وأنا عبدها. كيف أجعل حريتي حُرّةً
دون أن نفترقْ؟

∿

قليلٌ من المُطْلَق الأزرقِ اللانهائيِّ
يكفي
لتخفيف وَطْأة هذا الزمانْ
وتنظيف حَمْأَة هذا المكانْ

∿

سيمتدُّ هذا الحصارُ إلى أنْ
نُقلّم أشجارنا
بأيدي الأطّباء، والكَهَنَةْ

∿

سيمتدُّ هذا الحصارُ، حصاري المجازيُّ،
حتى أُعلّم نفسيَ زُهْدَ التأمُّل:
ما قبل نفسي ـــ بكتْ سَوْسَنَةْ
وما بعد نفسي ـــ بكتْ سَوْسَنَةْ
والمكانُ يُحَمْلقُ في عَبَث الأزمنةْ

146 MAHMOUD DARWISH

How do I carry my freedom, how does she carry me? Where
would we live after the nuptials, and what
would I tell her in the morning: Did you sleep as you should
sleep beside me? Did dreaming of the sky's land
distress your being? Did you rise safely from your sleep?
Would you drink with me some tea, or coffee with milk?
Do you prefer fruit juice, or my kisses?
(How do I make my freedom free?) O stranger!
I am not your stranger. This bed is your bed. Be
licentious, free, endless, and scatter my body
flower by flower with your gasp. My freedom! make me
accustomed to you. Take me beyond meaning
for us to become two in one!
How do I carry her, how does she carry me, how do I become her master
when I am her slave. How do I make my freedom free
without us parting?

A little of the endless blue
is enough
to make the footstep of this time lighter
and to clean up the mud of this place

This siege will extend until
we trim our trees
with the hands of doctors and oracles

This siege, my metaphorical siege, will extend
until I teach myself the ascetics of meditation:
before myself—an iris cried
after myself—an iris cried
and the place is staring at the futility of the ages

~

على الروح أن تَتَرجَّلْ
وتمشي على قَدَمَيْها الحريريَّتَيْن
إلى جانبي، ويداً بيد، هكذا صاحبَيْن
قدمين يَقْتَسمان الرغيفَ القديمَ
وكأسَ النبيذ القديمِ
لنقْطَعَ هذا الطريقَ معاً
ثم تذهَبُ آيّامُنا في اتجاهَيْن مُخْتَلفَيْن:
أنا ما وراءَ الطبيعة. أمّا هِيَ
فتختار أن تجلس القرفصاءَ
على صخرةٍ عاليةْ

~

[إلى شاعر:] كُلَّما غاب عنك الغياب
تورَّطْتُ في عُزْلَة الآلهةْ
فكن «ذاتَ» موضوعكَ التائهةْ
و«موضوعَ» ذاتكَ،
كُنْ حاضراً في الغيابْ

~

[إلى الشعر:] حاصِرْ حصاركَ

~

[إلى النثر:] جُرَّ البراهينَ من
مُعْجَم الفُقَهاء إلى واقعٍ دَمَّرتْهُ
البراهينُ. وأشَرَحْ غُباركَ.

~

[إلى الشعر والنثر:] طيرا معاً
كجناحَيْ سُنُونُوَّةٍ تحملان الربيعَ المُباركْ

❧

The soul must dismount
and walk on her two silken feet
beside me, hand in hand, as two old friends
sharing old bread
and vintage wine
to traverse the road together
then our days can go in two separate directions:
I beyond nature. As for the soul
she sits on a high rock
crouching

❧

(To a poet:) Whenever absence is your absentee
you get mixed up in the solitude of the gods
so be the bewildered "self" of your subject
and the "subject" of your self,
be present in absence

❧

(To poetry:) Besiege your siege

❧

(To prose:) Drag the evidence
out of the scholar's encyclopedia to a present
that the evidence destroyed. And explain your dust

❧

(To poetry and prose:) Fly together
as the wings of a swallow carry the blessed spring

෴

كتبتُ عن الحُبِّ عشرين سطراً
فخُيِّلَ لي
أنَّ هذا الحصارَ
تراجَعَ عشرين متراً!...

෴

يجدُ الوقتَ للسخريةِ:
هاتفي لا يرنُّ
ولا جَرَسُ الباب أيضاً يَرِنُّ
فكيف تيَّقنْت من أنَّني
لم أكُنْ ههُنا؟

෴

يجد الوقتَ للأغنيةِ:
في انتظارِك، لا أستطيعُ انتظارَك
لا أستطيعُ قراءةَ دوستويفسكي
ولا الاستماعَ إلى «أُمّ كلثوم» أو «ماريّا كالاس»
وغيرهما. في انتظارِك تمشي العقاربُ في
ساعة اليد نحو اليسار، إلى زَمَنٍ
لا مكانَ لَهُ،
في انتظارِك لم أنتظِرْك، انتظرتُ الأزَلْ

෴

يقولُ لها: أيَّ زهرٍ تُحِبِّينَهُ؟
فتقول: أحبُّ القُرُنْفُلَ... أَسْودْ
يقولُ: إلى أين تَمْضينَ بي،
والقرنفلُ أسودْ؟
تقول: إلى بُؤْرةِ الضوء في داخلي
وتقولُ: وأبْعَدَ... أبعدَ.. أبْعَدْ.

෴

᷂

I wrote twenty lines about love
and imagined
this siege
has withdrawn twenty meters! ...

᷂

He finds time for sarcasm:
My phone doesn't ring
and neither does the doorbell
so how were you certain that I
wasn't here?

᷂

He finds time for song:
While I wait for you, I can't wait for you
I can't read Dostoevsky
or listen to Om Kalthoum or Maria Callas
or anyone else. While I wait for you the hands
in my wristwatch move to the left, to a time
that has no place, while I wait for you
I didn't wait for you, I waited for eternity

᷂

He says: What flowers do you love?
She says: I love carnations ... black
He says: Where are you taking me
while the carnations are black?
She says: To the seat of light inside me
And she says: And farther ... farther ... farther

᷂

[إلى الحُبِّ:] يا حُبُّ، يا طائر الغَيب!
دَعْنا من الأزرق الأبديّ وحُمّى الغياب.
تعال إلى مطبخي لنُعدَّ العَشاءَ معاً.
سوف أطهو، وأنتَ تَصُبُّ النبيذ،
وتختارُ ما شئتَ من أُغنياتٍ تُذَكِّرنا
بحياد المكان وفَوْضَى العواطف: إنْ
قيلَ إنَّكَ جِنْسٌ من الجنِّ... صَدِّقْ!
وإن قيلَ إنَّكَ نوعٌ من الأنفلونزا... فصدِّق!
وحدِّقْ إليكَ ومَزِّقْ حجابك. لكنَّك الآن
قُرْبي أليفٌ لطيفٌ تُقَشِّرُ ثُوماً، وبعد العشاء
ستختارُ لي فيلماً عاطفيّاً قديماً،
لنشهدَ كيف غَدا البطلان هناك
هُنا شاهِدَيْنْ

_ح_

في الصباح الذي سوف يعقبُ هذا الحصار
سوف تمضي فتاةٌ إلى حُبِّها
بالقميص المُزَركَش، والبَنطَلُونِ الرماديِّ
شَفّافَةَ المَعْنَويّات كالمشمشيّات في
شهر آذار: هذا النهارُ لنا كُلُّهُ
كُلُّهُ، يا حبيبي، فلا تتأخَّرْ كثيراً
لئلاّ يَحُطَّ غرابٌ على كتفي...
وستقضمُ تُفّاحَةً في انتظار الأمَلْ
في انتظار الحبيب الذي
رُبَّما، رُبَّما لن يَصِلْ

_ح_

«أنا، أو هُوَ»
هكذا تبدأ الحربُ. لكنها
تنتهي بلقاءٍ حَرِجْ:
«أنا و هُوَ»

_ح_

(To Love:) O love, O bird of the unseen!
free us from the eternal blue and the fever of absence.
Come to my kitchen and let us prepare dinner together.
I will cook, and you'll pour the wine,
and choose what you like of songs that remind us
of the neutrality of place and the mayhem of emotions: if
it were said that you are a kind of jinn ... believe it!
and if it were said that you are a kind of flu ... believe it!
Stare at yourself and tear your veil. But you are now here
near me, pleasant and domestic peeling garlic, and after dinner
you'll choose for me a romantic movie,
we can witness how the two heroes over there
became two viewers

On the morning that will follow this siege
a girl will walk to her love
in an ornate shirt, and ashen pants,
transparent in spirit like apricots
in March: Today is all ours,
all of it, my love, don't be too late
lest a raven alight on my shoulder ...
And she'll bite an apple waiting for hope
waiting for a lover who,
perhaps, might not arrive

"Me, or him"
that's how war starts. But
it ends in an awkward stance:
"Me and him"

«أنا هيَ حتى الأَبَد»
هكذا يبدأ الحُبّ. لكنه
عندما ينتهي
ينتهي بوداعٍ حَرِجٍ:
«أنا و هيَ»

ﺨ

لا أحبُّكَ، لا أكرهُكَ
قال مُعْتَقَلٌ للمحقِّقِ: قلبي مَلِيءٌ
بما ليس يَعْنيك. قلبي يفيضُ برائحةِ المَرْمِيَّةِ،
قلبي بريءٌ، مُضيءٌ، مَلِيءٌ،
ولا وَقْتَ في القلب للامتحان. بلى،
لا أحبُّكَ. مَنْ أَنْتَ حتَّى أحبَّكَ؟
هل أنت بعضُ أنايَ، وموعدُ شايٍ
وَبُحَّةُ نايٍ، وأغنيةٌ كي أُحبَّكَ؟
لكنني أكرهُ الاعتقال ولا أكرهُكَ.
هكذا قال مُعتقلٌ للمحقِّق: عاطفتي
لا تَخُصُّكَ. عاطفتي هي لَيْلي الخصوصيُّ...
لَيْلي الذي يتحرَّكُ بين الوسائد حُرّاً
من الوزن والقافيةُ!

ﺨ

سيمتدُّ هذا الحصار إلى أَنْ يُنَقِّحَ
سادةُ «أولمب» إلياذةَ الخالدةُ

ﺨ

سيولَدُ طفلٌ، هنا الآن،
في شارع الموت... في الساعة الواحدةُ

ﺨ

سيلعب طفلٌ بطائرةٍ من وَرَقْ
بألوانها الأَربعة

154   MAHMOUD DARWISH

"I am she until the end"
that's how love begins. But
when it ends
it's an awkward farewell:
"She and I"

&

I don't love you, I don't hate you
the detainee told the interrogator: My heart is filled
with what doesn't concern you. My heart overflows with sage scent,
my heart is innocent, illuminated, full,
and there is no time in the heart for cross-examination. Yes,
I don't love you. Who are you that I should love you?
Are you some of my I, and a meeting over tea
and a năy's hoarseness, and a song that I should love you?
But I hate detainment and I don't hate you.
This is what the detainee told the interrogator: My passion
does not concern you. My passion is my private night ...
my night that moves between the pillows free
of meter and rhyme!

&

This siege will extend until the gods
at Olympus are done pruning the Iliad Immortal

&

A boy is about to be born, here and now,
in the street of death ... at one o'clock

&

A boy will play with a kite
of four colors

[أحمر، أسود، أبيض، أخضر]
ثم يدخلُ في نجمةٍ شاردةْ

઼

جَلَسْنا بعيدينَ عن / مصائرنا كطيورٍ
تُؤَثِّثُ أعشاشَها في ثُقُوب التماثيل،
أو في المداخنِ،
أو في الخيام التي نُصبَتْ
في طريقِ الأميرِ إلى رِحْلة الصَّيْدْ...

઼

[إلى حارس:] سأُعلِّمُكَ الانتظارْ
على بابٍ موتي المؤَجَّلِ
تمهَّلْ، تمهَّلْ
لعلّك تسأمُ منِّي
وترفعُ ظلَّكَ عنِّي
وتدخُلُ ليلَكَ حُرّاً
بلا شَبَحي!

઼

[إلى حارس آخر:] سأُعلِّمُكَ الانتظارْ
على بابِ مَقْهى
فتسمع دقّاتِ قلبِكَ أبطأ، أسْرَعَ
قد تعرفُ القشعريرةَ مثلي
تمهَّلْ،
لعلّكَ مثلي تُصفِّر لحناً يُهَاجِرُ
أندلسيَّ الأسى، فارسيَّ المدارْ
فيوجِعُكَ الياسمينُ، وترحَلْ

઼

[إلى حارس ثالث:] سأُعلِّمك الانتظارْ
علَى مقْعدٍ حَجَريٍّ، فقَدْ

(red, black, white, green)
then he'll enter a fugitive star

⌒

We sat far from / our destinies like birds
that furnish their nests inside the cavities of statues,
or in chimneys,
or in tents pitched
on the prince's way to a hunt ...

⌒

(To a guard:) I'll teach you waiting
at my postponed death's door
be patient, be patient
maybe you'll get bored with me
and lift your shadow off me
and enter your night free
without my ghost!

⌒

(To another guard:) I'll teach you waiting
at a café entrance
for you to hear your heart slow down, speed up
you might know shuddering as I do
be patient,
and you might whistle as I do a migrant tune
Andalusian in sorrow, Persian in orbit
then the jasmine hurts you, and you leave

⌒

(To a third guard:) I'll teach you waiting
on a stone bench, perhaps

نتبادلُ أسماءنا. قد ترى
شَبَهاً طارئاً بَيْنَنا:
لَكَ أمٌّ
ولي والدةٌ
ولنا مَطَرٌ واحدٌ
ولنا قَمَرٌ واحدٌ
وغيابٌ قصيرٌ عن المائدةْ

مح

على طَلَلي يَنْبُتُ الظلُّ أخْضَرَ،
والذئبُ يغفو على شَعْرِ شاتي
ويحلُمْ مثلي،
ومثل الملاكْ
بأنَّ الحياةَ هنا
لا هُناكْ...

مح

الأساطيرُ ترفض تَعْديلَ حَبْكتها
رُبّما مَسَّها خَلَلٌ طارىءٌ
رُبّما جَنَحَتْ سُفُنٌ نحو يابسةٍ
غيرِ مأهولة،
فأُصيبَ الخياليُّ بالواقعيِّ...
ولكنها لا تُغَيِّر حَبْكَتَهَا.
كلّما وَجَدَتْ واقعاً لا يلائمُها
عدَّلَتْهُ بجرأفة،
فالحقيقةُ جاريةُ النصّ، حَسْناءُ
بيضاءُ، من غير سُوء...

مح

[إلى شبه مستشرق:] ليكُنْ ما تَظُنُّ
لنفترض الآن أني غبيٌّ، غبيٌّ، غبيٌّ
ولا ألعبُ الجولف،
لا أفهمُ التكنولوجيا،

we would exchange our names. You might see
an urgent simile between us:
you have a mother
and I have a mother
and we have one rain
and we have one moon
and a brief absence from the dining table

༄

On my ruins the shadow sprouts green,
and the wolf dozes off on my sheep's wool
and dreams as I do,
and as an angel does,
that life is here
not there ...

༄

The myths refuse to adjust their plot.
They may suffer a sudden malfunction
and some of the ships may drift to a dry
unpopulated land
where the imaginary becomes afflicted with the real ...
but they don't change their plot.
Whenever they find a reality that doesn't suit them
they alter it with a bulldozer,
because reality is an ongoing text, lovely
white, without malady ...

༄

(To a quasi-Orientalist:) Suppose what you think is true
suppose now that I'm an idiot, idiot, idiot
and I don't play golf,
and I don't comprehend technology,

ولا أستطيعُ قيادةَ طَيَّارة!
ألهذا أخذتَ حياتي لتصنع منها حياتَكَ؟
لو كُنْتَ غيرَكَ، لو كُنْتُ غيري
لكُنَّا صديقَيْنِ يعترفانِ بحاجتنا للغباء...
أما للغبيِّ، كما لليهوديّ في
«تاجر البندقية» قَلْبٌ، وخبزٌ
وعينانِ تغرورقان؟

۵

في الحصار، يصيرُ الزمانُ مكاناً
تحجَّرَ في أبده
في الحصار، يصيرُ المكانُ زماناً
تخَلَّفَ عن مَوْعِدهِ

۵

المكانُ هُوَ الرائحةْ
عندما أتذكَّرُ أرضاً
أشُمُّ دَمَ الرائحة
وأحِنُّ إلى نَفْسِيَ النازحةْ

۵

هذه الأرضُ واطئةٌ، عاليةٌ
أو مُقَدَّسَةٌ، زانيةٌ
لا نُبالي كثيراً بفقه الصفاتِ
فقد يصبحُ الفَرْجُ،
فَرْجُ السمواتِ،
جغرافيةٌ!

۵

ألشهيدُ يحاصرني كُلَّما عِشْتُ يوماً جديداً
ويسألني: أين كُنْتَ؟
أعِدْ للقواميس كُلَّ الكلام الذي

and I can't fly a plane!
Is that why you took my life and made of it your life?
If you were another, if I were another
we would be two friends who confess a need for idiocy ...
Doesn't the idiot, as the Jew
in the *Merchant of Venice*, have a heart, and bread,
and eyes that well up?

In siege, time becomes place
petrified in its eternity.
In siege, place becomes time
late for its appointment

Place is the scent.
When I recall a land
I smell the blood of scent
and long for my displaced self

This land is low, high
or holy, fornicator
we don't care much for the jurisprudence of adjectives
because the orifice,
the heavens' orifice, might become
a geography!

The martyr besieges me whenever I live a new day
and asks: Where were you?
Give back to the dictionaries all the talk

كُنْتَ أهْدَيْتَنِيه،
وخفِّفْ عن النائمين طنينَ الصدى!

Ꙭ

ألشهيدُ يُوَضِّحُ لي: لم أُفتِّشْ وراء المدى
عن عذارى الخلود، فإني أُحبُّ الحياةَ
على الأرض، بين الصنوبر والتين، لكنني
ما استطعتُ إليها سبيلاً،
ففتَّشْتُ عنها بآخرِ ما أملكُ:
الدمُ في جَسَدِ اللازوردْ

Ꙭ

ألشهيدُ يُعَلِّمني: لا جماليَّ خارجَ حُرِّيتي

Ꙭ

ألشهيدُ يحذِّرني: لا تُصَدِّقْ زغاريدهُنَّ
وصدِّقْ أبي حين ينظر في صورتي باكياً:
كيف بَدَّلْتَ أدوارنَا، يا بُنَيَّ،
وسِرْتَ أمامي؟
أنا أوَّلاً
وأنا أوَّلاً!

Ꙭ

ألشهيدُ يُحاصرُني: لم أغيِّرْ سوى مَوقعي
وأثاثي الفقير،
وَضَعْتُ غزالاً على مخدعي
وهلالاً على إصبعي
كي أخفِّفَ من وَجَعي

Ꙭ

you gave to me as gift,
and ease the drone of echo off the sleeping!

✏

The martyr clarifies for me: I didn't search beyond the expanse
for immortal virgins, because I love life
on earth, among the pines and figs, but
I couldn't find a way to it,
so I looked for it with the last thing I owned:
blood in the lapis body

✏

The martyr teaches me: no aesthetic outside my freedom

✏

The martyr cautions me: Don't believe the women's zaghareed
and believe my father when he looks into my picture tearfully:
How did you swap our roles, my son,
and walk ahead of me?
Me first
and me first!

✏

The martyr besieges me: I only changed my position
and my impoverished furniture,
I placed a gazelle in my bedroom
and a crescent on my finger
to ease my pain

✏

ألشهيدُ يحاصرني: لا تَسِرْ في الجنازةِ
إلاَّ إذا كُنْت تعرفُني.
لا أُريدُ مجاملةً من أحَدْ

~

سَيَشْتَدُّ هذا الحصارُ
لِيُقْنِعَنا
باختيارِ عَبوديّةٍ لا تَضُرُّ،
ولكنْ بحريّةٍ كاملةْ

~

أن تُقاوِمَ يعني: التأكُّدَ مِنْ
صِحّةِ القلبِ والخُصْيَتَيْنِ،
ومن دائكَ المتأصِّلِ:
داءِ الأمَلْ

~

وفي ما تبقَّى من الفجرِ أمشي إلى خارجي
وفي ما تبقَّى من الليلِ أَسمعُ وَقْع الخُطى داخلي

~

إذا مَرِضَ الحُبُّ عالجتُهُ
بالرياضةِ والسخريةْ
وبِفَصْلِ المُغنِّي عن.. الأغنيةْ

~

ألحصارُ يُحوِّلني من مُغَنٍّ إلى...
وَتَرٍ سادِسٍ في الكمانْ

~

The martyr besieges me: Don't walk in my funeral
unless you had known me.
I need courtesy from no one

~

This siege will intensify
to convince us
to choose a harmless slavery,
but with total freedom of choice

~

To resist means: to be certain
of the well-being of the heart and testicles,
and of your chronic illness:
the illness of hope

~

And in what remains of dawn I walk to my exterior
and in what remains of night I hear the fall of footsteps inside me

~

When love falls ill I treat it
with sports and sarcasm
and with separating the singer ... from the song

~

The siege transforms me from a singer into ...
a sixth string on the violin

~

[إلى قارىء:] لا تثقْ بالقصيدةِ،
بِنْتِ الغياب،
فلا هيَ حَدْسٌ
ولا هيَ فكرٌ
ولكنها حاسَّة الهاويةْ

~

الكتابة جَرْوٌ صغيرٌ يَعَضُّ العَدَمْ
الكتابةُ تجرحُ من دون دَمْ

~

أصدقائي يُعِدُّون لي دائماً حَفلَةً
للوداع، وقبراً مريحا يُظَلِّلُهُ السنديانُ
وشاهدةً من رُخام الزَمَنْ
فأسبقهم دائماً في الجنازة:
مَنْ ماتَ... مَنْ؟

~

ألشهيدةُ بنتُ الشهيدة بنتُ الشهيد
وأختُ الشهيد وأختُ الشهيدة كنَّةُ
أمِّ الشهيد حفيدةُ جدٍّ شهيد
وجارةُ عمِّ الشهيد [الخ... الخ...]
ولا شيء يحدَثُ في العالم المتمدِّن،
فالزمنَ البربريُّ انتهى،
والضحيّةُ مجهولةُ الإسم، عاديّةٌ
والضحيّةُ.. مثل الحقيقة.. نسبيّةٌ
[الخ... الخ...]

~

هدوءاً، هدوءاً، فإن الجنودَ يريدون
في هذه الساعة الاستماعَ إلى الأغنيات
التي استَمع الشُهداءُ إليها، وظلَّتْ
كرائحة البُنِّ في دَمِهِمْ... طازجَة

166   MAHMOUD DARWISH

(To a reader:) Don't trust the poem,
this daughter of absence,
she's neither speculation
nor intellect,
she's chasm's sense

⟡

Writing is a small puppy biting void
writing wounds without drawing blood

⟡

My friends always prepare a farewell party
for me, a comfortable grave shaded with holm oak
and a tombstone made of time's marble
but in the funeral I'm always ahead of them:
Who died ... who?

⟡

The martyr is the daughter of a martyr who is the daughter of a martyr
and her brother is a martyr and her sister is a martyr and a daughter-in-law
of a martyr's mother who's the grandchild of a martyr's grandfather
and a martyr's uncle's neighbor etc., etc.
And nothing happens in this civilized world,
the age of barbarism is over,
and the victim is nameless, ordinary
and the victim ... like truth ... is relative
etc., etc.

⟡

Quiet, quiet, the soldiers want
in this hour to listen to the songs
the martyrs listened to, the songs that remained
like the aroma of coffee in their spilled blood ... fresh

هُدْنةٌ، هدنةٌ لاختبار التعاليم:
هل تصلحُ الطائراتُ محاريثَ؟
قُلْنا لهم: هدنةٌ، هدنةٌ لامتحان النوايا،
فقد يتسرَّبُ شيءٌ من السِلْم للنفس!
عندئذ نتبارى على حُبِّ أشيائنا
بوسائلَ شعريّة.
فأجابوا: ألا تعلمون بأنَّ السلامَ مَعَ النَفْس
يفتحُ أبوابَ قَلْعَتَنا
لِمَقامِ الحجازِ أو النَهَوَنْد؟
فقلنا: وماذا؟... وبَعْد؟

هـ

فناجينُ قهوتنا. والعصافيرُ. والشَجَرُ الأخضَرُ
الأزرقُ الظلِّ. والشمسُ تقفزُ من
حائط نحو آخَرَ مثلَ الغزالة...
والماءُ في السُحُبِ اللانهائيّة الشكلِ
في ما تبقَّى لنا من سماء،
وأشياءُ أخرى مُؤَجَّلَةُ الذكريات
تدلُّ على أن هذا الصباح قويٌّ بهيٌّ،
وأنَّا ضيوفٌ على الأبديّةِ.

هـ

بلادٌ على أُهْبَة الفجرِ،
عمَّا قليلْ
تنامُ الكواكبُ في لُغَة الشعْر.
عمَّا قليلْ
نودِّعُ هذا الطريقَ الطويلْ
ونسألُ: من أين نبدأ؟
عمَّا قليلْ
نُحذِّرُ نرجِسَنا الجَبليَّ الجميلْ
من الافتتان بصورته: لم تَعُدْ
صالحاً للقصيدةِ، فانظرْ
إلى عابرات السبيلْ

168 MAHMOUD DARWISH

Truce, truce to test the instructions:
Would fighter jets work as plows?
We said to them: Truce, truce to test the will,
some peace might leak into the self!
Then we can compete over how to love our things
with poetic methods.
They answered: Don't you know that peace with self
opens our citadel doors
to the hejaz and the nahawand?
We said: So what? ... What then?

Our coffee cups. And birds. And the green trees
with blue shadows. And the sun leaping from
one wall to another like a gazelle ...
and the water in clouds with endless shapes
in what is left to us of sky,
and other things of postponed memory
indicate this morning is strong and beautiful,
and that we are eternity's guests

A country on the verge of dawn,
in a little while
the planets will sleep in poetry's language.
In a little while
we will bid this long road farewell
and ask: Where do we begin?
In a little while
we will caution our beautiful mountain narcissus
against infatuation with its image: You are no longer
fit for the poem, so look
toward the passersby

سلامٌ على مَنْ يُشَاطِرُني الانتباهَ إلى
نَشْوَة الضوء، ضوء الفراشةِ، في
لَيْل هذا النَفَقْ!

෨

سلامٌ على مَنْ يُقَاسِمُني قَدَحي
في كثافة لَيْلٍ يفيضُ من المقعدَيْن:
سلامٌ على شَبَحي!

෨

ألسلامُ كلامُ المُسَافر في نَفْسِه
للمسافر في الجِهَةِ الثانِيَةْ...

ألسلامُ حَمَامُ غَريبَيْنِ يقتسمان الهديلَ
الأخيرَ، على حافَّة الهاويةْ

෨

ألسلامُ حنينُ عَدُوَّين، كُلٌّ على حِدَةٍ
للتثاؤُبِ فوق رصيف الضَجَرْ

ألسلامُ أنينُ مُحبَّيْنِ يغتسلان
بضوء القَمَرْ

෨

ألسلامُ اعتذارُ القويِّ لمن هُوَ
أضعفُ منه سلاحاً، وأقوى مَدى

ألسلامُ انكسارُ السيوف أمام الجمالِ
الطبيعيِّ، حيث يَفُلُّ الحديدَ الندى

✑

Salaam upon whoever splits with me the attention to
light's ecstasy, the butterfly light, in
this tunnel's night!

✑

Salaam upon whoever shares with me my glass
in the density of a night that overflows two seats:
salaam upon my ghost!

✑

Salaam is what a traveler says to himself
to another traveler on the other side ...

Salaam is the doves of two strangers sharing their last
cooing, on the edge of the chasm

✑

Salaam is two enemies longing, each separately,
to yawn on boredom's sidewalk

Salaam is two lovers moaning to bathe
in moonlight

✑

Salaam is the apology of the mighty to the one
with weaker weapons and stronger range

Salaam is the sword breaking in front of natural
beauty, where dew smelts the iron

ᗝ

ألسلامُ نهارٌ أليفٌ، لطيفٌ، خفيفُ
الخُطَى، لا يُعَادي أَحَدْ

ألسلامُ قطارٌ يُوحِّدُ سُكّانَهُ العائدينَ
أو الذاهبينَ إلى نُزْهَةٍ في ضواحي الأَبَدْ

ᗝ

ألسلامُ هو الاعترافُ، علانيّةً، بالحقيقة:
ماذا صَنَعْتُمْ بطيف القتيلْ؟

ألسلامُ هُوَ الانصرافُ إلى عَمَلٍ في الحديقة:
ماذا سنزرَعُ عمّا قليلْ؟

ᗝ

ألسلامُ هُوَ الانتباهُ إلى الجاذبيّةِ في
مُقْلَتَيْ ثَعْلَبٍ تُغْوِيان الغريزةَ في امرأةٍ خائفةْ

ألسلامُ هُوَ الآه تُسْندُ مُرْتَفَعَاتِ
المُوَشَّح، في قلب جيتارةٍ نازفةْ

ᗝ

ألسلامُ رثاءُ فتىً ثَقَبَتْ قلبَهُ شامَةُ
امرأةٍ، لا رَصاصٌ ولا قُنْبُلَةْ

ألسلامُ غناءُ حياةٍ هنا، في الحياةِ،
على وَتَر السُّنْبُلَةْ

Salaam is a friendly day, pleasant, light-
footed, enemy of no one

Salaam is a train that unites all its passengers
who are coming from or going to a picnic in eternity's suburbs

Salaam is the public confession of truth:
What have you done with the murdered's ghost?

Salaam is the turning toward an errand in the garden:
What will we plant in a little while?

Salaam is the caution against a fox's attractive
eyes that lure the instinct of a frightened woman

Salaam is the aah strutting the crescendo
of a muwashah, in the heart of a bleeding guitar

Salaam is the lament of a young man whose heart a woman's beauty
mark pierced, not a bullet or a bomb

Salaam is the singing of life here, in life,
on the string of an ear of wheat

لا تعتذر
عما فعلت

۲۰۰۳

توارد خواطر، أو توارد مصائر:
لا أنتَ أنت
ولا الدِيارُ ديارُ
[أبو تمام]

والآن، لا أَنا أَنا
ولا البيتُ بيتي
[لوركا]

Don't Apologize for What You've Done

2003

A telepathy of minds, or a telepathy of destinies:

> Neither you are you
> nor home is home
> ABU TAMMAM

> And now, I am not I
> and the house is not my house
> FEDERICO GARCÍA LORCA

I. في شهوة الإيقاع

I. IN THE LUST OF CADENCE

يختارني الإيقاع

يَخْـتَارُني الإيقاعُ، يَشْرَقُ بي
أنا رَجْعُ الكمان، ولستُ عازِفَهُ
أنا في حضرة الذكرى
صدى الأشياء تنطقُ بي
فأنطقُ ...
كُلَّما أصغيتُ للحجرِ استمعتُ إلى
هديلِ يَمَـامَةٍ بيضاءَ
تشهَـق بي:
أخي! أنا أُخْـتُـكَ الصُّغرى،
فأذرف باسمها دَمْعَ الكلام
وكُلَّما أبْصَرْتُ جذْعَ الـزَّنزَلَخْت
على الطريق إلى الغمامِ،
سمعتُ قلبَ الأُمّ
يخفقُ بي:
أنا اُ مرأة مُطَلَّقَةٌ،
فألعن باسمها زِيزَ الظلام
وكُلَّما شاهَدْتُ مرآةً على قمرٍ
رأيتُ الحبّ شيطاناً
يُحَمْلقُ بي:
أنا ما زِلْتُ موجوداً
ولكن لن تعود كما تركتُكَ
لن تعود، ولن أعودَ
فيكملُ الإيقاعُ دَوْرَتَهُ
ويْشَرَقُ بي ...

Cadence Chooses Me

Cadence chooses me, it chokes on me
I am the violin's regurgitant flow, and not its player
I am in the presence of memory
the echo of things pronounces through me
then I pronounce ...
Whenever I listen to the stone I hear
the cooing of a white pigeon
gasp in me:
My brother! I am your little sister,
so I cry in her name the tears of speech
And whenever I see the zanzalakht trunk
on the way to the clouds,
I hear a mother's heart
palpitate in me:
I am a divorced woman,
so I curse in her name the cicada darkness
And whenever I see a mirror on a moon
I see love a devil
glaring at me:
I am still here
but you won't return as you were when I left you
you won't return, and I won't return
Then cadence completes its cycle
and chokes on me ...

لي حكمة المحكوم بالإعدام

لِـيَ حِكْمَةُ المحكوم بالإعدامِ:
لا أشياءَ أملِكُها لتملكني،
كتبتُ وصيّتي بدمي:
«ثِقُوا بالماء يا سُكّانَ أغنيتي!»
وَنِمْتُ مُضَرَّجاً ومُتَوَّجاً بغدي ...
حَلِـمْتُ بأنَّ قلب الأرض أكبرُ
من خريطتها،
وأوضحُ من مراياها وَمِشْنَقَتي.
وَهمْتُ بغيمةٍ بيضاءَ تأخذني
إلى أعلى
كأنني هُـدْهُدٌ، والريحُ أجنحتي.
وعند الفجر، أيقظني
نداءُ الحارس الليليِّ
من حُلمي ومن لغتي:
ستحيا مِيتةً أخرى،
فَعَدِّلْ في وصيّـتكَ الأخيرة،
قد تأجَّل موعدُ الإعدام ثانيةً
سألت: إلى متى؟
قال: انتظر لتموت أكثَر
قُلْتُ: لا أشياء أملكها لتملكني
كتبتُ وصيّتي بدمي:
«ثِقُوا بالماء
يا سُكّان أغنيتي!»

I Have the Wisdom of One Condemned to Death

I have the wisdom of one condemned to death:
I own nothing for anything to own me,
I wrote my will with my blood:
"Trust in water O dwellers of my song!"
Then I slept smeared and crowned with my tomorrow ...
I dreamt that the land's heart is bigger
than its map,
and clearer than its mirrors and my gallows.
I dreamt up a white cloud that takes me
higher
as if I were a hoopoe, and the wind my wings.
And by dawn, the calling
of the night guard woke me
from my dream and from my language:
You will live another death,
alter your last will,
execution has been postponed a second time
I asked: Until when?
He said: Wait to die some more
I said: I own nothing for anything to own me
I wrote my will with my blood:
"Trust in water
O dwellers of my song!"

سيجيءُ يوم آخرُ

سيجيءُ يَوْمٌ آخَرٌ، يومٌ نسائيٌّ
شفيفُ الاستعارة، كاملُ التكوين،
ماسيّ زَفَافِ الزيارة، مُشْمسٌ،
سَلِسٌ، خَفيفُ الظلّ. لا أحدٌ يُحسُّ
برغبةٍ في الانتحار أو الرحيل. فكلّ
شيءٍ، خارج الماضي، طبيعيٌّ حقيقيٌّ،
رديفُ صفاته الأولى. كأنَّ الوقتَ
يرقد في إجازته... «أطيلي وقت زينتك
الجميلَ. تشمّسي في شمس نَهْدَيْك الـحَريريّين،
وانتظري البشارةَ ريثما تأتي. وفي ما
بعد نكبرُ. عندنا وقتٌ إضافيٌّ
لنكبر بعد هذا اليوم...»/
سوف يجيء يومٌ آخرٌ، يومٌ نسائيٌّ
غنائيُّ الإشارة، لازورديُّ التحيةِ
والعبارة. كُلُّ شيءٍ أُنثويٌّ خارج
الماضي. يَسيلُ الماءُ من ضرع الحجارةِ.
لا غُبَارَ، ولا جَفَافَ، ولا خسارةَ.
والحمامُ ينامُ بعد الظهر في دبّابة
مهجورةٍ إن لم يجد عُشّاً صغيراً
في سرير العاشِقَيْن ...

Another Day Will Come

Another day will come, a womanly day
diaphanous in metaphor, complete in being,
diamond and processional in visitation, sunny,
flexible, with a light shadow. No one will feel
a desire for suicide or for leaving. All
things, outside the past, natural and real,
will be synonyms of their early traits. As if time
is slumbering on vacation ... "Extend your lovely
beauty-time. Sunbathe in the sun of your silken breasts,
and wait until good omen arrives. Later
we will grow older. We have enough time
to grow older after this day ..." /
Another day will come, a womanly day
songlike in gesture, lapis in greeting
and in phrase. All things will be feminine outside
the past. Water will flow from rock's bosom.
No dust, no drought, no defeat.
And a dove will sleep in the afternoon in an abandoned
combat tank if it doesn't find a small nest
in the lovers' bed ...

وأنا، وإن كنت الأخير

وأنا، وإن كُنْتُ الأخيرَ،
وَجَدْتُ ما يكفي من الكلماتِ ...
كُلُّ قصيدة رَسْمٌ
سأرسم للسنونو الآن خارطةَ الربيع
وللمُشَاة على الرصيف الزيزفونَ
وللنساء اللازوردْ ...
وأنا، سيحملُني الطريقُ
وسوف أحملُهُ على كتفي
إلى أنْ يستعيدَ الشيءُ صورتَهُ،
كما هـيَ،
واسمَهُ الأصليَّ في ما بعد/
كُلُّ قصيدة أُمٌّ
تفتِّشُ للسحابة عن أخيها
قرب بئر الماء:
«يا وَلَدي! سأعطيك البديلَ
فإنني حُبْلى ...»/
وكُلُّ قصيدة حُلْمٌ:
«حَلِمْتُ بأنَّ لي حلماً»
سيحملني وأحملُهُ
إلى أن أكتب السَّطْرَ الأخيرَ
على رخام القبرِ:
«نِمْتُ ... لكي أطير»

... وسوف أعمل للمسيح حذاءهُ الشتويَّ
كي يمشي، كـكُلِّ الناس،
من أعلى الجبال ... إلى البحيرةُ

And I, Even if I Were the Last

And I, even if I were the last,
have found enough of words ...
Every poem is a sketch
I'll sketch now for the swallow the map of spring
and for the pedestrians on the sidewalk some jujube
and for the women the lapis lazuli ...
As for me, the road will carry me
and I will carry it on my shoulder
until each thing regains its image,
as it was,
and its original name later on /
Every poem is a mother
searching for the cloud's brother
near the well:
"My son! I'll give you a replacement
I'm pregnant ..." /
And every poem is a dream:
"I dreamt that I have a dream"
that will carry me and that I will carry
until I write the final line
on the grave's marble:
"I slept ... so that I can fly"

... and I will carry for Christ his winter shoes
so he can walk, like all people,
from the highest mountain ... down to the lake

في بيت أمّي

في بيت أمّي صُورَتي ترنو إليّ
ولا تكفُّ عن السؤال:
أأنت، يا ضَيفي، أنا؟
هل كنتَ في العشرينَ من عُمري،
بلا نظّارة طبّيةٍ،
وبلا حقائبَ؟
كان ثُقْبٌ في جدار السور يكفي
كي تعلّمك النجومُ هوايةَ التحديقِ
في الأبديِّ ...
[ما الأبديُّ؟ قُلْتُ مخاطباً نفسي]
ويا ضيفي ... أأنتَ أنا كما كنا؟
فَمَنْ منّا تنصَّلَ من ملامحه؟
أتذكرُ حافرَ الفَرَس الحرونِ على جبينكَ
أم مَسَحْتَ الـجُرْحَ بالمكياج كي تبدو
وسيمَ الشكل في الكاميرا؟
أأنتَ أنا؟ أتذكرُ قلبَكَ المثقوبَ
بالناي القديم وريشة العنقاء؟
أم غيّرْتَ قَلْبَكَ عندما غيّرتَ دَرْبَكَ؟

قلت: يا هذا، أنا هُوَ أنت
لكني قفزتُ عن الجدار لكي أرى
ماذا سيحدث لو رآني الغيبُ أقطفُ
من حدائقه الـمُعَلّقة البنفسجَ باحترامٍ ...
رُبّما ألقى السلام، وقال لي:
عُدْ سالماً ...
وقفزت عن هذا الجدار لكي أرى
ما لا يُرى
وأقيسَ عُمْقَ الهاويةْ

In My Mother's House

In my mother's house my photo gazes at me
and doesn't cease asking:
Are you, my dear guest, me?
Were you once twenty of my years,
without medical glasses,
and without suitcases?
A hole in the wall was enough
for the stars to teach you the hobby of staring
into the eternal ...
(What's the eternal? I said to myself)
And my dear guest ... are you me as we once were?
Which one of us renounced his features?
Do you remember that stubborn horse's hoofprint on your forehead
or did you blend the wound in with makeup to appear
handsome for the camera?
Are you me? Don't you remember your heart punctured
with the old flute and with the phoenix feather?
Or did you change your heart when you changed your path?

I said: Listen you, I am he you
but I jumped down from the wall to see
what would happen if fate saw me picking
purple flowers from its hanging gardens respectfully ...
It might greet me and say:
Get back safe ...
And I jumped down from this wall to see
what can't be seen
and to measure the depth of the abyss

لا تعتذر عمَّا فعلت

لا تعتذرْ عمَّا فَعَلْتَ ـــ أقول
في سرّي. أقول لآخَري الشخصيِّ:
ها هـيَ ذكرياتُكَ كُلُّها مرئيّةٌ:
ضَجَرُ الظهيرة في نُعَاس القطّ/
عُرْفُ الديك/
عطرُ المريمَّيَّة/
قهوةُ الأُمّ/
الحصيرةُ والوسائدُ/
بابُ غُرْفَتِكَ الحديديُّ/
الذبابةُ حول سقراطَ/
السحابةُ فوق أفلاطونَ/
ديوانُ الحماسةِ/
صورةُ الأب/
مُعْجَمُ البلدان/
شيكسبير/
الأشقَّاءُ الثلاثةُ، والشقيقاتُ الثلاثُ،
وأصدقاؤك في الطفولة، والفضوليُّون:
«هل هذا هُوَ؟» اختلف الشهودُ:
لعلّه، وكأنه. فسَألْتُ: «مَنْ هُوَ؟»
لم يُجيبوني. هَمَسْتُ لآخري: «أهو
الذي قد كان أنتَ ... أنا؟» فغضَّ
الطرف. والتفتوا إلى أُمِّي لتشهد
أنني هُوَ ... فاستعدَّتْ للغناء على
طريقتها: أنا الأُمُّ التي ولدتُهُ،
لكنَّ الرياحَ هيَ التي ربَّتْهُ.
قلتُ لآخري: لا تعتذر إلاَّ لأُمِّكَ!

Don't Apologize for What You've Done

Don't apologize for what you've done—I say
to myself. To my personal other I say:
Here they are, your memories, all visible:
The noon boredom in a cat's drowsiness /
The rooster's crest /
The sage fragrance /
Mother's coffee /
The straw mat and the pillows /
Your room's metal door /
The fly around Socrates /
The cloud above Plato /
The *Hamassa Diwan* /
Father's picture /
The Encyclopedia of Countries /
Shakespeare /
The three brothers, and the three sisters,
and your childhood friends, and the nosy people:
Is that him? The witnesses disagree:
Perhaps! he looks like him. I asked: Who?
They didn't reply. So I whispered to my other self: Is the one
who was once you … me? But he moved his eyes
away from me. Then people turned to my mother to confirm
that I am he … so she got ready to sing
in her own style: I am the mother who gave birth to him,
but the winds are the ones that raised him.
Then I told my other self: Apologize only to your mother!

في مثل هذا اليوم

في مثل هذا اليوم، في الطَّرَف الخفيِّ
من الكنيسةِ، في بهاءِ كاملِ التأنيثِ،
في السنة الكبيسة، في التقاء الأخضر
الأبديّ بالـكُحْليّ في هذا الصباح، وفي
التقاء الشكل بالمضمون، والحسيّ بالصُّوفيّ،
تحت عريشة فَضْفَاضَة في ظلّ دوريٍّ
يوتّرُ صورةَ المعنى، وفي هذا المكان
العاطفيِّ/
سألتقي بنهايتي وبدايتي
وأقولَ: ويحكما! خذاني و أ تركا
قلبَ الحقيقة طازَجاً لبنات آوى الجائعاتِ،
أقول: لَسْتُ مواطناً
أو لاجئاً
وأُريد شيئاً واحداً، لا غير،
شيئاً واحداً:
موتاً بسيطاً هادئاً
في مثل هذا اليوم،
في الطرف الخفيِّ من الزَّنَابقِ،
قد يُعَوِّضُني كثيراً أو قليلا
عن حياةٍ كنت أُحْصيها
دقائقَ
أو رحيلا
وأُريد موتاً في الحديقةِ
ليس أكْثَرَ أو أَقَلّ!

On a Day like Today

On a day like today, in the hidden corner
of the church, in full feminine adornment,
in a leap year, in the meeting of endless
green with kohl darkness on this morning, and in
the meeting of shape with substance,
and the sensory with the Sufi,
beneath a spacious grapevine trellis
in a house sparrow's shadow
that distresses meaning's image, and in this
sentimental place /
    I will meet with my end and my beginning
    and say: Damn you! take me and leave
the heart of truth fresh for the jackals' daughters,
I'll say: I am not a citizen
or a refugee
and I want only one thing, nothing else,
one thing:
a quiet simple death
on a day like today,
in the hidden corner of irises,
which might compensate me a lot or a little
for a life I used to measure
in minutes
or departures
and I want a death in the garden
no more and no less!

أَنزلْ، هنا، والآن

أنزلْ، هنا، والآن، عن كتفَيْكَ قَبْرَكَ
وأعط عُمرَكَ فُرْصَةً أخرى لترميم الحكايةِ
ليس كُلُّ الـحُبِّ موتاً
ليست الأرضُ اغتراباً مزمناً،
فلرما جاءت مناسبةٌ، فتنسى
لَسْعَةَ العَسَل القديم، كأنْ تحبَّ
وأنتَ لا تدري فتاةً لا تحبُّكَ
أو تحبُّكَ، دون أن تدري لماذا
لا تحبُّكَ أو تحبُّكَ/
أو تحسَّ وأنت مُسْتَندٌ إلى دَرَج
بأنك كنتَ غيرك في الثنائياتِ/
فاخرج من «أنا» كَ إلى سواكَ
ومن رُؤَاكَ إلى خُطَاكَ
ومُـدَّ جسركَ عالياً،
فاللامكانُ هُـوَ المكيدةُ،
والبَعُوضُ على السياج يَـحُكُّ ظَهْرَكَ،
قد تذكّركُ البَعُوضةُ بالحياة!
فجرِّب الآن الحياةَ لكي تُدَرِّبَكَ الحياةُ
على الحياةِ،
وخفِّف الذكرى عن الأنثى
و أ نزلْ
ها هنا
والآن
عن كتفيكَ ... قَـبْـرَكْ!

Set Down, Here, and Now

Set down, here, and now, from your shoulders your grave
and give your life another chance to renovate the story.
Not all love is death
land is not a chronic exile,
because an occasion might come, and you might forget
the old honey sting, and love
without knowing it a girl who loves you not
or loves you, without knowing why
she loves you or loves you not /
Or you might feel while leaning on the staircase
that you were another in the duality of things /
So get out of your "I" to your else
and from your vision to your steps
and extend your bridge high,
because nonplace is a ruse,
and the mosquitoes on the fence might scratch your back,
a mosquito might remind you of life!
So try life now for life to train you
to live,
and ease a woman's memory
and set down
right here
and now
from your shoulders ... your grave!

إن عدت وحدك

إن عُـدْتَ وَحدَكَ، قُلْ لنفسك:
غيَّر المنفى ملامحه ...
ألم يفجعْ أبو تـمّام قَبْلَكَ
حين قابل نفسَهُ:
«لا أنتِ أنتِ
ولا الديارُ هيَ الديارُ»...

ستحمل الأشياءُ عنك شعورَكَ الوطنيَّ:
تنبتُ زهرةٌ بريّةٌ في ركنك المهجور/
ينقُرُ طائرُ الدوريّ حَرْفَ «الحاء»،
في اسمكَ،
في لحاء التّينَة المكسورِ/
تلسَعُ نَحْلَةٌ يَدَكَ التي امتدَّتْ
إلى زَغَبِ الإوزّةِ خلف هذا السورِ/

أمّا أنت،
فالمرآةُ قد خَذَلَتْكَ،
أنْتَ ... ولَسْتَ أنتَ، تقولُ:
«أين تركت وجهي؟»
ثم تبحثُ عن شعورك، خارج الأشياء،
بين سعادةٍ تبكي وإحْبَاطٍ يُقَهْقِهُ ...
هل وجدت الآن نفسك؟
قل لنفسك: عُدْتُ وحدي ناقصاً
قَمَرَيْنِ،
لكنَّ الديارَ هي الديار!

If You Return Alone

If you return alone, tell yourself:
Exile has changed its features …
Wasn't Abu Tammam before you harrowed
when he met himself:
"Neither you are you
nor home is home" …

Things will carry for you your patriotic feeling:
A wildflower will sprout in your abandoned corner /
The house sparrow will pick at the letter "h"
in your name
in the fig tree's broken husk /
A bee will sting your hand as you reach
for the goose fuzz behind this fence /

As for you,
the mirror has failed you,
and you are … and aren't you:
Where did I leave my face? you say
then search for your feeling, outside the things,
between a crying happiness and a guffawing depression …
Have you found yourself now?
Tell yourself: I returned alone missing
two moons,
but home is home!

لم أَعتذر للبئر

لم أعتَذرْ للبئر حين مَرَرْتُ بالبئرِ،
استَعَرْتُ من الصَّنَوْبَرة العتيقة غيمةً
وعَصرْتُها كالبرتقالة، وانتظرتُ غزالة
بيضاءَ أسطوريَّةً. وأمَرْتُ قلبي بالتريّث:
كُنْ حياديّاً كأنَّكَ لَسْتَ مني! ها هنا
وقف الرُّعاةُ الطيّبون على الهواء وطوَّروا
النايات، ثم استدرجوا حَجَلَ الجبال إلى
الفخاخ. وها هنا أسْرَجْتُ للطيران نحو
كواكبي فَرَساً، وطرتُ. وها هنا قالت
لي العرَّافةُ: احذرْ شارع الإسفلت
والعربات وامشِ على زفيرك. ها هنا
أرخيتُ ظلّي وانتظرتُ، إخْتَرْتُ أصغرَ
صخرة وَسَهِرْتُ. كَسَّرْتُ الخرافة وانكسرتُ.
ودُرْتُ حول البئر حتى طِرْتُ من نفسي
إلى ما ليس منها. صاح بي صوتٌ
عميقٌ: ليس هذا القبرُ قَبركَ، فاعتذرت.
قرأت آيات من الذكر الحكيم، وقُلْتُ
للمجهول في البئر: السلام عليك يوم
قُتِلْتَ في أرض السلام، ويَوْمَ تصعَدُ
من ظلام البئر حيّا!

I Didn't Apologize to the Well

I didn't apologize to the well when I passed the well,
I borrowed from the ancient pine tree a cloud
and squeezed it like an orange, then waited for a gazelle
white and legendary. And I ordered my heart to be patient:
Be neutral as if you were not of me! Right here
the kind shepherds stood on air and evolved
their flutes, then persuaded the mountain quail toward
the snare. And right here I saddled a horse for flying toward
my planets, then flew. And right here the priestess
told me: Beware of the asphalt road and the cars
and walk upon your exhalation. Right here
I slackened my shadow and waited, I picked the tiniest
rock and stayed up late. I broke the myth and I broke.
And I circled the well until I flew from myself
to what isn't of it. A deep voice shouted at me:
This grave isn't your grave. So I apologized.
I read verses from the wise holy book, and said
to the unknown one in the well: Salaam upon you the day
you were killed in the land of peace, and the day you rise
from the darkness of the well alive!

لا راية في الريح

لا رايةٌ في الريح تخفقُ/
لا حصانٌ سابحٌ في الريح/
لا طَبْلَ يُبَشِّرُ بارتفاع الموج
أو بهبوطه،
لا شيءَ يحدثُ في التراجيديَّات هذا اليومَ/
أُسدلَت الستارةُ/
غادَرَ الشعراءُ والمتفرِّجونَ،
فلا أرزَّ/
لا مظاهرةٌ/
ولا أغصانُ زيتونٍ تُحيّي الهابطينَ
من المراكب مُتَعبينَ من الرُّعافِ
وخفَّة الفصل الأخيرِ/
كأنَّهُمْ يأتون من قَدَرٍ إلى قَدَرٍ/
مصائرُهُمْ مُدَوَّنةٌ وراء النصِّ،
إغريقيَّةٌ في شكل طُروادِيَّةٍ،
بيضاءَ، أو سوداءَ/
لا انكسروا ولا انتصروا
ولم يتساءلوا: ماذا سيحدثُ في صباح غدٍ
وماذا بعد هذا الانتظار الهوميريّ؟/
كأنه حُلْمٌ جميلٌ يُنصف الأسرى
ويُسعفُهُمْ على الليل المحليّ الطويل،
كأنهم قالوا:
« نُداوي جرحنا بالملح
« نحيا قرب ذكرانا
« نجرِّبُ موتنا العاديَّ
« ننتظر القيامةَ، ههنا، في دارها
في الفصل ما بعد الأخيرَ...»

No Banner in the Wind

No banner in the wind fluttering /
No horse swimming in the wind /
No drums promising the rise of the waves
or their fall,
nothing happens in today's tragedies /
The curtains are down /
The poets and the spectators have gone,
so there is no rice /
No demonstration /
And no olive branches greeting those coming down
off the boats worn out from their nosebleeds
and from the levity of the final act /
As if they were going from one fate to another /
Their destinies already prescribed behind the text,
Greek in a Trojan shape,
white, or black /
They were neither broken nor triumphant
and they didn't ask: "What will happen tomorrow morning
and what now after this long Homeric waiting?" /
As if it were a beautiful dream that treated the captives justly
and aided them through the long local night,
as if they had said:
"We treat our wounds with salt"
"We live near our memories"
"We try out our ordinary death"
"We wait for judgment day, right here, in its house
in the act after the last …"

سقط الحصان عن القصيدة

سَقَطَ الحصانُ عن القصيدةِ
والجليليّاتُ كُنَّ مُبَلَّلاتٍ
بالفَراش وبالندى،
يَرْقُصْنَ فوق الأقحوانْ

الغائبان: أنا وأنتِ
أنا وأنتِ الغائبانْ

زوجا يمام أبيضانْ
يَتَسَامران على غُصون السنديانْ

لا حُبَّ، لكني أُحبُّ قصائدَ
الحبّ القديمةَ، تحرسُ
القَمَرَ المريضَ من الدخانْ

كرٌّ وفرٌّ، كالكَمَـنْجَةِ في الرباعيّاتِ
أنْأى عن زماني حين أدنو
من تضاريس المكانْ ...

لم يَبْقَ في اللغة الحديثةِ هامشٌ
للاحتفاء بما نحبُّ،
فكُلُّ ما سيكونُ ... كانْ

سقط الحصان مُضَرَّجاً
بقصيدتي
وأنا سقطتُ مُضَرَّجاً
بدَم الحصانْ ...

The Horse Fell Off the Poem

The horse fell off the poem
and the Galilean women were wet
with butterflies and dew,
dancing above chrysanthemum

The two absent ones: you and I
you and I are the two absent ones

A pair of white doves
chatting on the branches of a holm oak

No love, but I love ancient
love poems that guard
the sick moon from smoke

I attack and retreat, like the violin in quatrains
I get far from my time when I am near
the topography of place ...

There is no margin in modern language left
to celebrate what we love,
because all that will be ... was

The horse fell bloodied
with my poem
and I fell bloodied
with the horse's blood ...

لبلادنا

لبلادنا،
وَهِيَ القريبةُ من كلام اللهِ،
سَقْفٌ من سحابْ
لبلادنا،
وهي البعيدةُ عن صفاتِ الاسم،
خارطةُ الغيابْ
لبلادنا،
وهي الصغيرة مثل حبّة سُمْسُمٍ،
أُفْقٌ سماويٌّ ... وهاويةٌ خفيَّةٌ
لبلادنا،
وهي الفقيرةُ مثل أجنحة القَطَا،
كُتُبٌ مُقَدَّسَةٌ ... وجرحٌ في الهويّةْ
لبلادنا،
وهي المطوَّقَةُ الممزَّقةُ التلال،
كمائنُ الماضي الجديد
لبلادنا، وهي السَّبِيّةْ
حُريّةُ الموت اشتياقاً واحتراقا
وبلادُنا، في ليلها الدمويِّ
جَوْهَرَةٌ تشعُّ على البعيد على البعيد
تُضيء خارجَها ...
وأمَّا نحن، داخلها،
فنزدادُ اختناقا!

To Our Land

To our land,
and it is the one near the word of god,
a ceiling of clouds
To our land,
and it is the one far from the adjectives of nouns,
the map of absence
To our land,
and it is the one tiny as a sesame seed,
a heavenly horizon ... and a hidden chasm
To our land,
and it is the one poor as a grouse's wings,
holy books ... and an identity wound
To our land,
and it is the one surrounded with torn hills,
the ambush of a new past
To our land, and it is a prize of war,
the freedom to die from longing and burning
and our land, in its bloodied night,
is a jewel that glimmers for the far upon the far
and illuminates what's outside it ...
As for us, inside,
we suffocate more!

ولنا بلاد

ولنا بلادٌ لا حُدُودَ لها، كفكرتنا عن
المجهول، ضيّقةٌ وواسعةٌ. بلادٌ ...
حين نمشي في خريطتها تضيقُ بنا،
وتأخذنا إلى نَفَقٍ رمادي، فنصرخ
في متاهتها: وما زلنا نحبُّك. حُبُّنا
مَرَضٌ ورائيٌّ. بلادٌ ... حين
تتنبّذُنا إلى المجهول ... تكبُرُ. يكبُرُ
الصفصافُ والأوصافُ. يكبُرُ عُشْبُها
وجبالُها الزرقاءُ. تَتّسعُ البحيرةُ في
شمالِ الروح. ترتفعُ السنابلُ في جنوب
الروح. تلمعُ حبّةُ الليمون قنديلاً
على ليل الـمُهاجرِ. تسطعُ الجغرافيا
كُتُباً مُقَدَّسَةً. وسلسلةُ التلال
تصير معراجاً، إلى الأعلى ... إلى الأعلى.
«لو أنّـيَ طائرٌ لحرقتُ أجنحتي» يقول
لنفسه المنفيُّ. رائحةُ الخريف تصيرُ
صورةَ ما أحبُّ... تسرّبَ المطرُ
الخفيفُ إلى جفاف القلب، فانفتح الخيالُ
على مصادره، وصار هو المكانَ، هو
الحقيقيَّ الوحيدَ. وكُلُّ شيء في
البعيد يعود ريفيّاً بدائيّاً، كأنَّ الأرضَ
ما زالت تكوّن نفسها للقاء آدَمَ، نازلاً
للطابق الأرضيِّ من فردوسه. فأقول:
تلك بلادنا حُبْلى بنا ... فمتى وُلِدْنا؟
هل تزوّج آدمُ أُ مرأتين؟ أم أنّا
سَنُولَدُ مرةً أخرى
لكي ننسى الخطيئةَ؟

And We Have a Land

And we have a land without borders, like our idea
of the unknown, narrow and wide. A land ...
when we walk in its map it becomes narrow with us,
and takes us to an ashen tunnel, so we shout
in its labyrinth: And we still love you, our love
is a hereditary illness. A land ... when
it banishes us to the unknown ... it grows. And
the willows and adjectives grow. And its grass grows
and its blue mountains. The lake widens
in the soul's north. Wheat rises in the soul's
south. The lemon fruit gleams like a lantern
in the emigrant's night. Geography glistens
like a holy book. And the chain of hills
becomes an ascension place to higher ... to higher.
"If I were a bird I would have burned my wings," someone says
to his exiled self. The scent of autumn becomes
the image of what I love ... The light rain leaks
into the heart's drought, and the imagination opens up
to its sources, and becomes place, the only
real one. And everything from the faraway
returns as a primitive countryside, as if earth
were still creating itself to meet Adam, descending
to the ground floor from his paradise. Then I say:
That's our land over there pregnant with us ... When was it
that we were born? Did Adam get married twice? Or will we
be born a second time
to forget sin?

لا شيء إلّا الضوء

لا شيءَ إلّا الضوء،
لم أوقفْ حصاني
إلّا لأقطف وردةً حمراءَ من
بُستان كَنْعَانيّة أغْوَتْ حصاني
وتحصَّنَتْ في الضوء:
«لا تدخُلْ ولا تخرجْ» ...
فلم أدخلْ، ولم أخرجْ
وقالت: هل تراني؟
فهمستُ: ينقصني، لأعرف، فارقٌ
بين المسافر والطريق، وفارقٌ
بين المغنّي والأغاني ...
جَلَسَتْ أريحا، مثل حرف
من حروف الأبجدية، في إسمها
وكَبوْتُ في إسمي
عند مُفْتَرَق المعاني ...
أنا ما أكونُ غداً
ولم أوقفْ حصاني
إلّا لأقطفَ وردةً حمراءَ من
بستان كَنْعَانيّة أغوتْ حصاني
ومضيتُ أبحثُ عن مكاني
أعلى وأبْعَدَ،
ثم أعلى ثم أبعَدَ،
من زماني ...

Nothing but Light

Nothing but light,
I only stopped my horse
to pick a red rose from
the garden of a Canaanite who had seduced my horse
and fortified in the light:
Don't come in and don't get out ...
So I didn't go in, and I didn't get out
Then she said: Do you see me?
I whispered: I need, to be certain, a difference
between the traveler and the road, and a difference
between the singer and the song ...
Jericho sat, like a letter of the alphabet, within her name
and I tumbled in mine
at the crossroads of meaning ...
I am what I become tomorrow
and I only stopped my horse
to pick a red rose from
the garden of a Canaanite who had seduced my horse
then I went searching for my place
higher and farther,
then higher and farther,
than my time ...

نزَف الحبيبُ شقائق النعمان

نزَفَ الحبيبُ شقائقَ النُّعْمانِ،
أرضُ الأرجوان تلألأتْ بجروحِه،
أولى أغانيها: دَمُ الـحُبِّ الذي سفكته آلهةٌ،
وآخرُها دَمٌ ...
يا شعبَ كَنْعَانَ احتفلْ
بربيع أرضك، واشتعلْ
كزهورها، يا شعب كنعان الـمُجَرَّدَ من
سلاحك، واكتملْ!
من حُسْن حَظِّكَ أنَّكَ أ خترتَ الزراعةَ مِهْنَةً
من سوء حظك أنَّكَ اخترتَ البساتينَ
القريبةَ من حدود الله،
حيث السيفُ يكتب سيرةَ الصَّلْصَال...
فلتَكُنِ السنابلُ جَيْشَكَ الأبديِّ،
وليكنِ الخلودُ كلابَ صيدٍ
في حقول القمح،
ولتكن الأيائلُ حُـرَّةً
كقصيدةٍ رعويةٍ ...

نزَفَ الحبيبُ شقائقَ النعمان،
فاصفرَّتْ صخورُ السَّفْحِ من
وَجَع المخاض الصعبِ،
واحمرَّتْ،
وسال الماءُ أحمرَ
في عروق ربيعنا ...
أولى أغانينا دَمُ الـحُبِّ الذي
سفكته آلهةٌ،
وآخرُها دَمٌ سَفَكَتْهُ آلهةُ الحديد...

The Beloved Hemorrhaged Anemones

The beloved hemorrhaged anemones,
the purple land glittered with his wounds,
the first of its songs: the blood of love shed by gods,
and the last of it is blood ...
O people of Canaan celebrate
your land's spring and set yourself aflame
like its flowers, O people of Canaan stripped
of your weapons, and become complete!
It's your good luck that you chose agriculture as a profession.
It's your bad luck that you chose the gardens
near god's borders,
where the sword writes clay's tale ...
So let the grain spikes be your eternal army,
and let immortality be hunting dogs
in wheat fields,
and let the stags be free
like a pastoral poem ...

The beloved hemorrhaged anemones,
and the rocks on the slope yellowed from
prolonged labor contractions,
then turned red,
then water flowed red
in our spring's veins ...
The first of our songs is the blood of love
that gods shed,
and the last is the blood shed by iron gods ...

في القدس

في القدس، أعني داخلَ السُّور القديمِ،
أسيرُ من زَمَنٍ إلى زَمَنٍ بلا ذكرى
تُصوِّبُني. فإن الأنبياءَ هناك يقتسمون
تاريخَ المقدَّس ... يصعدون إلى السماء
ويرجعون أقلَّ إحباطاً وحزناً، فالمحبَّة
والسلامُ مُقَدَّسَان وقادمان إلى المدينة.
كنت أمشي فوق مُنْحَدَرٍ وأُهجِسُ: كيف
يختلف الرُّواةُ على كلام الضوء في حَجَرٍ؟
أَمِنْ حَـجَرٍ شحيح الضوء تندلعُ الحروبُ؟
أسير في نومي. أحملق في منامي. لا
أرى أحداً ورائي. لا أرى أحداً أمامي.
كلُّ هذا الضوء لي. أمشي. أخفُّ. أطيرُ
ثم أصير غيري في التَّجَلِّي. تنبُتُ
الكلماتُ كالأعشاب من فم أشعيا
النَّبويِّ: «إنْ لم تُؤْمنوا لن تَـأْمَنُوا».
أمشي كأنِّي واحدٌ غيري. وجُرحي وَرْدَةٌ
بيضاءُ إنجيليَّةٌ. ويدايَ مثل حمامتَيْن
على الصليب تُحلِّقان وتحملان الأرضَ.
لا أمشي، أطيرُ، أصيرُ غَيْري في
التجلِّي. لا مكانَ ولا زمانَ. فمن أنا؟
أنا لا أنا في حضرة المعراج. لكنِّي
أفكِّرُ: وَحدهُ، كان النبيّ محمَّدٌ
يتكلَّمُ العربيَّة الفُصْحَى. «وماذا بعد؟»
ماذا بعد؟ صاحت فجأة جنديَّةٌ:
هُـوَ أنتَ ثانيةً؟ ألم أقتلْكَ؟
قلت: قَتَلْتِني ... ونسيتُ، مثلك، أن أموت.

In Jerusalem

In Jerusalem, and I mean within the ancient walls,
I walk from one epoch to another without a memory
to guide me. The prophets over there are sharing
the history of the holy ... ascending to heaven
and returning less discouraged and melancholy, because love
and peace are holy and are coming to town.
I was walking down a slope and thinking to myself: How
do the narrators disagree over what light said about a stone?
Is it from a dimly lit stone that wars flare up?
I walk in my sleep. I stare in my sleep. I see
no one behind me. I see no one ahead of me.
All this light is for me. I walk. I become lighter. I fly
then I become another. Transfigured. Words
sprout like grass from Isaiah's messenger
mouth: "If you don't believe you won't be safe."
I walk as if I were another. And my wound a white
biblical rose. And my hands like two doves
on the cross hovering and carrying the earth.
I don't walk, I fly, I become another,
transfigured. No place and no time. So who am I?
I am no I in ascension's presence. But I
think to myself: Alone, the prophet Muhammad
spoke classical Arabic. "And then what?"
Then what? A woman soldier shouted:
Is that you again? Didn't I kill you?
I said: You killed me ... and I forgot, like you, to die.

بغيابها كَوّنْت صورتها

بغيابها، كوّنْتُ صُورتَها: مِنَ الأرضِ
يبتدىء السماويُّ الخفيُّ. أنا هُنا أزنُ
المدى بمعلّقات الجاهليّين ... الغياب هُوَ
الدليلُ هُـوَ الدليلُ. لكُلِّ قافيةٍ أُقيمتْ
خيمةٌ. ولكُلِّ شيء في مهبِّ الريح
قافيةٌ. يُعَلّمني الغيابُ دروسه: «لولا
السرابُ لَـمَا صَمَدْتَ...» وفي الفراغ
فَكَكْتُ حرفاً من حروف الأبجديّات القديمة،
واتّكَأْتُ على الغياب. فَمَنْ أنا بعد
الزيارةِ؟ طائرٌ، أم عابرٌ بين الرموز
وباعةِ الذكرى؟ كأني قِطْعَةٌ أثريَّةٌ،
وكأنني شَبَحٌ تسلّلَ من يَبوسَ، وقلْتُ لي:
فلنذهبْنَ إلى تلالٍ سَبْعَة. فوضعْتُ
أقْنِعَتي على حَجَرٍ، وسرْتُ كما يسير
النائمون يقودُني حُلمي. ومن قَمَرٍ إلى
قمرٍ قَفَزْتُ. هناك ما يكفي من اللاوعي
كي تَتحرَّر الأشياءُ من تاريخها. وهناك
ما يكفي من التاريخ كي يتحرَّر اللاوعيُّ
من معراجه. «خذني إلى سنواتنا
الأولى» ـــ تقول صديقتي الأولى. «دَعي
الشُّبّاكَ مفتوحاً ليدخل طائرُ الدوريّ
حُلمَكِ» ... ثم أصحو، لا مدينةَ في
المدينة. لا «هُنا» إلّا «هناك». ولا
هناك سوى هنا. لولا السرابُ
لَما مَشَيْتُ إلى تلالٍ سَبْعَةٍ...
لولا السراب!

In Her Absence I Created Her Image

In her absence I created her image: out of the earthly
the hidden heavenly commences. I am here weighing
the expanse with the Jahili odes … and absence
is the guide, it is the guide. For each rhyme a tent
is pitched. And for each thing blowing in the wind
a rhyme. Absence teaches me its lesson: If it weren't
for the mirage you wouldn't have been steadfast …
Then in the emptiness, I disassembled a letter from one
of the ancient alphabets, and I leaned on absence. So who am I
after the visitation? A bird, or a passerby amid the symbols
and the memory vendors? As if I were an antique piece,
as if I were a ghost sneaking in from Yabous, telling myself:
Let's go to the seven hills. Then I placed
my mask on a stone, and walked as the sleepless
walk, led by my dream. And from one moon
to another I leapt. There is enough of unconsciousness
to liberate things from their history. And there
is enough of history to liberate unconsciousness
from its ascension. Take me to our early
years—my first girlfriend says. Leave
the windows open for the house sparrow to enter
your dream—I say … then I awaken, and no city is in
the city. No "here" except "there." And no there
but here. If it weren't for the mirage
I wouldn't have walked to the seven hills …
if it weren't for the mirage!

الأربعاء، الجمعة، السبت

الأربعاء
الـجُمْعَةُ/
السَّبْتُ/
الأساطيرُ، ألبلادُ، تشابَهَتْ ...
لو كان لي قلبان لم أُندم على
حبّ، فإنْ أخطأتُ قُلْتُ: أسأتَ
يا قلبي الجريحَ الاختيارَ!... وقادني
القلبُ الصحيحُ إلى الينابيع/

الخميسُ
السَّوْسَنُ/
الاثنين/
أسماءُ المكان تشابَهَتْ. أرْهَقْتُ أُغنيتي
بوصف الظلَّ. والمعنى يَرَى قَلْبَ
الظلام ولا يُرَى. قال الكلامُ كلامَهُ،
فبكت إلهاتٌ كثيراتٌ على أدوارهنَّ/

ألحكمةُ/
الأَحَـدُ/
الـغَدُ/
الطُّرُقُ، الثلاثاءُ، السماء، تشابهت ...
لو كان لي دربان لاخترتُ البديلَ
الثالثَ. انكشَفَ الطريقُ الأوَّلُ،
انكشَفَ الطريقُ الآخَرُ،
انكَشَفَتْ دُروبُ الهاوية

Wednesday, Friday, Saturday

Wednesday /
Friday /
Saturday /
The myths, the land look alike …
If I had two hearts I wouldn't regret
a single love, so that when I erred I'd say: You chose
poorly my wounded heart! … then the right
heart would lead me to the springs /

Thursday
The lily /
Monday /
The names of the place sound alike. I exhausted my song
describing shadow. And meaning sees the heart
of darkness and is not seen. Speech said its words,
then many gods wept over their roles /

Wisdom /
Sunday /
Tomorrow /
The roads, Tuesday, the heavens are alike …
If I had two paths I would choose
the third. The first path has been exposed,
the other path has been exposed,
all the paths to the abyss have been exposed

زيتونتان

زيتونتانِ عتيقتان على شمال الشرقِ،
في الأولى اختبأتُ لأخدَعَ الراوي
وفي الأخرى خَبَّأتُ شقائق النعمانْ

إن شئتُ أن أنسى ... تذَكَّرْتُ
امتلأتُ بحاضري، واخترتُ يومَ
ولادتي ... لأرتّب النسيانْ

تَتَشَعَّبُ الذكرى. هُنَا قَمَرٌ يُعِدُّ
وليمةً لغيابه. وهناك بئرٌ في
جنوبيّ الحديقة زفّتِ امرأةً إلى شيطانْ

كُلُّ الملائكة الذين أحبُّهُمْ
أخذوا الربيعَ من المكان، صباح
أمسِ، وأورثوني قمّة البُركانْ

أنا آدمُ الثاني. تَعَلَّمْتُ القراءةَ
والكتابةَ من دروس خطيئتي،
وغدي سيبدأ من هنا، والآنْ

إن شئتُ أن أنسى... تذكّرتُ
انتقيْتُ بدايةً، وَوُلِدْتُ كيف أردتُ
لا بطلاً ... ولا قُرْبانْ

تَتَشَعَّبُ الذكرى وتلعَبُ. ها هنا
زيتونتان عتيقتان على شمال الشرقِ
في الأولى وَجَدْتُ بُذورَ أُغنيتي

وفي الأخرى وَجَدْتُ رسالةً
من قائد الرومانْ:

Two Olive Trees

Two olive trees in the northeast,
in the first I hid to trick the narrator
and in the other I hid the anemones

If I want to forget … I recall
I become filled with my presence, I choose the day
I was born … to arrange forgetfulness

Memory branches out. Here a moon prepares
a feast for its absence. And there a well in the garden's
south has processioned a woman to a devil

All the angels that I love
took spring away from the place, yesterday
morning, and bequeathed me the volcano summit

I am the second Adam. I learned to read
and write through my sins' lessons,
and my tomorrow starts from here, and now

If I want to forget … I recall
I select a beginning, I become born as I desire
not as a hero … nor as an offering

Memory branches out and plays. Right here
are two ancient olive trees in the northeast
in the first I found my song's seeds

and in the other I found a letter
from the commander of the Romans:

يا إخوَةَ الزيتونِ
أطلُبُ منكمُ الغفران،
أطلب منكمُ الغفران...

O olive brothers
I ask for your forgiveness,
I ask for your forgiveness ...

لا ينظرون وراءهم

لا ينظرونَ وراءهمْ ليودِّعوا منفى،
فإنَّ أمامهم منفى، لقد ألْفُوا الطريق
الدائريَّ، فلا أمامَ ولا وراء، ولا
شمالَ ولا جنوبَ. «يهاجرون» من
السياج إلى الحديقة. يتركون وصيَّةً
في كل مترٍ من فناء البيت:
«لا تتذكَّروا من بعدنا
إلّا الحياة» ...
«يسافرون» من الصباح السنديّ إلى
غبارٍ في الظهيرة، حاملين نُعوشَهُمْ ملأى
بأشياء الغياب: بطاقة شخصيّةٍ، ورسالةٍ
لحبيبة مَجْهولَةِ العُنْوانِ:
«لا تتذكَّري من بعدنا
إلّا الحياة»
و«يرحلون» من البيوت إلى الشوارع،
راسمينَ إشارةَ النصر الجريحةَ، قائلين
لمن يراهُمْ:
«لم نَزَلْ نحيا، فلا تتذكَّرُونا»!
يخرجون من الحكاية للتنفُّس والتشمُّسِ.
يحلُمُون بفكرةِ الطَّيَرَانِ أعلى... ثم أعلى.
يصعدون ويهبطون. ويذهبون ويرجعون.
ويقفزون من السيراميك القديم إلى النجوم.
ويرجعون إلى الحكاية ... لا نهايةً للبدايةِ.
يهربون من النُّعَاس إلى مَلَاك النوم،
أبيضَ، أحْمَرَ العينين من أثَرِ التأمُّل
في الدم المسفوكِ:
«لا تتذكروا من بعدنا
إلّا الحياة» ...

They Don't Look Behind Them

They don't look behind them to bid exile farewell,
since ahead of them is exile, and they've intimated the circular
road, so there's no ahead and no behind, and no
north and no south. "They emigrate"
from the fence to the garden. They leave a will
in every meter of the courtyard:
    "Remember after us
    only life" ...
"They travel" from the silken morning
to the dust at noon, carrying their caskets filled
with things of absence: an identity card, and a letter
to a lover with an unknown address:
    "Remember after us
    only life" ...
And "they depart" from the houses to the streets,
sketching out the wounded victory sign, telling
whoever sees them:
    "We're still alive, so don't remember us!"
They get out of the story to breathe and to sunbathe.
They dream how to fly higher ... then higher.
They ascend and descend. Come and go.
And leap from ancient ceramics to the stars.
And they return to the story ... endless is the beginning.
They escape from sleepiness to the angel of sleep,
who is white, red-eyed from contemplating
the shed blood:
    "Remember after us
    only life" ...

لم يسألوا: ماذا وراء الموت

لم يسألوا: ماذا وراء الموت؟ كانوا
يَحفظُون خريطةَ الفردوس أكثرَ من
كتاب الأرض، يُشْغِلُهُمْ سؤال آخر:
ماذا سنفعل قبل هذا الموت؟ قرب
حياتنا نحيا، ولا نحيا. كأنَّ حياتنا
حصَصٌ من الصحراء مُخْتَلَفٌ عليها بين
آلهة العقار، ونحن جيرانُ الغبار الغابرونَ.
حياتنا عبءٌ على ليل الـمُؤرّخ: «كُلَّما
أخفيتُهم طلعوا عليَّ من الغياب»...
حياتنا عبء على الرسام: «أرسُمُهُمْ،
فأصبح واحداً منهم، ويحجبني الضباب».
حياتنا عبء على الجنرال: «كيف يسيل
من شَبَح دم؟» وحياتنا
هي أن نكون كما نريد. نريد أن
نحيا قليلاً، لا لشيء ... بل لـنَـحْتَرَم
القيامَةَ بعد هذا الموت. واقتبسوا،
بلا قَصْد كلامَ الفيلسوف: «الموت
لا يعني لنا شيئاً. نكونُ فلا يكونُ.
الموت لا يعني لنا شيئاً. يكونُ فلا
نكونُ»
ورتّبوا أحلامهُمْ
بطريقةٍ أخرى. وناموا واقفين!

They Didn't Ask: What's After Death

They didn't ask: What's after death? They were
memorizing the map of paradise more than
the book of earth, consumed with another question:
What will we do before this death? Near
our lives we live, and don't live. As if our lives
are desert lots disputed by the gods
of real estate, and we are dust's bygone neighbors.
Our lives are a burden to the historian's night: "Whenever
I hide them they come into my view out of absence …"
Our lives are a burden to the artist: "I paint them,
then I become one of them, and fog veils me."
Our lives are a burden to the general: "How does blood
flow from a ghost?" And our lives
should be as we wish. We want to
live a little, not for anything … other than to respect
resurrection after this death. And they quoted,
unintentionally, the philosopher's words: "Death
means nothing to us. We are and it isn't.
Death means nothing to us. It is and
we aren't."
Then they rearranged their dreams
in a different manner. And slept standing!

قتلى ومجهولون

قتلى، ومجهولون. لا نِسْيانَ يجمعُهُمْ
ولا ذكرى تفرِّقهُمْ ... ومنسيّون في
عُشْبِ الشتاء على الطريق العامِّ بين
حكايتين طويلتين عن البُطُولة والعذابِ.
«أنا الضحيّةُ». «لا. أنا وحدي
الضحية». لم يقولوا للمؤلِّف: «لا
ضحيّةً تقتل الأخرى. هنالك في
الحكاية قاتلٌ وضحيّةٌ». كانوا صغاراً
يقطفون الثلج عن سَرْوِ المسيح،
ويلعبون مع الملائكة الصغار، فإنَّهُمْ
أبناءُ جيلٍ واحد .... يتسرَّبُون من
المدارس هاربيـنَ من الرياضيّات والشعرِ
الحماسيّ القديم، ويلعبون مَعَ الجنود،
على الحواجز، لُعْبَةَ الموت البريئةَ.
لم يقولوا للجنود: دعوا البنادقَ
وافتحوا الطرقاتِ كي تجدَ الفراشةُ
أمَّها قرب الصباح، وكي نطير مع
الفراشة خارج الأحلام، فالأحلامُ
ضيِّقَةٌ على أبوابنا. كانوا صغاراً
يلعبون، ويصنعون حكايةً للوردة
الحمراء تحت الثلج، خَلْفَ حكايَتَيْنِ
طويلَتيْنِ عن البطولة والعذاب، ويهربون
مَعَ الملائكة الصغار إلى سماء صافيةٍ.

Murdered and Unknown

Murdered, and unknown. No forgetfulness gathers them
and no remembrance scatters them ... they're forgotten in
winter's grass on the public highway between
two long stories about heroism and suffering.
"I am the victim." "No. I alone am
the victim." They didn't tell the author: "No
victim kills another. There is in
the story a victim and a killer." They were young
picking the snow off Christ's cypress,
and playing with cherubs, since they were
of one generation ... they used to leak out
of schools to escape math and ancient
Hamassa poetry, then play with soldiers,
by the roadblocks, the innocent game of death.
They didn't tell the soldiers: "Drop your rifles
and open up the roads for the butterfly to find
its mother by morning, and for us to fly with
the butterfly outside dreams, since dreams
are narrow at our doors." They were young
playing, and making a story for the red
rose beneath the snow, behind two long
stories about heroism and suffering, and they were
running away with cherubs toward a clear sky.

السروة انكسرت

«السروة شجن الشجرة وليس
الشجرة، ولا ظل لها
لأنها ظل الشجرة»
بسام حجار

ألسروةُ أ نْكَسَرَتْ كمئذنة، ونامت في
الطريق على تَقَشُّف ظلّها، خضراءَ، داكنةٌ،
كما هيَ. لم يُصَبْ أحدٌ بسوء. مَرّت
العَرَباتُ مُسْرِعَةً على أغصانها. هَبَّ الغبارُ
على الزجاج .../ ألسروةُ انكسرت، ولكنَّ
الحمامةَ لم تغيّر عُشَّها العَلَنيَّ في دارٍ
مُجَاورةٍ. وحلّق طائران مهاجران على
كَفَاف مكانها، وتبادلا بعضَ الرموز.
وقالت امرأةٌ لجارتها: تُرَى، شاهَدْتِ عاصفةً؟
فقالت: لا، ولا جرَّافةً.../ والسروةُ
انكسرتْ. وقال العابرون على الحُطام:
لعلّها سَئِمَتْ من الإهمال، أو هَرِمَتْ
من الأيّام، فَهْيَ طويلةٌ كزرافة، وقليلةُ
المعنى كمكنسة الغبار، ولا تُظَلِّلُ عاشِقَيْن.
وقال طفلٌ: كنتُ أرسمها بلا خطأ،
فإنَّ قوامَها سَهْلٌ. وقالت طفلةٌ: إن
السماءَ اليوم ناقصةٌ لأن السروة انكسرت.
وقال فتىً: ولكنَّ السماءَ اليوم كاملةٌ
لأن السروةَ انكسرتْ. وقُلْتُ أنا
لنفسي: لا غُموضَ ولا وُضوحَ،
السروة انكسرتْ، وهذا كُلُّ ما في
الأمرِ: إنَّ السروة انكسرتْ!

The Cypress Broke

> The cypress is the tree's grief and not
> the tree, and it has no shadow because it is
> the tree's shadow
>
> BASSAM HAJJAR

The cypress broke like a minaret, and slept on
the road upon its chapped shadow, dark, green,
as it has always been. No one got hurt. The vehicles
sped over its branches. The dust blew
into the windshields … / The cypress broke, but
the pigeon in a neighboring house didn't change
its public nest. And two migrant birds hovered above
the hem of the place, and exchanged some symbols.
And a woman said to her neighbor: Say, did you see a storm?
She said: No, and no bulldozer either … / And the cypress
broke. And those passing by the wreckage said:
Maybe it got bored with being neglected, or it grew old
with the days, it is long like a giraffe, and little
in meaning like a dust broom, and couldn't shade two lovers.
And a boy said: I used to draw it perfectly,
its figure was easy to draw. And a girl said: The sky today
is incomplete because the cypress broke.
And a young man said: But the sky today is complete
because the cypress broke. And I said
to myself: Neither mystery nor clarity,
the cypress broke, and that is all
there is to it: the cypress broke!

رجل وخشف في الحديقة

[إلى سليمان النجاب]

رَجُلٌ وخِشْفٌ في الحديقة يلعبان معاً...
أقول لصاحبي: مِنْ أين جاءَ ابْنُ الغزالِ؟
يقول: جاء من السماء. لعلّهُ «يَحْيَى»
رُزِقْتُ به ليُؤنِسَ وحشتي. لا أمّ
تُرْضِعُهُ فكُنْتُ الأمَّ، أسقيه حليبَ
الشاة ممزوجاً بمِلعَقة مِنَ العَسَلِ
الـمُعَطَّر. ثم أحمِلُهُ كغيمَةِ عاشقٍ في
غابة البَلّوطِ ...
قُلْتُ لصاحبي: هل صار يأْلَفُ بيتَكَ
المأهولَ بالأصوات والأدوات؟
قال: وصار يرقُدُ في سريري حين يمرضُ...
ثُمَّ قال: وصِرْتُ أمرَضُ حين يمرض.
صِرْتُ أهذي: «أيّها الطفلُ اليتيمُ!
أنا أبوك وأُمُّكَ، انهض كي تعلّمني
السكينة»/

بعد شهرٍ زُرْتُهُ في بيته الريفيّ.
كان كلامُهُ يبكي. لأوّل مرّة يبكي سُلَيْمانُ
القويُّ، يقول لي متهدِّج الصوت: «ابنُ
الغزال، ابنُ الغزالة مات بين يديَّ.
لم يألف حياةَ البيت. لكنْ لم يَمُتْ
مثلي ومثلكَ...»

لم أقل شيئاً لصاحبيَ الحزيـن. ولم
يودِّعني، كعادته، بأبياتٍ من الشعر
القديم. مشى إلى قبر الغزال الأبيض.
احتَضَنَ الترابَ وأجهش: «انهضْ
كي ينام أبوك، يا ابني، في سريرك.
ها هنا أجِدُ السكينةَ»/

A Man and a Fawn Are in the Garden

for Sulieman el-Najjab

A man and a fawn are in the garden playing together ...
I say to my friend: Where did this fawn come from?
He says: It came from heaven. Maybe it will "live."
It was sent to soothe my loneliness. No mother
to nurse it so I became the mother, I feed it sheep's milk
mixed with a spoonful of scented honey,
then I carry it like a lover's cloud
in the oak forest ...
I said: Is it domestic yet in your house
that is filled with sounds and instruments?
He said: And it now sleeps in my bed when it falls ill ...
Then he said: And I fall ill when it falls ill.
I even hallucinate: You orphan child!
I am your father and mother, get up and teach me
serenity /

A month later I visited him at his home in the countryside.
His speech was weeping. For the first time Sulieman
the strong weeps, and tells me in a trembling voice: The gazelle's
son, the fawn, died in my hands.
It didn't like the domestic life. But it didn't die
like you and I ...

I said nothing to my mournful friend. And he didn't
say goodbye to me, as usual, with stanzas of ancient
poetry. He walked to the little gazelle's white grave.
He embraced the dirt and sobbed: Get up, my son,
and let your father sleep in your bed.
Right here I'll find serenity /

نام في قبر الغزال، وصار لي
ماضٍ صغيرٌ في المكانْ:
رَجُلٌ وخِشْفٌ في الحديقة يرقدانْ!

He slept in the gazelle's grave, and a small past
in the place has now become mine:
a man and a fawn are in the garden sleeping!

هذا هو النسيان

هذا هُوَ النسيانُ حوَلكَ: يافطاتٌ
تُوقظُ الماضي، تحثُّ على التذكُّر. تكبح
الزَّمَنَ السريعَ على إشارات المرور،
وتُغلقُ الساحاتِ/

تمثالٌ رُخَاميٌّ هو النسيانُ. تمثالٌ
يُحَمْلقُ فيكَ: قفْ مثلي لتشبِهَني.
وَضَعْ ورداً على قدميَّ/

أغنيةٌ مُكرَّرَةٌ هو النسيانُ. أغنيةٌ
تطاردُ ربَّة البيت احتفاءً بالمناسبة
السعيدةِ، في السرير وغرفة الفيديو،
وفي صالونها الخاوي، ومطبخها/

وأنصابٌ هو النسيانُ. أنصابٌ على
الطرقات تأخذ هيئة الشَّجَر البُرونزيِّ
المرصَّع بالمدائح والصقورِ/

ومتحفٌ خالٍ من الغد، باردٌ،
يروي الفصولَ المنتقاةَ من البدايةْ
هذا هو النسيانُ: أن تتذكَّرَ الماضي
ولا تتذكرَ الغَدَ في الحكايةْ

This Is Forgetfulness

This is forgetfulness around you: billboards
awakening the past, urging remembrance. Reining in
the speeding time at traffic lights,
and closing up the squares /

A marble statue is forgetfulness. A statue
staring at you: Stand up as I do to look like me.
And place roses on my feet /

A hackneyed song is forgetfulness. A song
chasing the housewife in celebration of the happy
occasion, in the bed and in the VCR room,
and in her vacant salon, and in her kitchen /

And a monument is forgetfulness. Monuments
on the roads shaped like bronze trees
adorned with eulogies and eagles /

And a museum empty of tomorrow, cold,
narrating the seasons already chosen from the start.
This is forgetfulness: that you remember the past
and not remember tomorrow in the story

تُنْسى، كأنك لم تكن

تُنْسى، كأنَّكَ لم تَكُنْ
تُنْسَى كمصرع طائرٍ
ككنيسةٍ مهجورةٍ تُنْسَى،
كحبّ عابرٍ
وكوردةٍ في الليل ... تُنْسَى

أنا للطريق ... هناك من سَبَقَتْ خُطَاهُ خُطايَ
مَنْ أمْلَى رُؤاهُ على رُؤَايَ. هُناكَ مَنْ
نَثَرَ الكلام على سجيَّتِه ليدخل في الحكايةِ
أو يضيءَ لمن سيأتي بعدهُ
أثراً غنائياً ... وحدسا

تُنْسَى، كأنك لم تكن
شخصاً، ولا نصّاً ... وتُنْسَى

أمشي على هَدْيِ البصيرة، رُبَّما
أعطي الحكايةَ سيرةً شخصيَّةً. فالمفرداتُ
تَسوسُني وأسُوسُها. أنا شكلها
وهي التجلّي الـحُرُّ. لكنْ قيل ما سأقول.
يسبقني غدٌ ماض. أنا مَلِكُ الصدى.
لا عَرْشَ لي إلاّ الهوامش. والطريقُ
هو الطريقةُ. رُبَّما نَسِيَ الأوائلُ وَصْفَ
شيء ما، أُحرِّكُ فيه ذاكرةً وحسّا

تُنْسَى، كأنَّكَ لم تكن
خبراً، ولا أثراً ... وتُنْسى

أنا للطريق ... هناك مَنْ تمشي خُطَاهُ
على خُطَايَ، وَمَنْ سيتبعني إلى رؤيايَ.
مَنْ سيقول شعراً في مديح حدائقِ المنفى،
أمامَ البيْت، حراً من عبادَةِ أمس،

You'll Be Forgotten, As If You Never Were

You'll be forgotten, as if you never were.
Like a bird's violent death
or an abandoned church you'll be forgotten,
like a passing love
and a rose in the night ... forgotten

I am for the road ... There are those whose footsteps preceded mine
and those whose vision dictated mine. There are those
who scattered speech on their accord to enter the story
or to illuminate to others who will follow them
a lyrical trace ... and a speculation

You'll be forgotten, as if you never were
a person, or a text ... forgotten

I walk guided by insight, I might
give the story a biographical narrative. Vocabulary
governs me and I govern it. I am its shape
and it is the free transfiguration. But what I'd say has already been said.
A passing tomorrow precedes me. I am the king of echo.
My only throne is the margin. And the road
is the way. Maybe the forefathers forgot to describe
something, I might nudge in it a memory and a sense

You'll be forgotten, as if you never were
news, or a trace ... forgotten

I am for the road ... There are those whose footsteps
walk upon mine, those who will follow me to my vision.
Those who will recite eulogies to the gardens of exile,
in front of the house, free of worshipping yesterday,

حراً من كناياتي ومن لغتي، فأشهد
أنني حيٌّ
وحُـرٌّ
حين أُنسَى!

free of my metonymy and my language, and only then
will I testify that I'm alive
and free
when I'm forgotten!

أَما أَنا، فأقول لاسمي

أمّا أنا، فأقولُ لاسمي: دَعْكَ منِّي
وابتعدْ عنِّي، فإني ضِقتُ منذ نطقتُ
واتَّسَعَتْ صفاتُك! خذ صفاتك وامتحنْ
غيري ... حملتُك حين كنا قادرَيْن على
عبور النهر مُتَّحدين «أنت أنا»، ولم
أُخْتَرْكَ يا ظلّي السلوقيَّ الوفيَّ، اختار
الآباء كي يتفاءلوا بالبحث عن معنى.
ولم يتساءلوا عمّا سيحدُثُ للمُسَمَّى عندما
يقسو عليه الاسمُ، أو يُمْلي عليه
كلامَهُ فيصير تابعَهُ ... فأين أنا؟
وأين حكايتي الصُّغْرَى وأوجاعي الصغيرةُ؟
تجلس امرأةٌ مَعَ اُسْمي دون أن
تصغي لصوت أُخُوَّةِ الحيوان
والإنسان في جَسَدي، وتروي لي
حكاية حبها، فأقول: إن أعطيتني يَدَك
الصغيرة صرْتُ مثلَ حديقة .. فتقول:
لَسْتَ هُوَ الذي أعنيه، لكني أريد
نصيحةً شعريّةً. ويحملقُ الطلاب في
اسمي غير مكترثين بي، وأنا أمرّ
كأنني شخص فضوليٌّ. وينظر قارىء
في اسمي، فيبدي رأيه فيه: أحبُّ
مسيحَهُ الحافي، وأما شِعْرُه الذاتيُّ في
وَصْف الضباب، فلا! ... ويسألني:
لماذا كنت ترمقني بطَرْف ساخر. فأقول:
كنت أحاور اسمي: هل أنا صفةٌ؟
فيسألني: وما شأني أنا؟/

أمّا أنا، فأقول لاسمي: أعطِني
ما ضاع من حُرِّيَّتي!

As for Me, I Say to My Name

As for me, I say to my name: Let me be
and get away from me, I've been fed up since I spoke
and since your adjectives grew! Take your adjectives and test
another ... I carried you when we were able to
cross the river united, "you me," although I didn't
choose you my saluki loyal shadow, the fathers
chose you as a good omen to search for meaning.
But they didn't question what might happen to the one named
when the name becomes cruel, or when it dictates to him
his speech and makes him its subject ... so where am I?
And where are my little aches and my little tales?
A woman sits with my name without
listening to the fraternity between animal
and man in my body, and tells me
her love story, so I say: If you give me your little
hand I'll become like a garden. Then she says:
That's not what I mean, I wanted
a poetic advice. And the students stare
at my name, disinterested in me when I pass
as if I were the one prying. And a reader
looks into my name, then gives his opinion: I love
its barefooted Christ, but as for his personal poetry
of describing fog, I don't! ... Then he asks me:
Why were you glancing at me in mockery? I say:
I was in dialogue with my name: whether I'm an adjective?
So he says: How is that my concern?

As for me, I say to my name: Give me
back what's been lost of my freedom!

الحلم، ما هو؟

ألـحُلْمُ، ما هُوَ؟
ما هُـوَ اللاشيءُ هذا
عابرُ الزمن،
البهيُّ كنجمةٍ في أوّل الحبِّ،
الشَّهيُّ كصورةِ امرأةٍ
تدلُّكَ نهدها بالشَّمسِ؟/
ما هُـوَ، لا أكاد أراه حتى
يختفي في الأمسِ/
لا هُـوَ واقعٌ لأعيش وطأته وخفَّتَهُ
ولا هُـوَ عكسُهُ لأطير حُرّاً
في فضاء الـحَدْسِ/
ما هُـوَ، ما هُـوَ اللاشيءُ، هذا الـهَشُّ
هذا اللانهائيُّ، الضعيفُ، الباطنيُّ
الزائرُ، المتطايرُ، المتناثرُ،
المتجدِّدُ المتعدِّدُ اللاَّ شكلٍ؟
ما هُـوَ؟ لا يُجَسُّ ولا يُـمَسُّ/
ولا يَـمُـدُّ يداً إلى الـمُتَلهِّفين الحائرينَ
فما هُـوَ السريُّ هذا،
الحائرُ، الـحَذِرُ، المحيِّرُ
حين أنتظرُ الزيارةَ مطمئنَّ النفسِ/
يكسرني ويخرجُ مثل لؤلؤةٍ
تُـدَحْرجُ ضوءها،
ويقول لي: لا تنتظرني
إن أردتَ زيارتي
لا تنتظرني!

Dream, What Is It?

Dream, what is it?
What is it this nothing this
time's passerby,
this splendid as a star in the beginning of love,
delicious as a woman's image
massaging her breast in the sun? /
What is it? I can barely see it before
it disappears in yesterday /
It is neither a reality that I might live its gravity and its levity
nor the opposite that I might fly free
in the space of speculation /
What is it, what is it this nothing, this frail
this endless, the feeble, the internal
visitor, the volatile, the scattered,
the renewing and numerously shapeless?
What is it? Neither palpable nor touchable /
Nor does it extend a hand to the confused and yearning
so what is it this secretive,
this perplexed, cautious, and perplexing? /
When I await its visit self-assured
it breaks me and exits as a pearl
rolling its light,
and says to me: Don't wait for me
if you want me to visit
don't wait for me!

الآن، إذ تصحو، تذكَّر

الآن، إذ تصحو، تَذكَّرْ رَقْصَةَ البَجَع
الأخيرةَ. هل رَقَصْتَ مَعَ الملائكة الصغارِ
وأنت تحلُمُ؟ هل أضاءتك الفراشةُ عندما
احترقَّتْ بضوء الوردة الأبديِّ؟ هل
ظهرتْ لك العنقاءُ واضحةً ... وهل نادتك
باسمك؟ هل رأيتَ الفجرَ يطلع من
أصابع مَنْ تُحبُّ؟ وهل لَمَسْتَ الحُلم
باليد، أم تَرَكْتَ الحُلْمَ يحلُمُ وحْدهُ،
حين انتبهتَ إلى غيابكَ بَغْتَةً؟
ما هكذا يُخْلي المنامَ الحالمونَ،
فإنهم يتوهجون،
ويكملون حياتهم في الحُلْم ...
قل لي: كيف كنت تعيش حُلْمَك
في مكانٍ ما، أقلْ لك مَنْ تكونْ

والآن، إذ تصحو، تذكَّرْ:
هل أسَأْتَ إلى منامك؟
إن أسأت، إذاً تذكَّرْ
رقصةَ البجع الأخيرةَ!

Now, When You Awaken, Remember

Now, when you awaken, remember the swan's last
dance. Did you dance with cherubs
while you were dreaming? Did the butterfly illuminate you
when it burned with the eternal light of the rose? Did
the phoenix appear to you clearly ... and did it call you
by name? Did you see the dawn rise
out of your beloved's fingers? And did you touch the dream
by hand, or did you let the dream dream alone,
when you became aware of your absence suddenly?
This isn't how the dreamers vacate their sleep,
they become incandescent,
and complete their lives in the dream ...
Tell me how you lived your dream
in some place, and I'll tell you who you are

And now, when you awaken, remember:
did you mistreat your sleep?
If you did, then remember
the swan's last dance!

الظلّ

الظلُّ، لا ذَكَرٌ ولا أُنثى
رماديٌّ، ولو أشْعَلْتُ فيه النارَ ...
يتبعُني، ويكبُر ثُـمَّ يصغرُ
كُنْتُ أمشي. كان يمشي
كنت أجلسُ. كان يجلسُ
كنت أركضُ. كان يركضُ
قلت: أخدعُهُ وأخلَعُ معطفي الـكُحْليَّ
قلَّدني، وألقي عنه معطفَهُ الرماديَّ ...
استَدَرْتُ إلى الطريق الجانبيّة
فاستدار إلى الطريق الجانبيّة.
قُلْتُ: أخدعُهُ وأخرجُ من غروب مدينتي
فرأيتُهُ يمشي أمامي
في غروب مدينة أخرى ...
فقلت: أعود مُتَّكئاً على عُكّازتينِ
فعاد متكئاً على عكازتينِ
فقلت: أحمله على كتفي،
فاستَعْصَى ...
فقلتُ: إذن، سأتبعُهُ لأخدَعَهُ
سأتبعُ بَبّغاءَ الشكل سُخْرِيَةً
أقلّد ما يُقلّدني
لكي يَقَعَ الشبيهُ على الشبيه
فلا أراهُ، ولا يراني.

The Shadow

The shadow, neither male nor female,
ashen, even if I set it on fire ...
It follows me, it grows then shrinks.
I was walking. It was walking.
I sat. It sat.
I ran. It ran.
I said: Let me trick it and take off my kohl coat
it copied me, and took off its ashen coat ...
I turned onto the side road
it turned onto the side road.
I said: Let me trick it and walk out of my city's sunset
then I saw it walking ahead of me
into the sunset of another city ...
I said: I'll come back leaning on two crutches
then it returned leaning on two crutches.
So I said: I'll carry it on my shoulders,
but it resisted ...
I said: Then, I'll follow it to deceive it.
I'll follow this parrot of shapes and mock it
copying what copies me
for the like to stumble on the like
and I would not see it, nor it see me.

لا شيء يعجبني

«لا شيءَ يُعْجِبني»
يقول مسافرٌ في الباص ـــ لا الراديو
ولا صُحُفُ الصباح، ولا القِلاعُ على التلال.
أُريد أن أبكي/
يقول السائقُ: انتظرِ الوصولَ إلى المحطّةِ،
وأبْكِ وحدك ما استطعتَ/
تقولَ سيّدةٌ: أنا أيضاً. أنا لا
شيءَ يُعْجِبني. دَلَلْتُ ابني على قبري،
فأعْجَبَهُ ونامَ، ولم يُوَدِّعْني/
يقول الجامعيُّ: ولا أنا، لا شيءَ
يعجبني. دَرَسْتُ الأركيولوجيا دون أن
أجِدَ الهُويّةَ في الحجارةِ. هل أنا
حقاً أنا؟/
ويقول جنديٌّ: أنا أيضاً. أنا لا
شيءَ يُعْجِبني. أحاصِرُ دائماً شَبَحاً
يُحاصِرُني/
يقولُ السائقُ العصبيُّ: ها نحن
اقتربنا من محطتنا الأخيرة، فاستعدوا
للنزول ...٥/
فيصرخون: نريدُ ما بَعْدَ المحطّةِ،
فانطلق!
أمَّا أنا فأقولُ: أ نْزِلْني هنا. أنا
مثلهم لا شيء يعجبني، ولكني تعبتُ
من السَّفَرْ.

Nothing Pleases Me

Nothing pleases me
the traveler on the bus says—Not the radio
or the morning newspaper, nor the citadels on the hills.
I want to cry /
The driver says: Wait until you get to the station,
then cry alone all you want /
A woman says: Me too. Nothing
pleases me. I guided my son to my grave,
he liked it and slept there, without saying goodbye /
A college student says: Nor does anything
please me. I studied archaeology but didn't
find identity in stone. Am I
really me? /
And a soldier says: Me too. Nothing
pleases me. I always besiege a ghost
besieging me /
The edgy driver says: Here we are
almost near our last stop, get ready
to get off ... /
Then they scream: We want what's beyond the station,
keep going!
As for myself I say: Let me off here. I am
like them, nothing pleases me, but I'm worn out
from travel.

هو هادىءٌ، وأنا كذلك

هُـوَ هادِئٌ، وأنا كذلكَ
يَـحْتَسي شاياً بليمونٍ،
وأشربُ قهوةً،
هذا هُـوَ الشيءُ المغايرُ بَيْنَنَا.
هُـوَ يرتدي، مثلي، قميصاً واسعاً ومُخَطَّطاً
وأنا أطالعُ، مثلَهُ، صُـحُفَ المساءِ.
هُـوَ لا يراني حين أنظرُ خلسَةً،
أنا لا أراه حين ينظرُ خلسةً،
هو هادِئٌ، وأنا كذلكَ.
يسألُ الجرسونَ شيئاً،
أسألُ الجرسونَ شيئاً...
قطّةٌ سوداءُ تعبُرُ بَيْنَنَا،
فأجسّ فروةَ ليلها
ويجسُّ فَرْوَةَ ليلها ...
أنا لا أقول لَـهُ: السماءُ اليومَ صافيةٌ
وأكثُر زرقةً.
هو لا يقول لي: السماءُ اليومَ صافيةٌ.
هو المرئيُّ والرائي
أنا المرئيُّ والرائي.
أحرّكُ رِجلِيَ اليُسْرى
يحرك رِجلَهُ اليُمْنَى.
أدندنُ لَـحْنَ أُغنية،
يدندن لحنَ أُغنية مُشَابهة.
أفكّرُ: هل هو المرآةُ أبصر فيه نفسي؟

ثم أنظر نحو عينيه،
ولكنْ لا أراهُ ...
فأتركُ المقهى على عَجَلٍ.
أفكّرُ: رُبّمَا هو قاتلٌ، أو رُبّمَا
هو عابرٌ قد ظنَّ أني قاتلٌ

هو خائفٌ، وأنا كذلكَ!

He's Calm, and I Am Too

He's calm, and I am too
he's drinking tea with lemon,
and I'm drinking coffee,
this is the difference between us.
He's wearing, as I am, a baggy striped shirt
and I'm reading, as he is, the evening newspaper.
He doesn't see me when I steal a glance,
I don't see him when he steals a glance,
he's calm, and I am too.
He asks the waiter something,
I ask the waiter something ...
A black cat passes between us,
I pet its night's fur
and he pets its night's fur ...
I don't say to him: The sky was clear today
and more blue.
He doesn't say to me: The sky was clear today.
He's the seen and the seer
I'm the seen and the seer.
I move my left leg
he moves his right leg.
I hum a song's melody
he hums a song with a similar melody.
I think: Is he the mirror I see myself in?

Then I look toward his eyes,
but I don't see him ...
I leave the café in a hurry.
I think: Maybe he's a killer, or maybe
he's a passerby who thinks I'm a killer

He's frightened, and I am too!

وصف الغيوم

«لوصف الغيوم،
عليَّ أن أسرع كثيراً
فبعد هنيهة لن تكون ما هي
عليه، ستصير أخرى»
شيمبورسكا

وَصْفُ الغيوم مَهارةٌ لم أوتَها ...
أمشي على جَبَلٍ وأنظُرُ من عَلٍ
نحو الغيوم، وقد تدلَّتْ من مَدار اللازَوَرْدِ
خفيفةً وشفيفةً،
كالقطن تحلجه الرياحُ،
كفكرة بيضاءَ عن معنى الوجود.
لعلَّ آلهةً تنقِّحُ قصَّةَ التكوينِ
«لا شكلٌ نهائيٌّ لهذا الكون...
لا تاريخَ للأشكال..»
أنظُرُ من عَلٍ، وأرى انبثاق الشكلِ
من عَبَثيّة اللّاشكلِ:
ريشُ الطير يَنْبُتُ في قُرون الأيّل البيضاء،
وَجْهُ الكائن البشريِّ يطلع من
جناح الطائر المائيّ ...
ترسُمُنا الغيومُ على وَتيرتها
وتختلط الوجوه مع الرؤى
لم يكتمل شيء ولا أحد، فبعد هنيهة
ستصيرُ صورتُكَ الجديدةُ صُورةَ النَّمِرِ
الجريح بصولجان الريح ...
رسّامون مجهولون ما زالوا أمامك
يلعبون، ويرسمون الـمُطلَقَ الأبديَّ،
أبيضَ، كالغيوم على جدار الكونِ ...
والشعراءُ يبنون المنازلَ بالغيوم
ويذهبون...

Describing Clouds

I'd have to be really quick
to describe clouds,
because in a second
they become another

WISLAWA SZYMBORSKA

Describing clouds is a talent I wasn't given ...
I am walking on a mountain and looking from a height
toward the clouds, as they hang from the lapis orbit
light and diaphanous,
like cotton ginned by wind,
like a white idea about the meaning of existence.
Perhaps some gods would refine the story of creation
"No final shape for this universe ...
no history of shapes ..."
I am looking from a height, and I see the bursting of shape
out of the frivolity of no-shape:
the bird feathers sprout in the white stag horns,
the human face appears
out of a marine bird's wing ...
The clouds sketch us in their manner
and the faces get mixed up with the vision,
nothing is complete nor anyone, because in a moment
your new image will become the image of the tiger
wounded by the wind's scepter ...
Unknown painters are still in front of you
playing, and drawing the absolute eternal,
white, like clouds on the wall of the universe ...
And the poets build homes with clouds
then move on ...

لكُلِّ حسّ صورةٌ،
ولكُلِّ وقت غيمةٌ،
لكن أعمارَ الغيوم قصيرةٌ في الريح،
كالأبد المؤقت في القصائدِ،
لا يزول ولا يدوم ...

من حُسْن حظّي أنني أمشي على جَبَلٍ
وأنظر من علٍ
نحو الغيوم...

For each sense there is an image,
and for each time there is a cloud,
but clouds have short lives in the wind,
like the temporary eternal in poems,
which neither vanishes nor lasts ...

It's my good fortune that I am walking on a mountain
looking from a height
toward the clouds ...

هي جملة اسمية

هي جُمَلَةٌ إسميَّةٌ، لا فِعْلَ
فيها أو لها: للبحر رائحةُ الأَسِرَّةِ
بعد فِعْلِ الـحُبِّ ... عِطرٌ مالحٌ أو
حامضٌ. هيَ جملة إسميَّة: فرحي
جريحٌ كالغروب على شبابيك الغريبة.
زهرتي خضراءُ كالعنقاء. قلبي فائضٌ
عن حاجتي، مترِّدٌ ما بين بابَيْن:
الدخولُ هو الفُكاهَةُ، والخروج هُـوَ
الـمَتَاهَةُ. أينَ ظلِّي ـــ مرشدي وسط
الزحام على الطريق إلى القيامة؟ ليتني
حَـجَرٌ قديمٌ داكنُ اللونيْن في سور المدينة،
كستنائيٌّ وأسودُ، طاعنٌ في اللاشعور
تجاه زوّاري وتأويل الظلال. وليت
للفعل الـمُضَارع موطئاً للسير خلفي
أو أمامي، حافيَ القدمين. أين
طريقيَ الثاني إلى دَرَج المدى؟ أين
السُّدَى؟ أين الطريقُ إلى الطريق؟
وأين نَـحْنُ، السائرين على خُطَى الفعل
المضارع، أين نحن؟ كلامُنا خَبَرٌ
ومُبْتَدأٌ أمام البحر، والزَّبَدُ المراوغُ
في الكلام هُـوَ النقاطُ على الحروف،
فليت للفعل المضارع موطئاً فوق
الرصيف ...

A Noun Sentence

A noun sentence, no verb
to it or in it: to the sea the scent of the bed
after making love ... a salty perfume
or a sour one. A noun sentence: my wounded joy
like the sunset at your strange windows.
My flower green like the phoenix. My heart exceeding
my need, hesitant between two doors:
entry a joke, and exit
a labyrinth. Where is my shadow—my guide amid
the crowdedness on the road to judgment day? And I
as an ancient stone of two dark colors in the city wall,
chestnut and black, a protruding insensitivity
toward my visitors and the interpretation of shadows. Wishing
for the present tense a foothold for walking behind me
or ahead of me, barefoot. Where
is my second road to the staircase of expanse? Where
is futility? Where is the road to the road?
And where are we, the marching on the footpath of the present
tense, where are we? Our talk a predicate
and a subject before the sea, and the elusive foam
of speech the dots on the letters,
wishing for the present tense a foothold
on the pavement ...

قل ما تشاء

قُلْ ما تشاءُ. ضَع النقاطَ على الحروفِ.
ضَع الحروفَ مع الحروف لتُولَدَ الكلماتُ،
غامضةً وواضحةً، ويبتدىءَ الكلامُ.
ضَع الكلامَ على المجاز. ضَع المجازَ على
الخيال. ضَع الخيالَ على تَلفُّته البعيد.
ضَع البعيدَ على البعيد ... سَيُولَدُ الإيقاعُ
عند تَشَابُك الصُّوَر الغريبة من لقاء
الواقعيِّ مع الخياليِّ الـمُشَاكِس/
هل كَتَبْتَ قصيدةً؟
كلا!
لعلَّ هناك ملحاً زائداً أو ناقصاً
في المفردات. لعلَّ حادثةً أخلَّتْ بالتوازن
في مُعَادَلَة الظلال. لعلَّ نسراً
مات في أعلى الجبال. لعلَّ أرضَ
الرمز خفَّتْ في الكناية فاستباحتها
الرياحُ. لعلَّها ثَقُلَتْ على ريش الخيال.
لعلَّ قلبَكَ لم يفكِّرْ جيِّداً، ولعلَّ
فكرَكَ لم يُحسَّ بما يرجُّك. فالقصيدة،
زوجةُ الغد وابنةُ الماضي، تخيِّم في
مكانٍ غامضٍ بين الكتابة والكلام /
فهل كَتَبْت قصيدةً؟
كلا!
إذنْ، ماذا كتبتَ؟
كتبتُ درساً جامعيّاً،
واعتزلْتُ الشعر منذ عرفتُ
كيمياءَ القصيدة ... واعتزلتْ!

Say What You Want

Say what you want. Put the dots on the letters.
Put the letters with the letters for words to be born,
mysterious and clear, and for speech to begin.
Put speech on metaphor. Metaphor on
imagination. And imagination on its looking around the far.
Put the far on the far ... cadence will be born
when strange images interlace through the meeting
of the real with the peevish imaginary /
    Have you written a poem?
    No!
Perhaps there is too much or too little salt
in the vocabulary. Perhaps an incident created an imbalance
in the equation of shadows. Perhaps an eagle
died in mountainous heights. Or the land
of symbols weighed less in metonymy so it got pillaged
by the wind. Perhaps it became too heavy for imagination's feathers.
Perhaps your heart could have thought better, and perhaps
your thought didn't sense what shakes you. Because the poem,
tomorrow's wife and daughter of the past, camps out
in a mysterious place between writing and speech /
    So have you written a poem?
    No!
    What have you written?
    I have written a paper,
    then I retired from poetry when I knew
    the chemistry of the poem ... I withdrew!

لا تكتب التاريخ شعراً

لا تكتب التاريخَ شعراً، فالسلاحُ هُوَ
المؤرِّخُ. والمؤرّخ لا يُصَابُ برعشة
الـحُمَّى إذا سَمَّى ضحاياه ولا يُصْغي
إلى سرديّة الجيتار. والتاريخ يوميّاتُ
أسلِحَةٍ مُدَوَّنةٌ على أجسادنا. «إنَّ
الذكيَّ العبقريَّ هو القويُّ». وليس
للتاريخ عاطفةٌ لـنَشْعُرَ بالحنين إلى
بدايتنا، ولا قَصْدٌ لنعرف ما الأمام
وما الوراء ... ولا استراحاتٌ على
سكك الحديد لندفن الموتى، وننظُرَ
صَوْبَ ما فَعَلَ الزمانُ بنا هناك، وما
فَعَلْنا بالزمان. كأنّنا منهُ وخارجَهُ.
فلا هو منطقيٌّ أو بديهيٌّ لنكسرَ
ما تَبَقَّى من خرافتنا عن الزمن السعيد،
ولا خرافيٌّ لنرضى بالإقامة عند أبواب
القيامة. إنَّهُ فينا وخارجنا.. وتكرارٌ
جُنونيٌّ، من الـمِقْلاع حتى الصاعق النَّوويِّ.
يصنعُنا ونصنعه بلا هَدَفٍ ... هل
التاريخ لم يُولَدْ كما شئنا، لأن
الكائنَ البشريَّ لم يُوجَدْ؟
فلاسفةٌ وفنّانونَ مَرُّوا من هناك ...
ودوَّن الشعراءُ يوميّاتِ أزهار البنفسج
ثم مروا من هناك... وصدَّق الفقراءُ
أخباراً عن الفردوس وانتظروا هناك ...
وجاء آلهةٌ لإنقاذ الطبيعة من أُلوهيَّتِنا
ومَرُّوا من هناك. وليس للتاريخ
وَقْتٌ للتأمُّل، ليس للتاريخ مرآةٌ
وَوَجْهٌ سافرٌ. هو واقعٌ لا واقعيٌّ
أو خيالٌ لا خياليٌّ، فلا تكتبه.
لا تكتبه، لا تكتبه شعراً!

Don't Write History as Poetry

Don't write history as poetry, because the weapon is
the historian. And the historian doesn't get fever
chills when he names his victims, and doesn't listen
to the guitar's rendition. And history is the dailiness
of weapons prescribed upon our bodies. "The
intelligent genius is the mighty one." And history
has no compassion that we can long for our
beginning, and no intention that we can know what's ahead
and what's behind ... and it has no rest stops
by the railroad tracks for us to bury the dead, for us to look
toward what time has done to us over there, and what
we've done to time. As if we were of it and outside it.
History is not logical or intuitive that we can break
what is left of our myth about happy times,
nor is it a myth that we can accept our dwelling at the doors
of judgment day. It is in us and outside us ... and a mad
repetition, from the catapult to the nuclear thunder.
Aimlessly we make it and it makes us ... Perhaps
history wasn't born as we desired, because
the Human Being never existed?
Philosophers and artists passed through there ...
and the poets wrote down the dailiness of their purple flowers
then passed through there ... and the poor believed
in sayings about paradise and waited there ...
and gods came to rescue nature from our divinity
and passed through there. And history has no
time for contemplation, history has no mirror
and no bare face. It is unreal reality
or unfanciful fancy, so don't write it.
Don't write it, don't write it as poetry!

ماذا سيبقى؟

ماذا سَيَبْقَى من هبات الغيمة البيضاءِ؟
ـــ زَهْرَةُ بَيْلَسَانْ
ماذا سيبقى من رَذاذ الموجة الزرقاءِ؟
ـــ إيقاعُ الزمانْ
ماذا سيبقى من نزيف الفكرة الخضراءِ؟
ـــ ماءٌ في عُرُوق السنديانْ
ماذا سيبقى من دُمُوع الـحُبِّ؟
ـــ وَشْمٌ ناعمٌ في الأرجوانْ
ماذا سيبقى من غُبار البحث عن معنى؟
ـــ طريقُ العنفوانْ
ماذا سيبقى من طريقِ الرحلة الكبرى
إلى المجهولِ؟
ـــ أغنيةُ الـمُسَافر للحصانْ
ماذا سيبقى من سراب الـحُلْمِ؟
ـــ آثارُ السماء على الكَمَانْ
ماذا سيبقى من لقاء الشيء باللاشيءِ؟
ـــ إحساسُ الألوهة بالأمانْ
ماذا سيبقى من كلام الشاعر العربيِّ؟
ـــ هاويةٌ ... وخَيْطٌ من دخانْ
ماذا سيبقى من كلامكَ أنْتَ؟
ـــ نسيانٌ ضروريٌّ لذاكرة المكانْ!

What Will Remain?

What will remain of the white cloud's offering?
—An elderberry blossom
What will remain of the blue wave's drizzle?
—The cadence of time
What will remain of the hemorrhage of a green idea?
—Water in holm oak veins
What will remain of the tears of love?
—A soft tattoo in violet
What will remain of the dust of searching for a meaning?
—The path of ardor
What will remain of the road of the great journey to the unknown?
—The traveler's song to the horse
What will remain of dream's mirage?
—The sky's trace on the violin
What will remain of thing meeting with nothing?
—Divinity's sense of security
What will remain of the Arabic poet's speech?
—A chasm ... and a thread of smoke
What will remain of your own speech?
—A necessary forgetfulness of the memory of place!

لا أَعرف اسمك

ــ لا أعرفُ اسمَك
□ سَمّني ما شئتَ
ــ لَسْت غزالةً
□ كلا. ولا فَرَساً
ــ ولست حَمَامَةَ المنفى
□ ولا حُوريَّةً
ــ مَنْ أنت؟ ما اسمُك؟
□ سَمّني، لأكونَ ما سَمَّيْتني
ــ لا أستطيع، لأنني ريحٌ
وأنتِ غريبةٌ مثلي، وللأسماءِ أرضٌ ما
□ إذنْ، أنا «لا أَحَدْ»

□ لا أعرفُ اسمكَ، ما اسمُكَ؟
ــ اختاري من الأسماء أقْرَبَها
إلى النسيان. سَمّيني أكُنْ في
أهل هذا الليل ما سَمَّيْتني!
□ لا أستطيعُ لأنني امرأةٌ مسافرةٌ
على ريحٍ. وأنت مسافر مثلي،
وللأسماء عائلةٌ وبَيْتٌ واضحٌ
ــ فإذن، أنا «لا شيءَ» ...

قالت «لا أحدْ»:
سأعبّىء اسمك شَهْوَةً. جَسَدي
يلمُّكَ من جهاتكَ كُلِّها. جَسَدي
يضُمُّكَ من جهاتي كُلِّها، لتكون شيئاً ما
ونمضي باحِثَيْنِ عن الحياة...

فقال «لا شيء»: الحياةُ جميلةٌ
مَعَكِ ... الحياة جميلةٌ!

I Don't Know Your Name

—I don't know your name
—Call me whatever you want
—You're not a gazelle
—No. And not a mare either
—And you're not an exile dove
—Nor a mermaid
—Who are you? What's your name?
—Give me a name, and I'll become what you name me
—I cannot, because I am a wind
and you're a stranger like me, and names have lands
—Then, I am "No one"

—I don't know your name, what's your name?
—Choose among the names the closest
to forgetfulness. Give me a name and I'll become
in this night's lot what you name me!
—I cannot, because I am a woman traveling
on a wind. And you're a traveler like me,
and names have families and distinct homes
—Then, I am "Nothing"...

"No one" said:
I'll fill your name up with desire. My body
gathers you from all of your directions. My body
embraces you from all of my directions, for you to become something,
and we can go on searching for life ...

Then "Nothing" said: Life is beautiful
with you ... life is beautiful!

هي في المساء

هي في المساء وحيدةٌ،
وأنا وحيدٌ مثلها...
بيني وبين شموعها في المطعم الشتويِّ
طاولتان فارغتان [لا شيءٌ يعكِّرُ صَمْتَنا]
هي لا تراني، إذ أراها
حين تقطفُ وردةً من صدرها
وأنا كذلك لا أراها، إذ تراني
حين أرشفُ من نبيذي قُبْلَةً ...
هي لا تُفَتِّتُ خبزها
وأنا كذلك لا أريقُ الماءَ
فوق الشَّرْشَف الورقيِّ
[لا شيءٌ يكدِّر صَفْوَنا]
هي وَحْدها، وأنا أمامَ جَمَالها
وحدي. لماذا لا تُوَحِّدُنا الهَشَاشَةُ؟
قلت في نفسي ——
لماذا لا أذوقُ نبيذَها؟
هي لا تراني، إذ أراها
حين ترفعُ ساقَها عن ساقها ...
وأنا كذلك لا أراها، إذ تراني
حين أخلَعُ معطفي ...
لا شيء يزعجها معي
لا شيء يزعجني، فنحن الآن
منسجمان في النسيان ...
كان عشاؤنا، كلٌّ على حِدَةٍ، شهيّاً
كان صَوْتُ الليل أزرَقَ
لم أكن وحدي، ولا هي وحدها
كنا معاً نصغي إلى البلَّوْرِ
[لا شيءٌ يُكَسِّرُ ليلنا]
هيَ لا تقولُ:

She's Alone in the Evening

She's alone in the evening,
and I am alone as she is ...
Between her candles and me in the winter restaurant
are two vacant tables (nothing disturbs our silence).
She doesn't see me, when I see her
picking a rose from her chest
and I also don't see her, when she sees me
sipping from my wine a kiss ...
She doesn't crumble her bread
and I also don't spill the water
on the paper tablecloth
(nothing disturbs our clarity).
She's alone, and I am in front of her beauty
alone. Why doesn't delicacy unite us?
I say to myself—
Why don't I taste her wine?
She doesn't see me, when I see her
uncrossing her legs ...
And I also don't see her, when she sees me
taking off my coat ...
Nothing bothers her when she's with me
nothing bothers me, because we are now
harmonious in forgetfulness ...
Our dinner was, separately, delicious
the night sound was blue
I wasn't alone, and neither was she alone
we were together listening to the crystal
(nothing fractures our night).
She doesn't say:

الحبُّ يُولَدُ كائناً حيّا
ويُـمْسي فِكْرَةً.
وأنا كذلك لا أقول:
الحب أمسى فكرةً

لكنه يبدو كذلك ...

Love is born a living creature
before it becomes an idea.
And I also don't say:
Love has become an idea

But it seems like it ...

في الانتظار

في الانتظار، يُصيبُني هَوَسٌ برصد
الاحتمالات الكثيرة: رُبَّما نَسِيَتْ حقيبتها
الصغيرة في القطار، فضاع عنواني
وضاع الهاتفُ المحمولُ، فانقطعت شهيّتها
وقالت: لا نصيبَ له من المطر الخفيف/
ورُبَّما انشَغَلَتْ بأمرٍ طارىءٍ أو رحلة
نحو الجنوب لكي تزور الشمسَ، واتَّصَلَتْ
ولكن لم تَجِدْني في الصباح، فقد
خَرَجْتُ لأشتري غاردينيا لمسائنا وزجاجتينِ
من النبيذ/
وربما اختَلَفَتْ مع الزَّوْج القديم على
شُؤون الذكريات، فأقْسَمَتْ ألّا ترى
رجلاً يُهدِّدُها بصُنع الذكريات/
ورُبَّما اصطَدَمَتْ بتاكسي في الطريقِ
إليَّ، فانطفأتْ كواكب في مَجَرّتها.
وما زالت تُعَالَجُ بالمهدّىء والنعاسِ/
وربما نظرتْ إلى المرآة قبل خروجها
من نفسها، وتحسَّسَتْ أُجَّاصَتَيْنِ كبيرتينِ
تُـمَوِّجان حريرَها، فتنهَّدَتْ وتردّدتْ:
هل يستحقُّ أنوثتي أحدٌ سوايَ/
وربما عبرتْ، مُصَادَفَةً، بحبٌّ
سابقٍ لم تَشْفَ منه، فرافَقَتْهُ إلى
العشاءِ/
ورُبَّما ماتَتْ،
فإنَّ الموت يعشق فجأة، مثلي،
وإنَّ الموتَ، مثلي، لا يحبُّ الانتظار

While Waiting

While waiting, I become obsessed with observing
the many possibilities: maybe she forgot her small
suitcase on the train, and my address got lost
and her mobile phone got lost, so she lost her appetite
and said: No share of the light drizzle for him /
Or maybe she got busy with an urgent matter or a journey
to the south to visit the sun, and called
but didn't find me in the morning, because
I had gone to buy some gardenia for our evening
and two bottles of wine /
Or maybe she was in dispute with her ex-husband
over matters of memory, and she swore not to see
another man who might threaten her with making memories /
Or maybe she crashed into a taxi on the way
to see me, which extinguished some planets in her galaxy.
And she is still being treated with tranquilizers and sleep /
Or maybe she looked in the mirror before going out
of herself, felt two large pears
making waves on her silk, then sighed and hesitated:
Does anyone else other than myself deserve my womanhood /
Or maybe she ran, by coincidence, into an old
love she hadn't healed from, and joined him for dinner /
Or maybe she died,
because death loves suddenly, like me,
and death, like me, doesn't love waiting

لو كنتُ غيري

لو كُنْتُ غيري في الطريق، لما التفتُّ
إلى الوراء، لَقُلْتُ ما قال المسافرُ
للمسافرة الغريبةِ: يا غريبةُ! أيقظي
الجيتارَ أكْثَرَ! أرجئي غَدَنا ليمتدَّ الطريقُ
بنا، ويتَّسعَ الفضاءُ لنا، فننجو من
حكايتنا معاً: كمْ أنتِ أنتِ.. وكم أنا
غيري أمامك ها هنا!

لو كُنْتُ غيري لانتميتُ إلى الطريق،
فلن أعود ولن تعودي. أيقظي الجيتار
كي نتحسَّسَ المجهولَ والجهةَ التي تُغْوي
المسافرَ باختبار الجاذبيّة. ما أنا إلاّ
خُطَايَ، وأنت بوصلتي وهاويتي معاً.
لو كُنْتُ غيري في الطريق، لكُنْتُ
أخفيتُ العواطفَ في الحقيبة، كي
تكون قصيدتي مائيّةً، شَفَّافةً، بيضاءَ،
تجريديّةً، وخفيفةً... أقوى من الذكرى،
وأضْعَفَ من حُبَيْبات الندى، ولَقُلْتُ:
إنَّ هُويَّتي هذا المدى!

لو كُنْتُ غيري في الطريق، لَقُلْتُ
للجيتار: دَرِّبْني على وَتَرٍ إضافيٌّ!
فإنَّ البيتَ أبعدُ، والطريقَ إليه أجملُ ــ
هكذا ستقول أغنيتي الجديدةُ ــ كلما
طال الطريق تجدَّد المعنى، وصرتُ أُ ثنين
في هذا الطريق: أنا ... وغيري!

If I Were Another

If I were another on the road, I would not have looked
back, I would have said what one traveler said
to another: Stranger! awaken
the guitar more! Delay our tomorrow so our road
may extend and space may widen for us, and we may get rescued
from our story together: you are so much yourself ... and I am
so much other than myself right here before you!

If I were another I would have belonged to the road,
neither you nor I would return. Awaken the guitar
and we might sense the unknown and the route that tempts
the traveler to test gravity. I am only
my steps, and you are both my compass and my chasm.
If I were another on the road, I would have
hidden my emotions in the suitcase, so my poem
would be of water, diaphanous, white,
abstract, and lightweight ... stronger than memory,
and weaker than dewdrops, and I would have said:
My identity is this expanse!

If I were another on the road, I would have said
to the guitar: Teach me an extra string!
Because the house is farther, and the road to it prettier—
that's what my new song would say. Whenever
the road lengthens the meaning renews, and I become two
on this road: I ... and another!

شكراً لتونس

شكراً لتونسَ. أَرْجَعْتِني سالماً من
حُبِّها، فبكيتُ بين نسائها في المسرح
البلديِّ حين تملَّصَ المعنى من الكلمات.
كُنْتُ أودِّعُ الصيفَ الأخيرَ كما يودِّعُ
شاعرٌ أغنيةً غَزَلِيَّةً: ماذا سأكتبُ
بعدها لحبيبة أُخرى ... إذا أحببتُ؟
في لُغَتي دُوَارُ البحر. في لغتي رحيلٌ
غامضٌ من صُوَر. لا قرطاجَ تكبحُهُ، ولا
ريحُ البرابرة الجنوبيِّين. جئتُ على
وتيرة نَوْرَس، ونَصَبْتُ خيمتي الجديدة
فوق مُنْحَدَرٍ سماويٍّ. سأكتبُ ههنا فصلاً
جديداً في مديح البحر: أُسْطوريَّةٌ
لغتي، وقلبي مَوْجَةٌ زرقاءُ تخدشُ
صخرةً: «لا تُعْطِني، يا بحرُ، ما
لا أستحقُّ من النشيد. ولا تكن
يا، بحرُ، أكثرَ أو أقلَّ من النشيد!» ...
تطيرُ بيْ لُغَتي إلى مجهولنا الأبديِّ،
خلف الحاضر المكسور من جِهَتَيْن: إنْ
تنظرْ وراءك تُوقظْ سَدُومَ المكان على
خطيئته... وإن تنظرْ أمامَكَ توقظ
التاريخَ، فاحذرْ لَدْغَةَ الجهتين... واتبَعْني.
أقول لها: سأمكثُ عند تونس بين
مَنْزِلَتَيْن: لا بيتي هنا بيتي، ولا
منفايَ كالمنفى. وها أنذا أُودِّعُها،
فيجرحني هواءُ البحر ... مِسْكُ الليل يجرحني،
وعِقْدُ الياسمين على كلام الناس يجرحني،
ويجرحني التأمُّلُ في الطريق اللوبيِّ إلى ضواحي الأندلسْ ...

Thanks to Tunis

Thanks to Tunis. She brought me back safely
from her love, so I cried amid her women in the public
auditorium when meaning slipped out of the words.
I was bidding the last summer farewell as a poet bids
a love eulogy farewell: What will I write
after her to another lover ... if I love another?
In my language, there is seasickness. In my language there is
a mysterious departure from Tyre. Neither Carthage reins it in, nor
the wind of the southern barbarians. I came
in a seagull's fashion, and pitched my new tent
on a heavenly slope. Right here I'll write
a new chapter in the eulogies to the sea: mythic
is my language, and my heart a blue wave grazing
a rock: "Don't give me, O sea, what I don't deserve
of song. And don't be, O sea, more or less than song!" ...
My language takes me in flight to our eternal unknown,
behind a present broken on two sides: If
you look behind you Sodom will awaken the place
to its sin ... and if you look ahead you will awaken
history, so beware of the sting on either side ... and follow me.
I tell it: My stay in Tunis is between
two ranks: my home here is not my home, nor
is my exile like exile. So here I am bidding her farewell,
and the sea air wounds me ... the night's musk wounds me,
and the jasmine necklace in the words people say wounds me,
and also the contemplation in the spiral path to the suburbs of the Andalus
wounds me ...

لي مقعد في المسرح المهجور

ليَ مقْعدٌ في المسرح المهجور في
بيروتَ. قد أنسى، وقد أتذكُّر
الفصلَ الأخيرَ بلا حنينٍ ... لا لشيءٍ
بل لأنَّ المسرحيَّةَ لم تكنْ مكتوبةً
بمهارةٍ ...
فوضى
كيوميّات حرب اليائسين، وسيرةٌ ذاتيَّةٌ
لغرائز المتفرجين. مُمَثِّلون يُمَزِّقون نُصُوصَهُمْ
ويفتِّشون عن المؤلف بيننا، نحن الشهودَ
الجالسين على مقاعدنا.
أقول لجاريَ الفنَّان: لا تُشهِر سلاحك،
وانتظرْ، إلّا إذا كُنْتَ الـمُؤَلِّفَ!
— لا
ويسألني: وهل أنت المؤلِّفُ؟
— لا.
ونجلس خائفَيْن. أقول: كُنْ بَطَلاً
حياديّاً لتنجو من مصير واضح
فيقول: لا بَطَل يموت مُبَجَّلاً في المشهد
الثاني. سأنتظر البقيَّة. ربما أجريتُ
تعديلاً على أحد الفصول. وربما أصلحتُ
ما صَنَعَ الحديدُ بإخوتي
فأقول: أنتَ إذاً؟
يردُّ: أنا وأنتَ مؤلِّفان مُقَنَّعان وشاهدان
مُقَنَّعان.
أقول: ما شأني؟ أنا متفرِّجٌ
فيقول: لا متفرِّجٌ في باب هاويةٍ ... ولا
أحدٌ حياديّ هنا. وعليك أن تختار
دورك في النهايةُ
فأقول: تنقصني البداية، ما البداية؟

I Have a Seat in the Abandoned Theater

I have a seat in the abandoned theater
in Beirut. I might forget, and I might recall
the final act without longing ... not because of anything
other than that the play was not written
skillfully ...
Chaos
as in the war days of those in despair, and an autobiography
of the spectators' impulse. The actors were tearing up their scripts
and searching for the author among us, we the witnesses
sitting in our seats
I tell my neighbor the artist: Don't draw your weapon,
and wait, unless you're the author!
—No
Then he asks me: And you are you the author?
—No
So we sit scared. I say: Be a neutral
hero to escape from an obvious fate
He says: No hero dies revered in the second
scene. I will wait for the rest. Maybe I would
revise one of the acts. And maybe I would mend
what the iron has done to my brothers
So I say: It is you then?
He responds: You and I are two masked authors and two masked
witnesses
I say: How is this my concern? I'm a spectator
He says: No spectators at chasm's door ... and no
one is neutral here. And you must choose
your part in the end
So I say: I'm missing the beginning, what's the beginning?

في الشام

في الشام، أعرفُ مَنْ أنا وسط الزحام.
يَدُلّني قَـمَرٌ تَلألأ في يد أ مرأة... عليَّ.
يدلني حَجَرٌ تَوَضَّأ في دموع الياسمينة
ثم نام. يدلّني بَرَدَى الفقيرُ كغيمة
مكسورةٍ. ويَدُلّني شِعْرٌ فُروسيٌّ عليَّ:
هناك عند نهاية النفق الطويل مُحَاصَرٌ
مثلي سَيُوقِدُ شمعةً، من جرحه، لتراهُ
ينفضُ عن عباءَته الظلامَ. تَدُلّني رَيْحانةٌ
أرخت جدائلها على الموتِ ودفَّأت الرخام.
«هنا يكون الموتُ حبّاً نائماً» ويدُلّني
الشعراء، عُذريِّين كانوا أم إباحيِّيـنَ،
صُوفيِّين كانوا أم زَنَادِقَةً،
عليَّ: إذا
أ خْتَلَفْتَ عرفتَ نفسَكَ، فاختلفْ تجد
الكلامَ على زهور اللوز شفافاً، ويُقرِئْكَ
السماويُّ السلامَ. أنا أنا في الشام،
لا شَبَهي ولا شَبَحي. أنا وغدي يداً
بيدٍ نُرَفْرِفُ في جناحَيْ طائرٍ. في الشام
أمشي نائماً، وأنامُ في حِضْن الغزالةِ
ماشياً. لا فرق بين نهارها والليل
إلاَّ بعضُ أشغال الحمام. هناك أرضُ
الـحُلم عاليةٌ، ولكنّ السماء تسيرُ عاريةٌ
وتَسْكُنُ بين أهل الشام ...

In Syria

In Syria, I know who I am in the crowd.
A moon glittering in a woman's hand guides me ... to me.
A stone after ablution in the jasmine's tears guides me
then sleeps. The impoverished Barada guides me like a broken
cloud. And a heroic poetry guides me to me:
there at the end of the long tunnel besieged
like me he will light a candle, from his wound, so you can see him
shake the darkness off his aba. A basil plant that loosened
its braids over the dead guides me and warms up the marble.
"Here death is a sleeping love" and the poets
chaste be they or licentious,
Sufi or atheist,
guide me to me: If
you differ you know yourself, so differ to find
speech diaphanous on almond blossoms, and for the heavenly
to bestow on you salaam. I am me in Syria,
none is my like or my ghost. My tomorrow and I are hand
in hand fluttering in a bird's wings. In Syria
I walk in my sleep, I sleep in the gazelle's lap
walking. No difference between its night and day
except for some pigeons running their errands. There
the land of dream is high, but the sky walks naked
and resides among the people of Syria ...

في مصر

في مصرَ، لا تتشابَهُ الساعاتُ ...
كُلُّ دقيقة ذكرى تجدِّدُها طيورُ النيل.
كُنْتُ هناك. كان الكائنُ البشريُّ يبتكرُ
الإله/ الشمسَ. لا أَحَدَّ يُسَمِّي نفسَهُ
أحداً. «أنا اُبنُ النيل ـــ هذا الاسم
يكفيني». ومنذ اللحظة الأولى تُسَمِّي
نفسك «ابن النيل» كي تتجنَّب العَدَم
الثقيل. هناك أحياءٌ وموتى يقطفون
معاً غيومَ القُطْنِ من أرض الصعيد،
ويزرعون القمحَ في الدلتا. وبين الحيِّ
والـمَيْتِ الذي فيه تناوُبُ حارسين على
الدفاع عن النخيل. وكُلُّ شيء عاطفيٌّ
فيك، إذ تمشي على أطراف روحكَ في
دهاليز الزمان، كأنَّ أُمَّكَ مصرَ
قد وَلَدَتْكَ زَهْرَةَ لُوتس، قبل الولادة،
هل عرفت الآن نفسَكَ؟ مصرُ تجلسُ
خلسةً مَعَ نفسها: «لا شيء يشبهني».
وترفو معطفَ الأبديَّة المثقوب من
إحدى جهات الريح. كُنْتُ هناك. كان
الكائنُ البشريُّ يكتب حكمة الموت / الحياة.
وكُلُّ شيء عاطفيٌّ، مُقْمِرٌ ... إلاَّ القصيدةَ
في التفاتها إلى غدها تُفَكِّر بالخلود،
ولا تقول سوى هشاشتها أمام النيل...

In Egypt

In Egypt, the hours are never alike …
Each minute is a memory the Nile birds renew.
I was there. The Human Being was inventing
the God / the Sun. No one has a name
for himself. "I am the son of the Nile—this name
is enough for me." And from the first instance you call
yourself "Son of the Nile" to avoid the heavy void.
Over there the living and the dead
pick cotton clouds together in Upper Egypt,
and plant the wheat in the Delta. And between the living
and the dead there is the handover between two guards
defending the palm trees. And everything is sentimental
within you, when you walk on your soul's tiptoes
in time's corridors, as if your mother Egypt
had given birth to you as a lotus flower first, before birth,
so do you know now who you are? Egypt sits
with herself in secret: "Nothing resembles me."
And darns eternity's perforated cloak while facing
one of the paths of the wind. I was there. Mankind
was writing the wisdom of Death / Life.
And everything is sentimental, moonstruck … except the poem
attending to its tomorrow and thinking of immortality—
it speaks only of its frailty before the Nile …

أتذكّر السَّيّاب

أتذكّرُ السَّيّابَ، يصرخُ في الخليج سُدَىً:
«عراقٌ، عراقٌ، ليس سوى العراق...»
ولا يردّ سوى الصدى.
أتذكّرُ السَّيّابَ، في هذا الفضاء السوميّ
تغلّبتْ أُنثى على عُقْم السديم
وأوْرَثَتْنا الأرضَ والمنفى معاً
أتذكّرُ السَّيّابَ... إن الشِّعْرَ يُولَدُ في العراقِ
فكُنْ عراقيّاً لتصبح شاعراً يا صاحبي!
أتذكّرُ السَّيّابَ، لم يَجِدِ الحياةَ كما
تخيّلَ بين دجلةً والفراتِ، فلم يفكر
مثلَ جلجامشْ بأعشاب الخلودِ،
ولم يُفَكّر بالقيامة بعدها...
أتذكّرُ السَّيّابَ، يأخذُ عن حمورابي
الشرائعَ كي يُغَطّي سَوْءَةً،
ويسير نحو ضريحه متصوّفاً.
أتذكّرُ السَّيّابَ، حين أُصابَ بالـحُمّى
وأهذي: إخوتي كانوا يُعدُّون العَشَاءَ
لجيش هولاكو، ولا خَدَمٌ سواهُمْ ... إخوتي!
أتذكّرُ السَّيّابَ، لم نَحْلُمْ بما لا
يستحقّ النَّحْلُ من قُوتٍ. ولم نحلم
بأكثرَ من يدين صغيرتين تصافحان غيابنا.
أتذكّرُ السَّيّابَ. حدّادون موتى ينهضون
من القبور ويصنعون قيودنا.
أتذكّرُ السَّيّابَ. إنّ الشعرَ تجربةٌ ومنفى
توأمان. ونحن لم نحلُمْ بأكثرَ من
حياةٍ كالحياةِ، وأن نموت على طريقتنا
«عراقٌ
«عراقٌ
« ليس سوى العراقْ ...»»

I Recall al-Sayyab

I recall al-Sayyab, screaming at the Gulf in vain:
"Iraq, Iraq, nothing but Iraq ..."
and only echo replies.
I recall al-Sayyab: In this Sumerian space
a female overcame nebula's sterility
and bequeathed us land and exile together.
I recall al-Sayyab ... Poetry is born in Iraq,
be an Iraqi to become a poet, my friend!
I recall al-Sayyab, he didn't find life
as he imagined between the Tigris and the Euphrates,
but didn't think like Gilgamesh of immortality herbs,
and didn't think of the judgment day that follows ...
I recall al-Sayyab, taking from Hammurabi
the tablets to cover his loins,
then walking toward his tomb, a Sufi.
I recall al-Sayyab, when I am stricken with fever
and I hallucinate: My brothers were preparing dinner
for Hulagu's army, they were the only servants ... my brothers!
I recall al-Sayyab, we didn't dream of what
bees don't deserve of sustenance. And we didn't dream
of more than two handshakes that greet our absence.
I recall al-Sayyab. Dead blacksmiths rise
from the graves and forge our chains.
I recall al-Sayyab. Poetry is the twins, experience
and exile. And we didn't dream of more than
a life like life, and that we die in our own style
"Iraq,
Iraq,
nothing but Iraq ..."

II. طريق الساحل

II. THE COASTAL ROAD

طريقٌ يُؤدّي إلى مصرَ والشام

[قلبي يرنُّ من الـجهَتَيْن]

طريقُ المسافر منْ ... وإلى نفسه

[جَسَدي ريشةٌ والمدى طائرٌ]

طريقُ الصواب ... طريقُ الخطأ

[لعلّي أخطأتُ، لكنها التجربة]

طريقٍ الصعود إلى شُرُفات السماء

[وأعلى وأعلى، وأَبعدْ]

طريقُ النزول إلى أوّل الأرض

[إنّ السماء رماديّةٌ]

طريق التأمُّل في الحبّ

[فالحبُّ قد يجعلُ الذئبَ نادلَ مقهى]

طريقُ السنونو ورائحةُ البرتقال على البحر

[إنّ الحنيـنَ هُوَ الرائحةْ]

طريقُ التَّوَابل والملح والقمح

[والحرب أيضاً]

طريقُ السلام الـمُتَوَّج بالقُدْس

[بعد انتهاء الحروب صليبيّةِ الأقنعة]

طريقُ التجارة والأبجديّة، والحالمينَ

[بتأليف سيرةٍ تِزْغَلُّةٍ]

طريقُ غُزاةٍ يريدون ترميمَ تاريخهم

[بغدٍ مُودَعٍ في البنوك]

طريقُ التَّحَرُّش بالميثولوجيا

[فقد تَسْتَجيبُ إلى التكنولوجيا]

طريقُ التخلّي، قليلاً، عن الإيديولوجيا

[لمصلَحَة العَوْلَـمَةْ]

طريقُ الصراع على أيّ شيء

[ولو كان جِنْسَ الملاك]

طريقُ الوفاق على كُلِّ شيء

[ولو كان أنثى الحجر]

طريقُ الإخاء الـمُخَاتِل

[بين الغزالِ وصيّاده]

طريقٌ يدلُّ على الشيء أو عكسه

[لفرط التَّشابُه بين الكِنَايَة والاستعارة]

طريقُ الخيول التي صَرَعَتْها المسافات

[والطائرات ...]

A road that leads to Egypt and Syria
   (my heart rings on either side)
The traveler's road from ... and to himself
   (my body is a feather and the expanse is a bird)
The right road ... the wrong road
   (I might have been wrong, but it's the experience)
The road of ascension to heaven's balconies
   (and higher and higher, and farther)
The road of descent to the first of the earth
   (the sky is ashen)
The road of contemplating love
   (because love might turn a wolf into a waiter)
The road of the swallow and the orange scent by the sea
   (longing is the scent)
The road of spices and salt and wheat
   (and war too)
The road of peace crowned with Jerusalem
   (after the end of Crusader-masked wars)
The road of trade and alphabet, and of the dreamers
   (who dream of writing the biography of a turtledove)
The road of invaders who want to renovate their history
   (with a tomorrow deposited in the banks)
The road of provoking mythology
   (for it might respond to technology)
The road of slightly giving up ideology
   (for the sake of globalization)
The road of conflict over anything
   (even if it resembled an angel)
The road of agreement over everything
   (even if it were a female stone)
The road of wily brotherhood
   (between the gazelle and its hunter)
A road that guides to the thing or its opposite
   (due to hypersimile between metaphor and metonymy)
The road of horses perished by the distances
   (and by the planes ...)

طريقُ البريد القديم الـمُسَجّل
[كُلُّ الرسائل مُودَعَةٌ في خزائن قيصر]
طريقٌ يطول ويقصُر
[وَفْقَ مزاج أبي الطيِّب الـمُتَنَبّي]
طريقُ الإلهاتِ مُنْحَنياتِ الظُّهور
[كرايات جيشٍ تَقَهْقَرْ]
طريقُ فتاةٍ تُظَلِّلُ عانَتها بالفراشةِ
[فاللازَوَرْدُ يُجَرِّدُها من ملابسها]
طريقُ الذين يُحيِّرُهُمْ وَصفُ زهرة لوز
[لأَنَّ الكثافةَ شَفّافةٌ]
طريقٌ طويلٌ بلا أنبياء
[فقد آثَروا الطُّرُقَ الوَعِرَة]
طريقٌ يؤدّي إلى طَلَل البيتِ
[تحت حديقة مُسْتَوْطَنة]
طريقٌ يَسُدّ عليَّ الطريق
فيصرخُ بي شَبَحي:
إنْ
أردتَ
الوصولَ إلى
نفسك الجامحةْ
فلا
تَسْلُك
الطُّرُقَ الواضحةْ!

The road of ancient certified mail
        (all letters are deposited in Caesar's safe)
A road that lengthens and shortens
        (according to al-Mutanabbi's whims)
The road of goddesses with bent backs
        (like a retreating army's banners)
A road for a young girl who covers her pubes with a butterfly
        (because the lapis lazuli takes off her dress)
The road of those puzzled by describing an almond blossom
        (since density is transparent)
A long road without prophets
        (for they chose the rugged road)
A road that leads to the house rubble
        (below a settlement's garden)
A road that blocks the road for me
so my ghost screams at me:
If
    you want
        to get
to
your indomitable self
don't
    follow
        the obvious roads!

III. لا كما يفعل السائح الأجنبي

III. NOT AS A FOREIGN TOURIST DOES

مَشَيْتُ على ما تَبَقَّى من القلبِ،
صَوْبَ الشمال ...
ثلاثُ كنائسَ مهجورةٌ،
سنديانٌ على الجانبَيْنِ،
قُرىً كنقاطٍ على أَحْرُف مُحِيَتْ،
وفتاةٌ على العشب تقرأُ ما
يُشْبِهُ الشَّعَرَ: لو كُنْتُ أكبَرَ،
لو كُنْتُ أكبَرَ، لاسْتَسْلَمَ الذئبُ لي!

... لم أكُنْ عاطفياً، ولا «دون جوان»
فلم أتمدَّد على العشب، لكنني
قُلْتُ في السرِّ: لو كنتُ أصغرَ
لو كنتُ أصغرَ عشرين عاماً
لَشاركْتُها الماءَ والسندويشات،
وعلَّمتُها كيف تَلْمسُ قوس قُزَحْ

مَشَيْتُ، كما يفعل السائحُ الأجنبيُّ ...
معي كاميرا، ودليلي كتابٌ صغيرٌ
يضمُّ قصائدَ في وَصْف هذا المكانِ
لأكثرَ من شاعرٍ أجنبيٍّ،
أحسُّ بأني أنا المتكلِّمُ فيها
ولولا الفوارقُ بين القوافي لقُلْتُ:
أنا آخري

... كنت أتبعُ وصف المكان. هنا
شَجَرٌ زائدٌ، وهنا قمرٌ ناقصٌ
وكما في القصائد: ينبتُ عشبٌ
على حَجَرٍ يتوجَّعُ. لا هُوَ حُلْمٌ
ولا هُوَ رمزٌ يدلُّ على طائرٍ وطنيٍّ،
ولكنه غيمةٌ أينعَتْ...
خطوة، خطوتان، ثلاثٌ ... وَجَدْتُ الربيعَ
قصيراً على الـمشمِشِيَّات. ما كِدْتُ أرنو
إلى زَهْرة اللوز حتى تنائَرْتُ ما بينَ
غَـمازَتَيْن. مَشَيْتُ لأتبعَ ما تَرَكَتْه الطيورُ
الصغيرةُ من نَمَشٍ في القصائد/

I walked on what remains of the heart,
toward the north ...
three abandoned churches,
holm oak on either side,
villages like dots erased from their letters,
and a young girl on the grass reading what
looks like poetry: If I were older,
if I were older, the wolf would have surrendered to me!

... I wasn't sentimental, or a Don Juan
I didn't lie down on the grass beside her, but I did
say to myself: If I were younger
if I were twenty years younger
I would have shared the sandwiches and the water with her,
and taught her how to touch the rainbow

I walked, as a foreign tourist does ...
a camera with me, and my guide a little book
containing poems that describe this place
by a few foreign poets,
I feel as if I were the speaker in them
and had it not been for the difference in rhyme
I would have said: I am another

... I used to follow the description of the place. Here
are excess trees, and here is a missing moon
and as in poems, grass sprouts
over an aching stone. It is not a dream
nor is it a symbol that leads to a national bird,
it is a cloud that has ripened ...
I took one step, two steps, three ... I found spring
too short for the apricots. As soon as I gazed
into the almond blossom I scattered between
two dimples. I walked to follow what the little
birds had left of freckles in the poem /

ثُمَّ تساءلْتُ: كيف يصير المكانُ
انعكاساً لصورته في الأساطير،
أو صِفَةً من صفات الكلام؟
وهل صورةُ الشيء أقوى
من الشيء؟
لولا مخيَّلتي قال لي آخري:
أنتَ لَسْتَ هنا!

لم أكن واقعيّاً. ولكنني لا
أُصدِّقُ تاريخَ «إلياذة» العسكريِّ،
هُوَ الشِّعْرُ، أسطورةٌ خَلَقَتْ واقعاً...
وتساءَلْتُ: لو كانتِ الكاميرا والصحافةُ
شاهدةً فوق أسوار طروادةَ الآسيوية،
هل كان «هوميرُ» يكتبُ غيرَ الأوديسة؟/

... أُمْسِكُ هذا الهواء الشهيَّ،
هواءَ الجليل، بكلتا يديَّ
وأَمْضَغُهُ مثلما يمضغُ الماعزُ الجبليُّ
أعالي الشُّجَيْرات،
أمشي، أعرِف نفسي إلى نفسها:
أنتِ، يا نفسُ، إحدى صفات المكان

ثلاثُ كنائسَ مهجورةٌ
مآذنُ مكسورةٌ،
سنديانٌ على الجانبيـن،
قُرىً كنقاط على أحْرُفٍ مُحِيَتْ،
وفتاةٌ على العشب تسأل طيفاً:
لماذا كبرتَ ولم تنتظرني
يقول لها: لم أكنْ حاضراً
عندما ضاق ثوبُ الحرير بتُفَّاحَتَيْن.
فغنِّي، كما كنتِ قبل قليل، تُغَنِّين:
لو كُنْتُ أكبرَ، لو كنتُ أكبرَ ...

أمَّا أنا، فسأدخُلُ في شجر التوت
حيث تُحوِّلُني دُودةُ القزِّ خَيْطَ حريرٍ،

Then I wondered: How does a place become
a reflection of its image in myth,
or an adjective of speech?
And is a thing's image stronger
than the thing itself?
If it weren't for my imagination
my other self would have told me:
You are not here!

I wasn't realistic. But I don't believe
the Iliad's military history,
it is a poem, a myth creating reality ...
And I wondered: Had the camera and the media
been witnesses above the walls of Asian Troy,
would Homer have written other than the Odyssey?

... I hold this delicious air,
the Galilee air, with both of my hands
and I chew it as mountain goats chew
the tops of bushes,
I walk, I introduce myself to itself:
You, O self, are one of the adjectives of the place

Three abandoned churches,
broken minarets,
holm oak on either side,
villages like dots erased from their letters,
and a young girl on the grass asking a specter:
Why did you grow up and not wait for me?
He tells her: I wasn't present
when the silk robe got too tight for two apples,
so sing, as you were singing a while ago:
If I were older, if I were older ... /

As for me, I will enter the mulberry trees
where the silkworm makes me into a silk thread,

فأدخلُ في إبرة أ مرأةٍ من
نساء الأساطير،
ثم أطير كشالٍ مع الريح...

then I'll enter a woman's needle in
one of the myths
and fly like a shawl with the wind ...

VI. بيت من الشعر/
بيتُ الجنوبي

[في ذكرى أمل دنقل]

IV. A POETRY STANZA / THE SOUTHERNER'S HOUSE

in memory of Amal Donqul

واقفاً مَعَهُ تحت نافذة،
أتأمَّلُ وَشْمَ الظلال على
ضفَّة الأبديَّة، قُلْتُ له:
قد تغيَّرتَ يا صاحبي .... وَانْفَطَرْتَ
فها هِيَ دراجةُ الموت تدنو
ولكنها لا تحرِّكُ صرختك الخاطفةُ

قال لي: عِشْتُ قرب حياتي
كما هِيَ،
لا شيءَ يُثْبِتُ أنِّيَ حيٌّ
ولا شيءَ يثبتُ أنّيَ مَيْتٌ
ولم أتدخَّل بما تفعلُ الطيرُ بي
وبما يحملُ الليلُ مِنْ
مَرَضِ العاطفةْ

ألغيابُ يرفّ كزوجَيْ حمام على النيلِ...
يُنبِّئُنا باختلاف الـخُطَى حول فعل الـمُضارعِ...
كُنَّا معاً، وعلى حِدَة، نَسْتَحثُّ غداً
غامضاً. لا نريدُ من الشيء إلاّ
شفافيَّةَ الشيء: حدِّقْ تَرَ الوردَ
أسوَد في الضوء. واحلُمْ تَرَ الضوءَ
في العتمة الوارفةْ ...

ألجنوبيُّ يحفظ درب الصعاليك عن
ظهر قلبٍ. ويُشبِهُهُم في سليقتهم
وارتجالِ المدى. لا «هناك» له،
لا «هنا»، لا عناوينَ للفوضويّ
ولا مشجَبٌ للكلام. يقول: النظامُ
احتكامُ الصدى للصدى. وأنا صوتُ
نفسي المشاع: أنا هُوَ أنتَ ونحنُ أنا.
وينامُ على دَرَج الفجر: هذا هو
البيتُ، بيتٌ من الشعر، بيتُ الجنوبيِّ.
لكنَّهُ صارمٌ في نظام قصيدته. صانعٌ
بارعٌ يُنقذُ الوَزْنَ من صَخَب العاصفةْ

Standing together beneath a window,
contemplating the tattoos of shadows
on eternity's bank, I said to him:
You have changed, my friend ... and you have been cleft
because here is death's bicycle approaching
yet it doesn't move your rapid scream

He said to me: I lived near my life
as it is,
nothing proves me living
and nothing proves me dead
and I didn't interfere with what the birds do to me
and with what the night carries
of passion's ailment

Absence flutters like a pair of pigeons over the Nile ...
informing us of a disagreement among the footsteps
around the present tense ...
He and I were, together, and separately, prompting a mysterious
tomorrow. We wanted from the thing only
the transparency of the thing: stare and you will see the rose
black in the light. Dream and you will see the light
in the lush darkness ...

The southerner knows the path of vagabonds
like the back of his heart. And mimics their instinct
and their improvisation of space. No "there" for him,
no "here," no address for the chaotic
and no clothes rack for speech. He says: Discipline
is echo's appeal to echo, and I am my self's
radiant sound: I am he you and we are I.
And he sleeps on dawn's doorsteps: this is
the house, a house of poetry, the southerner's stanza.
Yet he is stern with his poem's form. A brilliant
craftsman who saves meter from the roar of the storm

ألغيابُ على حاله. قَمَرٌ عابرٌ فوق
خُوفُو يُذهِّبُ سَقْفَ النخيل. وسائحةٌ
تملأ الكاميرا بالغياب، وتسألُ: ما
الساعةُ الآن؟ قال لها: الساعةُ
الآنَ عَشرُ دقائقَ ما بعد سبعة
آلاف عام من الأبجديّة. ثم تنهَّد:
مصرُ الشهيّةُ، مصرُ البهيّةُ مشغولةٌ
بالخلود. وأمَّا أنا ... فمريضٌ بها، لا
أفكّرُ إلاّ بصحّتها، وبِكسْرَةِ خبزٍ
غدي الناشفة

شاعرٌ، شاعرٌ من سُلالَةِ أهل
الخسارة، و ابنٌ وفيٌّ لريف المساكيـن.
قرآنُهُ عربيٌّ، ومزمورهُ عربيٌّ، وقُربَانُهُ
عربيٌّ. وفي قلبه زَمَنانِ غريبان،
يبتعدان ويقتربان: غدٌ لا يكفُّ
عن الاعتذار: «نَسِيتُكَ، لا تنتظرني».
وأمس يجرُّ مراكبَ فرعونَ نحو الشمال:
«انتظرتُكَ، لكنْ تأخرتَ». قُلتُ لَهُ:
أين كُنْتَ إذاً؟ قال لي: كُنْتُ
أبحث عن حاضري في جَناحَيْ سُنُونُوَّةٍ
خائفةٌ ...

ألجنوبيُّ يحملُ تاريخَهُ بيَدَيْه، كحفنة قمحٍ،
ويمشي على نفسه واثقاً من يسوع
السنابلِ. إنَّ الحياةَ بديهيّةٌ... فلماذا
نفسّرها بالأساطير؟ إنَّ الحياة حقيقيّةٌ
والصفاتِ هيَ الزائفةُ

قال لي في الطريق إلى ليله:
كلَّما قُلْتُ: كلاَّ. تجلّى ليَ اللهُ
حريّةً ... وبلغتُ الرضا الباطنيَّ عن
النفس. قلتُ: وهل يُصْلحُ الشعرُ
ما أفسد الدهرُ فينا وجنكيزخان
وأحفادهُ العائدون إلى النهر؟
قال: على قَدْرِ حُلمكَ تتّسع الأرضُ.
والأرضُ أمّ المخيّلة النازفة

And absence is as it has been. A moon passing over
Khufu and gilding the roofs of palm trees. And a tourist
woman filling her camera with absence, and asking: What
time is it now? He said to her: It is now
ten minutes past seven
thousand years of the alphabet. Then he sighed:
Delicious Egypt, beautiful Egypt is preoccupied
with immortality. And I … am sick with her, I
think of nothing but her health, and my tomorrow's
piece of dried bread

A poet, and a descendant
of the kin of loss, a loyal son to the pacified in the countryside.
His Quran is Arabic, and his Psalms are Arabic, and his Eucharist
is Arabic. And in his heart are two strange times,
drawing near and going far: a tomorrow that doesn't cease
apologizing: "I forgot about you, don't wait for me."
And a yesterday dragging the pharaoh's boats toward the north:
"I waited for you, but you were late." I said to him:
Where were you then? He said: I was
looking for my present in a frightened swallow's wings …

The southerner carries his history with his hands, like a fistful of wheat,
and walks upon himself, confident of the Christ
in the grains: Life is intuitive … why then
do we explain it with myth? Life is real
and the adjectives are false

He told me on his way to his night:
Whenever I said: No! God transfigured before me
as freedom … and I attained the visceral contentment
with the self. I said: And can poetry fix
what the ages broke in us and in Genghis Khan
and in his grandchildren who are coming back to the river?
He said: The land expands as much as your dream's measure.
And the land is the mother of the bleeding imagination

قال في آخر الليل: خذني إلى البيتِ،
بيتِ المجاز الأخيرِ ...
فإني غريبٌ هنا يا غريبُ،
ولا شيءَ يُفْرِحُني قرب بيتِ الحبيبِ
ولا شيءَ يجرحني في «طريق الحليب» البعيدةِ
قلت: وماذا عن الروح؟
قال: سَتَجْلِسُ قُرْبَ حياتي
فلا شيءَ يُثْبِتُ أنِّيَ ميتٌ
ولا شي يثبتُ أنِّيَ حيٌّ
ستحيا، كما هِيَ
حائرة آسفةٌ ...

At the end of the night he said: Take me to the house,
the house of the last metaphor ...
for I am O stranger a stranger here
and nothing pleases me near my lover's house
and nothing wounds me in the distant Milky Way
I said: And what about the soul?
He said: It will sit near my life
for nothing proves me living
and nothing proves me dead
it will live, as it is
mystified and blue ...

٧. كحادثة غامضة

V. LIKE A MYSTERIOUS INCIDENT

في دار بابلو نيرودا، على شاطىء
الباسفيك، تذكَّرْتُ يانيس ريتسوس.
كانت أثينا ترحِّبُ بالقادمين من البحر،
في مَسْرحٍ دائريٍّ مُضاءٍ بصرخة ريتسوس:
«آه فلسطيـنُ،
يا آسْمَ التراب،
ويا آسْمَ السماء،
سَتَنْتَصِرين ...»
وعانَقَني، ثُمَّ قَدَّمني شاهراً شارةَ النصرِ:
«هذا أخي».
فَشَعَرْتُ بأني انتصرتُ، وأني انكسرتُ
كقطعة ماسٍ، فلم يَبْقَ منِّي سوى الضوء/

في مطعم دافىء، نتبادلُ بَعْضَ الحنين
إلى بَلَدَيْنا القديمين، والذكريات عن
الغد: كانت أثينا القديمةُ أجملَ.
أما يَبُوسُ، فلن تتحمّل أكثر. فالجنرال
استعار قناعَ النبيّ ليبكي ويسرق
دمعَ الضحايا: «عزيزي العَدُوُّ!
قَتَلْتُكَ من دون قصد، عدوِّي العزيزَ،
لأَنَّكَ أزعجتَ دبّابتي»/

قال ريتسوس: لكنَّ اسبارطةً انكسَرَتْ
في مهبِّ الخيال الأثينيِّ. إنَّ الحقيقةَ
والحقَّ صنوان ينتصران معاً. يا أخي
في القصيدة! للشعر جسْرٌ على
أمس والغد. قد يلتقي باعةُ السَّمَكِ
الـمُتْعَبون مع الخارجين من الميثولوجيا.
وقد يشربون النبيذ معاً.
قلتُ: ما الشعْرُ؟ ... ما الشعْرُ في
آخر الأمر؟
قال: هو الـحَدَثُ الغامضُ، الشعرُ
يا صاحبي هو ذاك الحنيـنُ الذي لا
يُفسَّرُ، إذ يجعلُ الشيءَ طيفاً، وإذْ
يجعلُ الطَّيْفَ شيئاً. ولكنه قد يُفَسِّرُ
حاجَتنا لاقتسامِ الجمالِ العُمُوميِّ...

In Pablo Neruda's home, on the Pacific
coast, I remembered Yannis Ritsos.
Athens was welcoming those who had come from the sea,
in an amphitheater illuminated with Ritsos's scream:
        "O Palestine,
            name of the soil,
                and name of the sky,
                    you will be victorious ..."
And he embraced me, then introduced me with a victory sign:
"This is my brother."
        So I felt that I had won, and that I had been broken
        like a diamond, that nothing but light remained of me /

In a cozy restaurant, we exchanged some affection
about our two old countries, and some memories about
tomorrow: Ancient Athens was more beautiful.
As for Yabous, it cannot take more. The general
has borrowed a prophet's mask to cry and steal
the victims' tears: "My dear enemy!
I killed you unintentionally, my dear enemy,
because you bothered my tank" /

Ritsos said: But Sparta broke
in the rise of the Athenian imagination. Truth
and justice are twin brothers that win together. My brother
in poem! poetry has a bridge over
yesterday and tomorrow. The tired fishermen might get together
with those who are exiting mythology.
And together they might have some wine.
        I said: What is poetry ... what is poetry in a nutshell?
He said: It is the mysterious incident, poetry,
my friend, is that inexplicable longing
that makes a thing into a specter, and
makes a specter into a thing. Yet it also might explain
our need to share public beauty ... /

لا بحر في بيته في أثينا القديمة،
حيث الإلهاتُ كنَّ يُدِرْنَ شؤون الحياة
مع البَشَر الطيّبين، وحيث إلكترا الفتاةُ
تناجي إلكترا العجوزَ وتسألها:
هل أنا أنت حقّاً؟

ولا لَيْلَ في بيته الضيّق الـمُتَقَشِّف
فوق سطوحٍ تطلُّ على الغابة المعدنيّة.
لَوْحَاتُهُ كالقصائد مائيّةٌ، وعلى أرض
صالونه كُتُبٌ رُصِفَتْ كالحصى الـمُنْتَقَى.
قال لي: عندما يحزنُ الشعرُ أرسُمُ
فوق الحجارة بَعْضَ الفِخاخ لصَيْد القَطَا.
قُلْتُ: من أين يأتي إلى صوتك
البحرُ، والبحر منشغلٌ عنك يا صاحبي؟
قال: من جهة الذكريات، وإن
كنت «لا أتذكر أنّيَ كُنْتُ صغيراً».
وُلدت ولي أخَوان عَدُوّان:
سجني ودائي.
— وأين وَجَدْتَ الطُّفُولَةَ؟
— في داخلي العاطفيّ. أنا الطفلُ
والشيخُ. طفلي يُعَلِّمُ شيخي المجازَ.
وشيخي يُعلّم طفلي التأمُل في خارجي.
خارجي داخلي
كُلّما ضاق سجني تَوزَّعْتُ في الكُلِّ،
واتّسَعَتْ لغتي مثل لُؤْلُؤةٍ كُلّما عَسْعَسَ
الليل ضاءتْ/

وقلت: تعلّمتُ منك الكثير. تعلّمت
كيف أدرِّبُ نفسي على الانشغال بحبّ
الحياة، وكيف أُجدِّفُ في الأبيض
المتوسّط بحثاً عن الدرب والبيت أو
عن ثُنائيّة الدرب والبيت/
لم يَكْتَرِثْ للتحيّة. قدّم لي قهوةً.
ثم قال: سيرجعُ أوديسُكُمْ سالماً،
سوف يَرْجعُ .../

No sea in his house in ancient Athens,
where the goddesses were managing life's matters
alongside the kind humans, and where Electra the youthful
summons Electra the old and asks her: Are you
really me?

And no night in his narrow ascetic home
above roofs that overlook the metal forest.
His paintings like the poems are watercolor, and on the floor
of his guest room books were paved like chosen pebbles.
    He said to me: When poetry is obstinate I sketch
a few traps on the rocks to hunt the grouse.
    I said: From where does the sea come
to your voice, when the sea is already preoccupied, my friend?
    He said: From the direction of memories, even though
"I don't remember that I was once young."
I was born to two enemy brothers:
    my prison and my ailment.
And where did you find childhood then, I asked?
    In my sentimental interior. I am the child
and the elderly. My child teaches my elderly metaphor.
And my elderly teaches my child contemplation in my exterior.
    My exterior is my interior.
    Whenever my prison becomes narrow I spread into everything,
and my language widens as a pearl that lights up
each time night is on patrol /

And I said: I learned a lot from you. I learned
how to train myself to love
life and how to row in the white
Mediterranean looking for the way and for home or
for the duality of way and home /
He didn't care for the compliment. He offered me coffee.
Then said: Your Odysseus will come back safe,
he'll come back ... /

في دار پابلو نيرودا، على شاطىء
الپاسفيك، تذكَّرْتُ يا نيس ريتسوس
في بيته. كان في ذلك الوقت يدخُلُ
إحدى أساطيره، ويقول لإحدى الإلهاتِ:
إنْ كان لا بُدَّ من رحلةٍ، فلتَكُنْ
رحلةً أبديّةً!

In Pablo Neruda's home, on the Pacific
coast, I remembered Yannis Ritsos
at his house. He was entering at that time
one of his myths, saying to one of the goddesses:
If there must be a journey, then let it be
an eternal one!

IV. ليس للكردي إلّا الريح

[إلى: سليم بركات]

VI. THE KURD HAS ONLY THE WIND

for Saleem Barakat

يَتَذكَّرُ الكرديُّ، حين أزورهُ، غَدهُ...
فيُبعدهُ بمُكنسة الغبار: إليكَ عنّي!
فالجبالُ هيَ الجبال. ويشربُ الفودكا
لكي يُبقي الخيالَ على الحياد: أنا
المسافر في مجازي، والكراكيُّ الشقيّةُ
إخوتي الـحَمْقَى. وينفُضُ عن هُويّتِه
الظلالَ: هُويَّتي لُغَتي. أنا... وأنا.
أنا لغتي. أنا المنفيٌّ في لغتي.
وقلبي جمرةُ الكُرْديِّ فوق جبالِه الزرقاء...∕

نيقُوسيا هوامشٌ في قصيدتِه،
ككلِّ مدينةٍ أخرى. على دراجةٍ
حمل الجهاتِ، وقال: أَسْكُنُ أينما
وَقَعَتْ بيَ الجهةُ الأخيرةُ. هكذا
اختار الفراغَ ونام. لم يَحْلُمْ
بشيءٍ مُنْذ حَلَّ الجِنُّ في كلماتِه،
[كلماتُهُ عضلاتُهُ. عضلاتُهُ كلماتُهُ]
فالحالمون يُقَدِّسون الأمسَ، أوْ
يَرُشُون بَابَ الغد الذهبيِّ ...
لا غَدَ لي ولا أمسٍ. الـهُنَيْهَةُ
ساحتي البيضاء ...∕

منزلُهُ نظيفٌ مثلُ عَيْن الديك ...
منسيٌّ كخيمة سيّد القوم الذين
تبعثروا كالريش. سَجّادٌ من الصوف
المجعّد. مُعجَمٌ مُتآكلٌ. كُتُبٌ مُجلَّدةٌ
على عَجَلٍ. مخدّاتٌ مطرّزةٌ بإبرة
خادم المقهى. سكاكيـنُ مُجَلَّخةٌ لذبح
الطير والخنزير. فيديو للإباحيات.
باقاتٌ من الشوك الـمُعَادِل للبلاغة.
شُرْفَةٌ مفتوحةٌ للاستعارة: ها هنا
يَتَبادَلُ الأتراكُ والإغريقُ أدوارَ
الشتائم. تلك تَسْلِيَتي وتَسْلِيَةُ
الجنود الساهرين على حدود
فُكاهةٍ سوداء ...∕

The Kurd remembers, when I visit him, his tomorrow …
so he sweeps it away with a broom: Take it away from me!
because the mountains are the mountains. Then he drinks
vodka for the imagination to remain neutral and says: I am
the traveler in my metaphor, and the mischievous cranes
are my foolish brothers. And he shakes the shadows
off his identity: My identity is my language. I … and I.
I am my language. I'm the exile in my language.
And my heart is the Kurd's ember over his blue mountains … /

Nicosia is in the margin of his poem,
like any other city. On a bicycle
he carried the directions, and said: I stay
wherever the last direction drops me. This
is how I choose space and sleep. He hasn't dreamt
of anything since the jinn materialized in his words
(his words are his muscles, his muscles are his words)
because the dreamers sanctify yesterday, or
bribe tomorrow's golden door …
No tomorrow for him and no yesterday.
The little while is his white plaza … /

His house is as clean as a rooster's eye …
as forgotten as the chieftain's tent pitched for those
who were scattered like feathers. A carpet of wrinkled
wool. A decaying encyclopedia. Books leather-bound
in a hurry. Flying cushions embroidered by a café waiter's
needle. Sharpened knives for the slaughter
of pigs and poultry. A licentious videotape.
Bouquets of thorn the equivalent of eloquence.
And an open balcony for metaphor: Right here
the Turks and the Greeks take turns
in cursing. This is my hobby and the hobby
of soldiers who guard at night the borders
of a black comedy … /

ليس مسافراً هذا المسافرُ، كيفما اتَّفَقَ ...
الشمالُ هو الجنوبُ، الشرقُ غَرْبٌ
في السراب. ولا حقائبَ للرياح،
ولا وظيفة للغبار. كأنه يُخفي
الحنينَ إلى سواهُ، فلا يُغنِّي ...
لا يُغَنِّي حين يدخُلُ ظلُّه شَجَرَ الأكاسيا،
أو يبلَلُ شَعرهُ مَطَرٌ خفيفٌ ...
بل يُناجي الذئبَ، يسأله النزالَ:
تعال يا ابن الكلب نَقْرَعْ طَبْلَ
هذا الليل حتى نوقظ الموتى. فإنَّ
الكُرْدَ يقتربون من نار الحقيقة،
ثم يحترقون مثل فراشة الشُّعَراء/

يعرفُ ما يريد من المعاني. كُلُّها
عَبَثٌ. وللكلمات حيلَتُها لصيد نقيضها،
عبثاً. يفضُّ بكارةَ الكلمات ثم يعيدها
بكراً إلى قاموسه. ويَسُوسُ خَيْلَ
الأبجدية كالخراف إلى مكيدته، ويحلقُ
عائَةً أُ للُغة: انتقمتُ من الغياب.
فَعَلْتُ ما فعل الضبابُ بـإخوتي.
وشَوَيْتُ قلبي كالطريدة. لن أكون
كما أريد. ولن أحبَّ الأرض أكثر
أو أقلَّ من القصيدة. ليس
للكرديِّ إلاّ الريح تسكنُهُ ويسكُنُها.
وتُدْمنُهُ ويُدمنُها، لينجوَ من
صفات الأرض والأشياء ...ِ/

كان يخاطب المجهولَ: يا ابني الـحُرِّ!
يا كبش المتاه السرمديّ. إذا رأيتَ
أباك مشنوقاً فلا تُنْزِلْهُ عن حبل
السماء، ولا تُكَفِّنْهُ بقطن نشيدك
الرَّعَويِّ. لا تدفنه يا ابني، فالرياحُ
وصيَّةُ الكرديِّ للكرديِّ في منفاهُ،
يا ابني... والنسورُ كثيرةٌ حولي
وحولك في الأناضول الفسيح.
جنازتي سريَّةٌ رمزيَّةٌ، فَخُذِ الهباه

This traveler isn't a traveler to wherever …
The north is the south, the east is the west
in the mirage. And the winds have no suitcases,
and no job for dust. As if he were hiding
his longing for another, he doesn't sing … doesn't
sing when the acacia enters his shadow
or when a light rain wets his hair …
Instead he summons the wolf to a duel:
Come here you son of a bitch and let's beat this night's
drum until we awaken the dead. Because
the Kurd approaches truth's fire,
then burns like a poet's butterfly /

He knows what he wants of meaning. All of it
in vain. And the words have their tricks in hunting their antitheses,
in vain. He tears the hymens of words then returns them
as virgins to his dictionary. And he leads the horses
of the alphabet to his ruse like sheep, and shaves
the pubes of language: I have taken my revenge on absence.
I did what fog did to my brothers.
And I grilled my heart like a captured prey. I won't be
as I want. And I won't love the land more
or less than the poem. The Kurd
has only the wind to dwell in him and he in it.
To become addicted to him and he to it, to be saved
from the adjectives of the land and of the things … /

He was addressing the unknown: My free son!
ram of the eternal labyrinth, if you see
your father hanging, don't cut him down from the sky's
rope, and don't shroud him in your pastoral song's
cotton. Don't bury him, my son, because the wind
is bequeathed from one Kurd to another Kurd in exile,
son … and the eagles around you and me
are many in spacious Anatolia.
My funeral is secretive and symbolic, so take the dust

إلى مصائره، وجُرَّ سماءك الأولى
إلى قاموسك السحريِّ. واحذرْ
لَدْغَةَ الأَمَلِ الجريح، فإنه وَحْشٌ
خرافيٌّ. وأنت الآن... أنت الآن
حُرٌّ، يا ابن نفسكَ، أنت حُـرٌّ
من أبيك ولعنة الأسماء../

باللغة انتصَرْتَ على الـهُوَيَّة،
قُلْتُ للكرديِّ، باللغة انتقمتَ
من الغيابِ
فقال: لن أمضي إلى الصحراءِ
قُلْتُ: ولا أنا ...
ونظرت نحو الريح/
ــ عِمْتَ مساء
ــ عمت مساء!

to its destiny, and drag your first sky
to your magical dictionary. And beware
of the sting of wounded hope, that mythical
monster. And you are now ... you are now
free, son of yourself, you are free
of your father and of the curse of the names ... /

With language you overcame identity,
I told the Kurd, with language you took revenge
on absence
He said: I won't go to the desert
I said: Neither will I ...
Then I looked toward the wind /
—Good evening
—Good evening!

Notes

WE WERE MISSING A PRESENT

The lines "so I am not of the east / and I am not of the west, / nor am I an olive tree shading two verses in the Quran" borrow from a famous verse in the twenty-fourth *sūra* in the Quran that describes the light of God: "… as a niche in a glass, the glass as if it were a brilliant star lit from a blessed tree, an olive, not of the east or of the west, whose oil is near lighting, although a fire never touched it …"

SONNET I

Darwish's actual "pronoun revealed to double the 'I' " is "to be the revelation of the *Ana*'s *nūn* in its dual form." The *Ana* is the "I." The dual form is a unique construct in Arabic: the letter *nūn* (equivalent to the letter N), when preceded by a vowel, forms a suffix that indicates whether the nominative case is dual or plural.

The *nūn* is also one of the constituents of the *taf'eelah*, the basic unit of Arabic prosody. And its phonic ring is frequently used as an affirmative accent, or inflection, added to the ends of words.

YOUR NIGHT IS OF LILAC

The word for night in Arabic is *lail:* Your *Lail* Is of Lilac.

"Jahili poetry," also known as *Al-Mu'allaqat* ("the suspended ones"), refers to the seven poems that were suspended from the walls of the Kaaba in Mecca, before the message of Islam. *Jahili* means "of-the-ignorant," and denotes the pre-Islamic tribal era. Imru' el-Qyss (500–540) is one of those seven poets, and arguably the best among them. He was a prince of Kinda who led a life of sensual pleasure, but when he failed to avenge the murder of his father, the king, he traveled to Constantinople to ask the Byzantine emperor for help. He was placated with the nominal governance of Palestine, but died shortly thereafter, wretchedly, of an ulcerative skin disease rumored to be the result of poison placed inside his aba/cloak. A famous section in Imru' el-Qyss's *mu'allaqah* begins: "And a night, like the sea waves, has slowly let down its veil over me," and ends four stanzas later with: "as if its stars were anchored with linen ropes to solid stone."

TAKE MY HORSE AND SLAUGHTER IT …

Andalus is Arabic for Andalusia, the region of southern Spain where Muslim Arabs created a pluralistic civilization throughout the Middle Ages which was pivotal for the Renaissance. The brutal expulsion and cleansing of the Muslims and Jews from the Andalus began in the thirteenth century, and was effectively completed by 1492. Darwish has frequently visited the Andalus in his poetry: "I was not a passerby in the words of singers … I was / the words of singers, the peace of Athens and Persia, an east embracing a west / in the departure to one essence" (from "Eleven Planets at the End of the Andalusian Scene," 1992).

INANNA'S MILK

Inanna is the foremost deity of ancient Mesopotamia, and perhaps the first goddess of recorded human civilization. In Sumerian she is the "Lady of Heaven." In Akkadian, she is Ishtar.

Nebuchadnezzar II is the king under whose reign Babylon's Hanging Gardens became one of the marvels of the world. He conquered Palestine and Syria and, in biblical narrative, was responsible for the Exodus.

NO MORE AND NO LESS

Qyss Ibn el-Mulawah and Laila were lovers in the seventh century. When Laila's family turned down Qyss's proposal for marriage, and she was married off to another man, Qyss became progressively mad (*majnoon*). His incessant, forthright, and sometimes explicit verse forced the tribe to ostracize him in order to protect Laila's honor. He died a wanderer in the desert. He is known primarily by his beloved's name: Qyss Laila or Majnoon Laila. The name Laila is a derivative of *lail* (night), and became a symbol of the beloved in Arabic and Islamic poetry and culture.

WEDDING SONG

The actual title is "Zafaf Song." *Zafaf* is the processional celebration of the bride and groom, the commencement ritual in a wedding.

TWO STRANGER BIRDS IN OUR FEATHERS

"Youssef" refers to the biblical character Joseph, son of Jacob.

THE SUBSISTENCE OF BIRDS

Muwashah is a form of postclassical Arabic poetry sung in stanzas. Its composition was a prominent art form in the Andalusian era. It is still popular today.

Samarkand is a city in Uzbekistan that dates back to before Alexander the Great, who conquered it. In the eighth century, the Muslim Arabs established it as a cultural center, before it was destroyed by the Mongol invasion in the thirteenth century.

MAYBE, BECAUSE WINTER IS LATE

Nahawand is one of the musical scales in Arabic, borrowed from the Persian; it is also the name of a region in Iran.

JAMEEL BOUTHAINA AND I

Jameel and Bouthaina lived in the seventh century. Their bloomless romance agitated Jameel into love verse. He persisted in composing chaste, tender poetry for Bouthaina until his death. Their story is known as "the virginal love." The narrative has its share of variations, although marriage is not one of them. And like his contemporary Qyss Laila (see "No More and No Less"), Jameel became known by his beloved's name.

The *nūn:* see notes on "Sonnet I."

A MASK ... FOR MAJNOON LAILA

Najd is a region in central Saudi Arabia and is, historically, the land of the renowned ancient Arabic tribes from which many of the pre-Islamic poets came.

"The prince of Damascus" represents the seat of power that the Muslim caliph of the Umayyad dynasty held, and under whose rule the traditional nomadic life of the Arabs became rapidly urban. Qyss Laila's verse (as well as Jameel Bouthaina's) reflected neither social milieu, and represented in Arabic poetry an early autonomy (from tribe or nation) of the self.

Early Islamic love poetry, especially of Jameel and Qyss, in its devotional configuration of the self, was a source of influence on mystic and Sufi verse, Andalusian, Turkish, and Persian literature, and, arguably, the troubadours.

THE DAMASCENE COLLAR OF THE DOVE

"The Collar of the Dove" is a famous manuscript on beauty and the art of love, written in the eleventh century by Ibn Hazm, a renowned Andalusian Muslim scholar. The Muslim reign in Andalusia began as an emirate of the Umayyad dynasty, whose central caliphate was in Damascus, but persisted independently for centuries after that dynasty's end.

Jahili: see notes on "Your Night Is of Lilac."

An oud is a stringed instrument resembling the lute.

The Lotus Tree of Heaven, *Sidrat al-Muntaha* ("the highest degree of attainment"), is a fantastic tree that rises from the Seventh Heaven and reaches God's throne.

Youssef: the biblical son of Jacob.

Barada is a small river that runs through Damascus.

Qasyoon Valley is one of the city's suburbs.

The "butterfly's burden" is an expression Darwish originally used in the title of his 1977 poem "And You'll Carry the Butterfly's Burden."

A STATE OF SIEGE

Khilafah: Arabic for caliphate.

Khosrau is the title of ancient Persian kings, often suggesting the king whose defeat at the hands of early Arab Muslims in the seventh century opened Persia to Islam.

Zaghareed: ululations of joy.

Om Kalthoum: Egyptian diva of Arabic song in the twentieth century.

Nǎy: wooden (often reed) flute.

Red, black, white, green: the colors of the Palestinian flag.

Nahawand and *hejaz* are two scales of Arabic music. The former is named after a region in western Iran, the latter after the western coastal region in Saudi Arabia, where Mecca is located.

Muwashah: see notes on "The Subsistence of Birds."

CADENCE CHOOSES ME

Zanzalakht: the China tree (*Melia azedarach*) is an abundant and shady tree in the Galilee, often a place for social gatherings.

DON'T APOLOGIZE FOR WHAT YOU'VE DONE

Hamassa Diwan is an anthology of classical Arabic poetry collected according to theme, by Abu Tammam (788–845; see notes for "If You Return Alone"). The *Diwan* (collection of poems) became known for its most popular chapter, the *Hamassa* (valor) chapter, which dealt with heroic poetry.

The Encyclopedia of Countries alludes to *Mu'jam Al-Buldan,* a geographical dictionary of the Middle East written in the eleventh century by Yaqut al-Hamawi.

IF YOU RETURN ALONE

Abu Tammam (Habib ibn Aus) lived in the ninth century and was an early master of post-Jahili (Islamic) Arabic poetry and letters. He studied Greek philosophy, and his poetry is known for its innovative language and complex metaphors.

I DIDN'T APOLOGIZE TO THE WELL

Darwish clearly revisits one of his earlier poems, "The Well" (1996). It begins with: "I choose an overcast day to pass by the old well. / Maybe it has filled up with sky. Maybe it has overflown meaning / and the shepherd's parable." Then the poem ends with Darwish speaking to his ghost: "And we will say to the dead around it: Salaam / upon you who are alive in the butterfly's water, / and upon you who are dead: Salaam!"

AND WE HAVE A LAND

The word Darwish uses for "ascension" is *Me'raj.* It suggests the prophet Muhammad's miraculous rise to the heavens from Jerusalem, which culminated in his meeting with God: accompanied by the archangel Gabriel, the prophet traveled from Mecca to Jerusalem overnight (*Issra'*) on the back of a hybrid steed called al-Boraq. When he reached the city, Muhammad led all previous prophets in prayer at the site of al-Aqsa mosque, before his ascension to heaven. The Rock (beneath the Dome of the Rock) is the accepted site of ascension. The narrative of the ascension in Arabic and Muslim literature is equally rich on either side of literalism and mysticism.

IN HER ABSENCE I CREATED HER IMAGE

Yabous is the original name for Jerusalem, when the Jebusites (Yabousians), a Canaanite tribe, first inhabited the region around 2500 B.C. "The seven hills" indicate the topography of the Jerusalem area. The name for Jerusalem in Arabic is al-Quds, "the Holy Place."

MURDERED AND UNKNOWN

Hamassa: see notes on "Don't Apologize for What You've Done."

THE CYPRESS BROKE

Bassam Hajjar is a contemporary Lebanese poet and a translator of French literature into Arabic.

A MAN AND A FAWN ARE IN THE GARDEN

Sulieman el-Najjab is a political activist, artist, and friend of the poet. In Arabic, the third-person address of the verb *to live* is also a masculine name, Yahya, which corresponds to John (mentioned in the Quran as John the Baptist). Sulieman is Arabic for Solomon.

AS FOR ME, I SAY TO MY NAME

Mahmoud, the poet's name, like Muhammad, is a derivative of the word-root *hamd* ("praise" or "laudation"). Mahmoud means praised.

A NOUN SENTENCE

Arabic has no copulative verbs, which allows for the construct of "A Noun Sentence."

THANKS TO TUNIS

In the aftermath of the 1982 Israeli invasion of Lebanon, the Palestinian Liberation Organization was forced to roam the Mediterranean, before settling on Tunisian shores and taking residence there.

The lines: "Don't give me, O sea, what I don't deserve / of song. And don't be, O sea, more or less than song!" echo, in the singular, a famous refrain in a 1986 Darwish poem from his collection *It's a Song, It's a Song:* "Do not give us, O sea, what we do not deserve of song!"

IN SYRIA

Barada is a small river that runs through Damascus.

"Chaste" love (courtly love) refers primarily to Jameel Bouthaina's poetry and the devotional verse of Qyss Laila (see notes for "No More and No Less," "Jameel Bouthaina and I," and "A Mask … for Majnoon Laila.").

I RECALL AL-SAYYAB

Badr Shakir al-Sayyab (1924–1964), an Iraqi poet, is considered by most to be the father of modern Arabic verse. The refrain "Iraq, Iraq, nothing but Iraq" is borrowed from the opening poem, "Stranger to the Gulf," of his very influential 1960 book, *The Rain Song.*

Gilgamesh: Sumerian hero of the *Gilgamesh* epic, probably the first recorded myth of man that tells a story of creation.

Hammurabi (1792–1750 B.C.), a Babylonian king who unified Mesopotamia and who codified and tabulated the first human laws.

Hulagu (1217–1265) is the grandson of Genghis Khan. He was responsible for the brutal destruction of Baghdad and of the Abbasid dynasty in 1258. He ordered the destruction of the libraries, until the Euphrates and the Tigris ran ink. He lost a crucial battle in Palestine at Goliath Spring (Ain Jaloot) at the hands of the Mamluks in 1260, which halted the westward invasion of the Mongols.

THE COASTAL ROAD

Al-Mutanabbi (Ahmad bin Hussein, 915–965) was a brilliant Arab poet. His poetry remained influential as recently as the nineteenth century. Al-Mutanabbi, meaning *the one claiming prophecy,* is a pseudonym he acquired when, it is said, he made such a declaration in one of his youthful poems. Adventurous and politically ambitious, he frequented the Syrian and Egyptian courts of the time. His brilliance won him many patrons and many enemies. He was killed as a consequence of his political whims.

A POETRY STANZA / THE SOUTHERNER'S HOUSE

A poetry *stanza* in Arabic is a *house* (*Bayt*) of poetry (or a home). Amal Donqul (1940–1983) was an Egyptian poet from southern (Upper) Egypt. He died young of cancer, but not before leaving his mark on Arabic poetry. Darwish's poem commemorates the twentieth anniversary of Donqul's death.

Khufu: Arabic for Cheops.

LIKE A MYSTERIOUS INCIDENT

Darwish's encounter with Yannis Ritsos occurred after the Israeli invasion of Lebanon in 1982. Athens, Greece, was the first port of arrival for the PLO and its members before Tunisia became a new headquarters in exile.

Yabous: see notes on "In Her Absence I Created Her Image."

THE KURD HAS ONLY THE WIND

Saleem Barakat, Darwish's contemporary, is an acclaimed Syrian-Kurd poet, translator, and novelist, writing in Arabic. His work has been translated into several languages.

About the Author

MAHMOUD DARWISH (1941–2008) was born in al-Birwa village in Galilee, Palestine. After the creation of Israel in 1948, he led a life of exile. He returned to Palestine in 1996, dividing his residence between Ramallah and Amman. Perhaps the most distinguished Arab poet of his generation, he published more than twenty books of poetry and ten of prose, and was the editor of the international literary journal *al-Karmel,* based in Ramallah. Among his many awards are the Lenin Peace Prize, the French medal for Knight of Arts and Letters, the Lannan Prize for Cultural Freedom, the Prince Claus Award from the Netherlands, and the Golden Wreath Award from Struga Poetry Evenings. Among his works that have appeared in English are *Memory for Forgetfulness* (prose); *The Adam of Two Edens; Unfortunately, It Was Paradise;* and *Why Did You Leave the Horse Alone?*

About the Translator

FADY JOUDAH was born in Austin, Texas, in a Palestinian refugee home. His poetry collection, *The Earth in the Attic,* was the winner of the Yale Series for Younger Poets in 2007, and he is the recipient of the 2008 Saif Ghobash–Banipal Prize for Arabic Literary Translation from the United Kingdom's Society of Authors. Joudah is a physician of internal medicine and a field member of Doctors Without Borders.

The Chinese character for poetry is made up of two parts: "word" and "temple." It also serves as pressmark for Copper Canyon Press. Founded in 1972, Copper Canyon Press remains dedicated to publishing poetry exclusively, from Nobel laureates to new and emerging authors. The Press thrives with the generous patronage of readers, writers, booksellers, librarians, teachers, students, and funders—everyone who shares the conviction that poetry invigorates the language and sharpens our appreciation of the world.

Major funding has been provided by:

THE **PAUL G. ALLEN**
FAMILY *foundation*

Anonymous (2)

The Paul G. Allen Family Foundation

Lannan Foundation

National Endowment for the Arts

NATIONAL
ENDOWMENT
FOR THE ARTS

Washington State Arts Commission

WASHINGTON
STATE ARTS
COMMISSION

For information and catalogs:

COPPER CANYON PRESS
Post Office Box 271
Port Townsend, Washington 98368
360-385-4925
www.coppercanyonpress.org

English text in this book is set in the digital version of Figural, designed by Oldřich Menhart in 1940, and redrawn for Letraset in 1992 by Michael Gills. The Arabic text is set in al-Bayan. Book design and English composition by Valerie Brewster, Scribe Typography. Arabic composition by Aissa Deebi. Printed on archival-quality Glatfelter Author's Text by McNaughton & Gunn, Inc.